The New York Times

SUNDAY AT HOME CROSSWORDS
75 Puzzles from the Pages of *The New York Times*

Edited by Will Shortz

ST. MARTIN'S GRIFFIN ⚞ NEW YORK

The New York Times
CROSSWORDS
SMART PUZZLES PRESENTED WITH STYLE

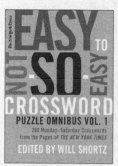

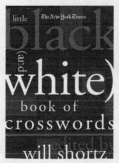

Available at your local bookstore or online at nytimes.com/nytstore.

 St. Martin's Griffin

ACROSS

1 Home of the Natl. Hollerin' Contest
5 Spicy cuisine
9 Beat ___ horse
14 Complain
18 Tenant's desire
20 Really rough
22 As a refutation
23 Acquirers of lost property
24 Part of New Eng.
25 Bit of cheer
26 Major source of the narcotic qat
28 Plain ___
29 Words under Washington's picture
32 "American Justice" network
33 International retailer whose name is an acronym
35 Stolen
36 Former German president Johannes
37 Major finale?
39 Desert attribute
43 Co-star of "Blow," 2001
44 Noisy celebration
46 Knock over
47 Writes without pen or pencil
50 Keys
51 Don who pitched a perfect game in the 1956 World Series
54 Lollobrigida and others
55 Tip for a calligrapher
56 Dandy
58 President who won by one electoral vote
59 Space shuttle supply
61 Locale for a vision of the Apostle Paul
64 Sicken
66 Candy treat
67 Basic infirmities
70 Cousin of a credit union
71 Friendly
74 Dimensions and tolerances, say
75 Taste
78 Tot minder
79 Major player in the movie biz?
81 Certain parallel: Abbr.
82 Some Sony computers
83 Apple product
85 Proclaims
88 Extends
89 The whole song and dance?
90 1999 "Star Wars" release
92 Subject of Cyrus the Great
93 Registers
96 Nickelodeon explorer
97 Fuss
98 Fairy queen, in Shakespeare
101 Underwriter's assessment
102 It's typically off base
103 Bottom line
106 Bistro adjunct
109 Round top
111 Long of "Boyz N the Hood"
112 Cease pleading
113 Building support
116 No matter what
119 Bruised
120 Nursery rhyme dish
121 "___I!"
122 Theodore of "The Defiant Ones"
123 Subject of una sinfonia
124 Prosperity

DOWN

1 "You're doing it all wrong!"
2 Cream-filled pastry
3 Doctor
4 Music category
5 Calculate, as the bill
6 Kind of yoga
7 Parseghian of Notre Dame
8 Without thinking
9 First two
10 Old "Romper Room" character with bouncing antennae
11 Actor McGregor
12 Newswoman Compton
13 Game with orcs and half-elves
14 Like the labyrinth of Knossos
15 Graded materials
16 Suit to ___
17 Financial inits.
18 Japanese electronics giant
19 Sack materials
21 Was overly nice
27 Choice at a restaurant
30 Unfinished threat
31 Breathe
33 Cause of a red face
34 German port
38 E Street Band's leader, informally
39 Ones with incendiary ideas
40 Simple
41 Equal alternative
42 Beyond understanding
43 Neither hor. nor vert.
45 Barker's attention-getter
47 Legend in one's own mind
48 Sign at a store clothing bin
49 Imminently
50 One way to take it
52 Contented responses
53 Arctic explorer John
57 Go for the gold?
60 Snare
62 Store chain since 1859
63 Part of a bee
65 ___ Enterprise
68 Year in the reign of Antoninus Pius
69 Like Longfellow's Evangeline
72 King's longtime home
73 Assent
76 Photographer Richard
77 Locks in a stable
80 Hi-___
84 Part of a conference sched.
86 Fishing gear
87 Have great affection for
88 Punches a new number in
91 Commercial ending with Water
92 English royal known as the Empress Maud

by Craig Kasper

94 "Cooks who know trust" this, in an old slogan
95 Tourist info spot
98 TV title role for Brandy Norwood
99 Beverage named for a Dutch river
100 Actress Blair
102 Idée ___ (accepted idea, in French)
104 Gird for battle, say
105 Oscar nominee for "The Insider"
106 Banned chemicals
107 1968 live folk album
108 Odious one
109 Shy
110 "The ability to describe others as they see themselves": Lincoln
114 Offerer of cozy accommodations
115 Baseball stat
117 Election day: Abbr.
118 Musical genre

2 "Ooh!"

ACROSS

1 Lays at the door of
7 One drawing sympathy
14 Tequila brand, for short
20 Any "Rock 'n' Roll High School" band member
21 Did some bookkeeping
22 Teamed up
23 Cuddly sheep?
25 Simple digs
26 TV remote, e.g.
27 Scout's find
29 Operatic prince
30 16th-century council city
31 Pen's end
33 Equinox mo.
34 Qum native
37 Eerie ability
39 Entre ___
41 Role-play, say
43 Those on the bench
46 Conservatives waiting in line?
50 Oater command
52 Wilhelm I ruled it
54 Pilot's vision problem
55 Idle, with "around"
57 A cabinet dept.
58 Blood: Prefix
60 Pro ___
61 Like a Miata
62 Expulsion from a court?
65 Treaty subject
68 Juilliard subj.
69 Necessitate
70 Mess up
73 Blasting aid
75 Carnaby Street types
77 Hillbillies' coif?
81 Hawkish
84 Test version
86 Biographer Leon
87 Ref. work with more than 300,000 entries
88 Be a fink
89 Lustrous fabric
91 Gave power to
93 Geom. solid
94 What van Gogh said regarding ears?
97 Reactor parts
98 Sinatra impersonator on "S.N.L."
100 Action film hero Williams
101 ___ Miguel (Azores island)
103 Cause of an intl. incident, maybe
104 Monokini's lack
106 ___ whim
108 Overshadow
112 Totally nuts
114 Taxco wrap
117 Edible spherule
119 Oscar-winning director of 2005
122 Sitting Bull being evasive?
124 Poverty-stricken
125 Downsize without layoffs
126 Timeless, in verse
127 Dedicated an ode to
128 Sonnet endings
129 Stopped arguing

DOWN

1 French port
2 Debussy opus
3 Go unhurriedly
4 State of increased quantity
5 Puts into effect
6 Shia, e.g.
7 Halloween activity
8 Clerical garment
9 Shoulder muscle, briefly
10 Vanilla-flavored treat
11 Cub leader
12 It may be found under a grate
13 Scene of a fall
14 1920's White House name
15 Kin of -kin
16 Lancelot lover
17 Calling the author of "In Cold Blood"?
18 Nix
19 Nose-wrinkler
24 Time on end
28 Makeshift swing
32 Nobelist Niels
35 Stays for another hitch
36 Really enjoyed
38 Druid, e.g.
40 In ___ (not yet born)
41 Wall Street option
42 Loses on purpose
43 Cross words
44 The munchies, for one
45 Swindle, slangily
47 2001 Sean Penn film
48 "___ chance"
49 Book size, in printing
51 Take a shot
53 Kick target
56 "Alfie" actress, 2004
59 Canton's home
63 Cereal box abbr.
64 Biddy
66 Pouty look
67 Insect-eating plant
71 Pool group
72 In ___ land
73 "The Sound of Music" name
74 Worthless African animal?
76 Genesis son
77 Novelist Binchy
78 Court plea, in brief
79 Thing to do
80 Some calculations
81 Carat divs.
82 Mrs. Theodore Roosevelt
83 New stylings
85 Rend
89 ___ Balls (Hostess brand)
90 Verne skipper
92 Chocolaty treats
95 Picks, with "for"
96 They're depressed during exams
99 Lost zip
102 Carol starter
104 Knuckle-dragger
105 Goes bonkers
107 Prince Valiant's son
109 Left on board
110 Alums do it
111 Sent, in a way
112 Journalist Sheehy
113 Ballerina Pavlova
115 History units
116 Jay Gould railroad
118 River of central Germany
120 Shoebox marking
121 Baseball Hall-of-Famer Roush
123 Polo Grounds legend

by Fred Piscop

3 FOOLS RUSH IN

ACROSS

1 Some people count by them
5 Potters' needs
10 Bits of Three Stooges violence
14 Instruction to a violinist
19 Overhead light?
20 Place for boats
21 Cut for a column
22 Ones undergoing transformation
23 Rock band whose first album was titled, appropriately, "High Voltage"
24 Announcer's cry at a hound race?
27 [Boo-hoo!]
29 Inconsistent
30 "___ Thou Now, O Soul" (Walt Whitman poem)
31 Jazz pianist Bill
33 Skirt feature
34 Flies, maybe
35 Minotaur's home
38 What priests on a space mission wear?
44 Pitch maker?
46 How sardines are often packed
47 Requirement for a hand, say
48 Receiver of donations
49 Take ___ (swing hard)
50 A celebrity carries one
52 Bldg. planner
53 Smart-mouthed
54 Prefix with -zoic
55 Classic Jaguar
56 Dr. Gregory of "ER"
59 Attack helicopter
61 King Frederick I's realm
63 Naps
65 Werner of "Ship of Fools," 1965
66 Mouthing off to police officers?
69 Informal head cover
72 Asylum seekers
73 Formally attired
77 Child actor discovered by Chaplin
79 Observe furtively
80 Atlanta-based health org.
81 Faux: Abbr.
82 Sheltered spot
83 They have big bills
85 Result of a slap, perhaps
86 ___ bean
87 Word with bitter or winter
88 Man ___
89 Abbott and Costello's "Here Come the ___"
92 Novelist Glyn who coined "It" as a euphemism
94 TV dog with its muzzle removed?
98 Teen problem
99 Chantilly seraph
100 "Norma Rae" director Martin
101 Consumer products giant, briefly
103 Fictional hero whose first words are "I was born in the Year 1632, in the City of York . . ."
106 Tissuelike
108 Tease
112 Marshes with libraries and opera houses?
115 Noted exile
116 Kitchen floor coverings, to a Brit
117 Fossey who did gorilla research
118 "The Wreck of the Mary ___"
119 Longtime NBC star
120 Dumb
121 Snafu
122 Turned up
123 Trails

DOWN

1 Sign of spring
2 City on the Brazos
3 ___ Towne
4 Debutante ball?
5 "Dreams From My Father" writer
6 Singer in the 1958 movie "Go, Johnny, Go!"
7 Night school subj.
8 His ___ (self-important man)
9 Stops daydreaming
10 "Hush!"
11 "Swan Lake" role
12 Terrible shame
13 Rte. parts
14 Lift
15 Habana or Cádiz
16 Grp. with lodges
17 Fall guys?
18 Horizontal thread in a fabric
25 Longtime Chicago Symphony conductor
26 Start of Kansas' motto
28 Cinematographer Nykvist
32 Common English place name ending
34 Big report
35 Surgical aid
36 Like triple plays compared to double plays
37 Aria that ends "O speranze d'amor!"
39 A, in Italy
40 Harvard student
41 ___ lit
42 Buckwheat groats
43 Drive . . . or part of a cattle drive
45 Horizontal line
51 Decree
52 Major extensions?
53 Backdrop for carolers?
56 "Wittle" toe
57 So out it's back in
58 Pasty
60 Foot specialist
62 Family history, e.g.
63 Short cuts
64 Stock market sell-off
67 "Without a doubt"
68 Word said with a hand behind one's back
69 1983 Mr. T film
70 Alley Oop's girl
71 Vagabond
74 Cyberchatting
75 Wheels for big wheels
76 Windows button
78 Crystal user
80 ___ number (ID on all stocks and registered bonds)
84 Symbol of royal power
85 Driller's deg.
88 Worthless
89 Some sunglasses
90 Many a John Ford film
91 Spanish road
93 Curtsier

by Paula Gamache

4 IN OTHER WORDS

ACROSS

1 Pot builder
9 Solitaire measure
14 Court marshal
21 Undying flower
22 Round window
23 Condition of the 85-Across
24 Peacemaker
25 Of yore
26 Boards
27 Something that goes for a quarter?
29 How Peter denied Jesus
31 The Marx Bros. left Paramount for it
32 Subj. of a library in Austin, Tex.
35 Opposite of protruding
36 Chaise place
38 Actress Andersson of "I Never Promised You a Rose Garden"
39 Delivered a stemwinder
41 Plant sci.
43 Unification Church member, slangily
44 Loaf
45 Threw out, as a question
46 Flip out
48 "Gold" Fonda role
49 Like Van Buren's presidency
50 123-Across or 96-Down?
53 It may be polar
54 Israeli political leader Peretz
56 Original finish?
57 Howe in the National Inventors Hall of Fame
58 Diana on the cover of "Sgt. Pepper's Lonely Hearts Club Band"
59 Snowboard alternative
61 Seize
62 Quadrille designs
64 Box ofc. buy
67 127-Across or 91-Down?
70 God who cuckolded Hephaestus
71 Seating areas
72 Cause of an explosion
73 Doofus
74 Put (down)
75 Old five-franc pieces
76 23-Across or 19-Down?
83 Not camera-ready?
84 1994 film with the tagline "Get ready for rush hour"
85 Really big
86 Bows
87 Wasn't straight
88 Mâcon's river
89 NNW's reverse
90 Big Southern department store chain
91 "The Trouble With Harry" co-star Edmund
93 24-Across or 5-Down?
97 Once across the Rio Grande?
98 Hamburger shack?
99 Caravaggio's "The Sacrifice of ___"
100 Neptune's closest moon
103 French textile city
104 Oxford lengths
106 Norse war god
107 Saloon habitués, slangily
108 Boarders board it
109 Bordeaux wine
111 On ___ (raging)
113 Wing
114 Tail
115 Like some stars
116 Reddish gem
119 Most drunken
121 Worth having
123 VX, e.g.
127 Secondary competitions, in some tennis tournaments
128 Piano's counterpart
129 Words before roof or flag
130 Tabasco and others
131 Let out
132 Course option

DOWN

1 Rude character
2 U.K. record label
3 Dorm leaders, for short
4 Smell ___
5 Wedded couples
6 Not forgotten
7 Flute parts
8 ___ Problem of celestial mechanics
9 Codger
10 Some toll units
11 Reverse mantra of "The Shining"
12 Salt agreement?
13 Circus props
14 "Don't fight"
15 It begins here
16 About
17 J.F.K. alternative
18 "Assuming it's O.K. with you . . ."
19 Impression of Count Dracula?
20 Second-largest city in Ark.
23 Cereal toppers
28 Leaf pore
30 Sharp fellow?
32 Cut (off)
33 Bud
34 "A Different World" actress
37 Candy bar fillings
38 Fake
40 Chinese bloomers
42 Person behind bars?
44 Some gowns
46 Welcome words to a hitchhiker
47 Dropped from the galleys
49 Undermine
51 Vandeweghe of the N.B.A.
52 Not final, at law
54 Strolls
55 Ancient deity mentioned 39 times in Allen Ginsberg's "Howl"
58 Slam
60 Serpentine signal
61 Overcaffeinated
62 "Six Degrees of Separation" playwright
63 Comedic spiel
64 A heart often has one
65 Place to keep toys?
66 "Shame!"
68 Nobel laureate between Hesse and Eliot
69 Heads to Harvard or Georgetown, maybe
70 It often features the quadratic formula
74 ___-10
76 An Ivy, briefly
77 Outlaw Kelly
78 Make rough
79 It's blown
80 Starbucks order
81 Unadorned
82 Rink athlete, informally
84 Trig ratios
87 Seesaw, e.g.

by Byron Walden

88 Flee like mice
89 Refurbish
91 Lack of gravity
92 Cry of relief
93 Months after Tebets
94 Real downer?
95 One-eyed leader
96 Makes a special invitation?

97 City on Lake Victoria
101 Tie indicator
102 Dial-up alternative, for short
104 Fancy homes
105 Land
107 Puppeteers Bil and Cora

109 Spanish sky
110 Liking
112 Dementieva of tennis
115 Texas metropolis nickname
117 Portland college
118 Maker of the game Dart Tag

120 Transfer ___
122 Pro
124 Indian state
125 What goes in your nose to make noise?
126 Pommes frites accompanier

5   RUBE GOLDBERG DEVICE

ACROSS

1 Audibly shocked
6 Bar
11 Two-seaters, maybe
19 Quaint opening for a note
20 Google's domain
22 Sailing
23 *First you . . .*
26 Nav. rank
27 ___ kwon do
28 Bit of athletic wear
29 *. . . which . . .*
34 Longevity
37 Explosion maker
38 Sound off
39 Smith Brothers competitor
41 Music box?
44 Super Mario Bros. player
45 You may put something on it at a bar
49 ___ Today (teachers' monthly)
50 High-altitude home
51 Not subject to any more changes
53 Shortly
54 Kind of help
55 Depilatory brand
56 *. . . that . . .*
59 Sot's woe
60 Didn't play
61 Suffix with hip
62 Mai ___
63 *After a while the . . .*
72 ___ soda
73 "Dream on!"
74 Spanish pronoun
75 Geom. figure
76 *. . . who . . .*
83 House or senate
84 Med. plans
85 Sick as ___
86 Glaswegian : Glasgow :: Loiner : ___
87 Waits
88 Foreign pen pal, maybe
89 Oil tanker cargoes
91 "Looky here!"
92 Bring in
93 Ship-to-shore transport
95 "Café-Concert" painter
97 Special
98 Additional, in commercialese
99 *. . . which . . .*
106 Replacing
108 "___ who?"
109 QB Grossman
110 *Next time . . .*
117 Aesthete
118 Trojan War hero
119 Capital nicknamed "City of Trees"
120 Back-of-book feature
121 Classic Harlem ballroom
122 Story subtitled "The Yeshiva Boy"

DOWN

1 Stock phrase
2 1977 biographical Broadway play starring Anne Bancroft
3 "Ditto"
4 [as is]
5 Make-believe
6 "I Love Lucy" neighbor
7 Any ship
8 Concert souvenir
9 Pained sounds
10 Glimpse
11 Classic setting for detective pulp fiction
12 Win by ___
13 "Don't take ___ seriously!"
14 Antitheft device
15 Stunk
16 Part of a windy road
17 Crack team?: Abbr.
18 Bloody 2004 thriller
21 It comes with strings attached
24 Class
25 Songwriter Washington
30 Stoop feature
31 Ancient region bordering Lydia
32 Rock singer Reznor
33 Homes on the Costa del Sol
35 Subject of a makeup exam?
36 Fishhook line
39 Tall and thin
40 On base
41 Music genre, briefly
42 End
43 Do-or-die time
46 Couldn't stand
47 Año nuevo time
48 Start of the title of many an ode
51 Party
52 Lascivious
54 Men-only
56 "2001" computer
57 Nos. on a scoreboard
58 Source of an explosion in Italy
60 French town of W.W. II
64 Lip
65 Lead character on TV's "The Pretender"
66 Plains tribe
67 Kind of lic.
68 Jupiter's counterpart
69 Belief
70 Senate staff
71 Assignation
76 Mississippi senator Cochran
77 Blend
78 Modulate
79 Internet address suffix
80 Long stretches
81 Shorten, maybe
82 "What did ___ deserve this?"
83 Beginning
87 Defeat easily
89 Handel's "___ Anthems"
90 With 101-Down, unwrinkle
92 Areas next to a great hall
94 Subjects to cross-x
96 Pitching figures
99 Roughage
100 Cautious
101 See 90-Down
102 Asking too much of someone?
103 Utah senator Hatch
104 Nadir amount
105 Dismiss
107 58-Down output
110 Capture

by Brendan Emmett Quigley

111 Link letters
112 Lance in law
113 Indianapolis's
___ Dome
114 "Punk'd" airer
115 Resetting
setting
116 Kicker?

ACROSS

1 Student's declaration
6 Restricted part of a street
13 Paul of pet food
17 1947 crime drama
21 Block in the Southwest
22 Golf club with a nearly vertical face
23 Love letters?
24 U.S. city in sight of two volcanoes
25 With 36-Across, "Poetry is . . ." (Osbert Sitwell)
27 Orange/yellow blooms
29 Feature of the villain in "The Fugitive"
30 Walk to the door
32 Single thread
33 Radisson alternative
36 See 25-Across
40 Hearty drink
43 Like the Uzbek and Kirghiz languages
47 Smog-watching grp.
48 Bagnell Dam river
49 Purplish
52 Ella of "Phantom Lady"
54 One way to be paid
58 Amount past due?
59 "Poetry is . . ." (Joseph Roux)
63 Oater locale
64 Where Springsteen was born, in song
65 Monte ___
66 Hyde Park stroller
68 Toil
71 Have on
75 Japanese band?
78 Like many pubs
81 With 89-Across, "Poetry is . . ." (Carl Sandburg)
85 Flat
88 Struggle
89 See 81-Across
93 QB Rodney
94 Banned spray
95 Russian city or oblast
96 Office gizmo
98 Soissons seasons
100 Baseball Hall-of-Famer Banks
104 Make an inauguration affirmation
107 Literary ending
111 "Poetry is . . ." (Edith Sitwell)
117 Took top honors
118 French city in W.W. II fighting
119 Title character in a "Sgt. Pepper" song
120 Grant maker
121 Hatch from Utah
123 15 years before the Battle of Hastings
125 Dead Sea Scrolls scribe
127 "___ gratias"
128 "Poetry is . . ." (Pablo Neruda)
133 Verges on
136 Sing "Gladly the cross-eyed bear," say
137 Tyro
141 ___ Mae
145 Elderly
148 "Poetry is . . ." (e. e. cummings)
151 English university V.I.P.s
152 Punjabi believer
153 No more
154 #24 of 24
155 As a result
156 Besides
157 Fall field worker
158 Snooped (around)

DOWN

1 Bueno's opposite
2 Tennis edge
3 It may start with someone entering a bar
4 West Indian sorcery
5 Prepare, as a side of beans
6 Beantown, on scoreboards
7 Durham sch.
8 Half of doce
9 Energy
10 Singer India ___
11 ___ this world
12 Nutrition drink brand
13 Belief
14 Up to one's ears (in)
15 Cuban patriot José
16 Go around
17 Beachwear
18 "Zounds," e.g.
19 Antiquity, quaintly
20 Denials
26 "This is where ___"
28 Alternative fuel
31 Halfhearted
34 Go bad
35 Red hair, e.g.
37 Arabian capital
38 Fairy-tale menace
39 G.P.A. spoilers
40 Mtn. stats
41 Trevi coin, once
42 Month after Ab
44 Friends
45 Not on the border
46 Poetic break: Var.
50 Sitting on
51 Tapas bar offering
53 Writer Sontag
55 Big spinner
56 Here, in Juárez
57 Camera inits.
60 Aligned
61 Main seating area
62 Namely
67 Perfect
69 N.C. State plays in it
70 Denny's alternative
72 Oklahoma city
73 Steinbeck's "To ___ Unknown"
74 Angry talk
75 Really, really
76 Physicist Niels
77 "Dies ___"
79 Arrived quietly
80 ". . . ___ great fall"
82 Exactly, after "to"
83 Parlor piece
84 Gridiron protection
86 Wasted gas
87 Inventor's place
90 Group of spies
91 Kind of check
92 Hundred Acre Wood donkey
97 Winter Olympics venues
99 It's raised on a farm
101 NASA homecoming
102 Tiny bite
103 "See ___ care!"
105 Two, in Lisbon
106 In many cases
108 Operatic Jenny
109 Early Nebraskan
110 Deli order
111 Old deferment classification
112 Beeper
113 Ticking off

by Victor Fleming

114 Pulled in
115 Poe's middle name
116 Surrealist Magritte
122 Reply to "No way!"
124 Old-style hangover remedy
126 League division
129 Mighty big
130 Swing wildly
131 Corner office and others
132 Gettysburg general under Lee
134 Household health hazard
135 Sportscast feature
138 Peevishness
139 TV's Swenson
140 Fashion's ___ von Furstenberg
142 "Here ___ . . ."
143 "Bus Stop" playwright
144 "Yikes!"
145 "___ on Melancholy"
146 Swe. abutter
147 Ma'am or dam
149 K.C.-to-Duluth dir.
150 "___ the fields . . ."

CIRCLE OF FRIENDS

ACROSS

1 Rude awakening
5 Frequent abbr. on sheet music for folk songs
9 Compound number?
14 Without an out
19 1998 Andrea Bocelli operatic album
20 DeSoto or LaSalle
21 Concentration thwarter
22 Something that might be tucked under the chin
23 . . . and 25-Across have "canine" surnames
25 . . . and 41-Across sang with their siblings
27 Ignore the alarm
28 "With any luck"
30 Shamed
31 Save one's own neck, maybe
32 Poet with a seemingly self-contradictory name
33 Bundle of nerves
34 Barely perceptible
36 Reach a settlement
37 Healing aid patented in 1872
41 . . . and 52-Across are Mormons
43 Matches
44 No Westminster contender
45 Compass point suffix
46 Not at all certain
47 Contest that leads to a draw

48 Loyal pooch
49 Census stats
51 Agassi partner
52 . . . and 69-Across have affiliations with "Jeopardy!"
55 Museum employee
57 The King of Pop, in headlines
58 1980s–'90s N.B.A. star Danny
59 Belligerent deity
60 Branches
61 He reached his peak in 1806
62 "Everybody Loves Raymond" role
64 News exec Roger
65 Glockenspiels' kin
69 . . . and 80-Across have mythological creatures as surnames
71 Mmes., across the Pyrenees
72 Symbol in el zodiaco
73 "Zip-__-Doo-Dah"
74 Have an in (with)
75 Stimulate
76 Kia model
77 "Didn't I tell you?!"
78 Faith in music
80 . . . and 99-Across starred in musicals and share their first names with a classic sitcom couple
84 Comment following a lucky guess
86 Pin site
87 Slippery as __

88 Taking care of the situation
89 France's Oscar
90 "The Most Happy Fella" song
91 Bailiwick of TV's Matlock
94 Country with a palm tree on its flag
95 Sophocles subject
99 . . . and 101-Across are known for their fancy footwork
101 . . . and 23-Across are Olympic gold medalists
103 Clan symbol
104 Makes
105 Xena's horse
106 Absence
107 Talked a blue streak?
108 Showed courage, old-style
109 In case
110 Caustic chemicals

DOWN

1 Fixes
2 Exam format
3 Erstwhile denaro
4 Cons
5 Access
6 Contrite
7 Long-distance letters
8 Exhibiting Ennui
9 Had fun with
10 Rogaine alternative
11 Cheryl of "Curb Your Enthusiasm"
12 Tongue's end?
13 Not totally disastrous
14 Flies

15 Strands in the winter?
16 This and that
17 Sheltered
18 Sale locale
24 Like hedgehogs
26 Bigger than big
29 Keratoid
34 Make a name for oneself?
35 Queen __ County, Md.
36 Elizabeth Taylor's pet charity, for short
37 Mission __, Calif.
38 Hockey infraction
39 Wink accompaniment
40 Asteroid discovered in 1898
41 Pricey
42 Donkeys, to mules
43 Discards
47 Casino supply
48 Police epithet, with "the"
50 Make fast
51 "The Female Eunuch" author
52 Singer/actress Akers
53 Performs perfectly
54 Puma rival
56 Before markdown: Abbr.
57 Half of Brangelina
60 Grant money?
61 Masterpiece
62 Jilted wife of myth
63 Staggering
64 "Is that __?"
65 Truculent
66 Leader of the Mel-Tones
67 Typeface akin to Helvetica

by Henry Hook

68 Expeditiously
69 Like il but not elle: Abbr.
70 Sore
71 Round all around
75 March honoree, familiarly
78 George Eliot, e.g.
79 Uses a Moviola, in film-making
80 Showing the least resistance
81 Close-fitting garment
82 Georgia of "The Mary Tyler Moore Show"
83 Erythrocyte
85 U.P.S. staffer, at times
86 Memorizes
89 Cicada sound
90 Baffin Bay sights
91 P.M. periods
92 Think way back?
93 Actor Jared
96 Bob of the P.G.A.
97 It may be served in a bed
98 Shows curiosity
100 Sports org. for nonprofessionals
102 "Chances __"

ACROSS

1 Tribe with a sun dance
6 Periods in contrast to global warming
13 Cuff
17 Rise and fall, as a ship
18 Team supporter's suction cup–mounted sign
19 Regardful
20 Where smart shoppers shop?
23 Ad ___
24 Lodges
25 Fake-out
26 Short-order cook's aid
27 A person doing a duck walk grasps these
29 Site of Napoleon's invasion of 1798–1801
31 Place for fish and ships
32 Tell
33 "___ me!"
34 Plight of an overcrowded orchestra?
38 Cat, at times
40 Computer file name extension
41 Camera inits.
42 Kind of sch.
43 Crew
46 Fit for dwelling
51 Blushing
52 Introduction to opera?
54 Epitome of blackness
55 Oodles
57 Frustrated
58 Gaynor of "South Pacific"
59 Common origami creations
61 Sought sanctuary, old-style
63 ___ "Inferno"
64 Lilylike plant
65 Actress Shire and others
66 Insider talk
67 Not exceeding
68 Locale of Hoosier beaches?
71 Bub
74 Leaving, slangily
76 Virus variety
77 "Essays of ___"
78 Bow
79 "___ now!"
81 Yes-men, maybe?
83 Bit of winter exercise?
89 Italian librettist Gaetano ___
90 Abbr. after many a military title
91 Match
92 Annual announcement from 13-Down
93 "Drink to me only with thine eyes" poet
94 Burmese gathering?
97 "Ciao"
98 Carolina university
100 Dog with a tightly curled tail
101 Geraldo rehearses his show?
105 Much-counterfeited timepiece
106 More run-down
107 Traction provider
108 ___ empty stomach
109 Mugs
110 Hopper of Hollywood

DOWN

1 Dish for an Italian racing champ?
2 Stimpy's TV pal
3 Most like a breeze
4 Dame Edith who was nominated for three Oscars
5 In stitches
6 "___ tree falls . . ."
7 Stephen King's first novel
8 Last
9 "Far out!"
10 Show fixation, maybe
11 Stowe girl
12 Composer Prokofiev
13 See 92-Across: Abbr.
14 French Bluebeard
15 Cultural/teaching facility
16 Una ___ (old coin words)
19 Calais confidant
20 Item on a chain, usually
21 Steers clear of
22 Passage
23 Nautical rope
28 Former Irish P.M. ___ Cosgrave
30 Québec traffic sign
31 Stole
34 ___ hammer (Viking symbol)
35 Show slight relief, maybe
36 Computer key
37 Kind of paper
39 Whoops
44 Basket material
45 Iowa and Missouri
47 A club, e.g.
48 Sandwich that can never be finished?
49 Be a couch potato
50 "___ Coming" (1969 hit)
52 Tiny annoyance
53 Gouges repeatedly
56 Overall
58 Jazz's Herbie
59 Thick-bodied fish
60 Cowboy's aid
61 Send out
62 Denver's ___ Gardens amusement park
63 Photographer Arbus
65 "Star Trek: ___"
66 German camera
68 Canine neighbor
69 Words often applied to 93-Across
70 Hen, at times
72 Freshens
73 Cover
75 Bug
77 School named in the Public Schools Act of 1868

by Charles M. Deber

80 Many urban dwellers
82 Like electrical plugs
83 Hall of Fame jockey Eddie
84 Become tiresome to
85 Loser at the Battle of Châlons, A.D. 451
86 Birthplace of Aaron Burr
87 "Happy Days" role
88 Lessener
93 Eponymous physicist
95 1932 skiing gold medalist Utterström
96 Bit of spelling?
97 King ___ tomb
99 ___ Lomond
102 Historic Heyerdahl craft
103 Prof.'s posting
104 Fooled

TWO TIMES THREE*

ACROSS

1 Like windows and geishas
7 Subject of a David McCullough political biography
12 Copper head?
15 Staying power
19 Chevy introduced in 1958
20 Time's 1977 Man of the Year
21 Strong draft horses
23 *What someone who looks at Medusa does
25 Act of putting into circulation
26 Private line
27 "___-La-La" (Al Green hit)
28 "A Lonely Rage" autobiographer
30 "Star Trek" series, to fans
31 Laws, informally
32 *1850 American literature classic
37 From ___ Z
39 Suffix with convention
40 Faulkner hero
41 Shakespearean question after "How now!"
42 *Demonstrate the method
48 Staying power?
50 Bus. card abbr.
51 Your highness?: Abbr.
52 ___-mo
53 Stuffs
54 Area of authority
56 It has gutters on each side
59 "The Lord of the Rings" creature
61 Mary of "Where Eagles Dare"
62 Cost of time or space
63 Without a break
65 Succeed
69 Agnus ___ (Mass prayers)
70 *Push aside
73 TV's "___-Team"
75 Meets, as a challenge
78 Kind of patch
79 Received, as a message
80 Eydie Gorme's "___ Es el Amor"
81 Hair-raising cry
84 Boxer Trinidad
85 Becker on "L.A. Law"
86 Verve
88 Run down
90 ___ 88
92 State with the fewest counties (three): Abbr.
93 John who hosted TV's "Talk Soup"
94 *Walk in the park, say
98 "Wouldn't ___ Loverly?"
99 House calls?
101 Battery size
102 High-school dept.
103 *Put at bay
108 Appointees confirmed by Cong.
112 Did not go fast?
113 Film noir, e.g.
114 ___ Schwarz
115 "Well, look ___!"
116 "Hamlet" setting
119 *Miami baseball list
122 British composer Robert
123 Have ___ in mind
124 Gertrude who swam the English Channel
125 Not included: Abbr.
126 9-1-1 grp.
127 Percolates
128 They may be light or free

DOWN

1 Relative of a mandolin
2 Tickle
3 Cutting
4 It goes back and forth in a workshop
5 Further
6 "Gimme ___!"
7 "Steady ___ goes"
8 Computer input
9 Big flap
10 Victorian roofs
11 Leather source
12 McMurry University site
13 Lays siege to
14 Mass transit choices
15 *Toothless South American animal
16 Seemed right
17 Money rival
18 Bisected fly?
22 "___ Nacht" (German words of parting)
24 Kyrgyzstan city
29 Support group
32 Diligent student, in slang
33 These: Fr.
34 Eases off
35 Head set
36 MapQuest request: Abbr.
38 English class assignment
42 Pricey strings
43 Attentive one
44 Sainted king called "the Stout"
45 Defeatees' comment
46 Son of Cedric the Saxon
47 Word of encouragement
49 Banjo-picker Scruggs
55 *Not so important
57 Opposite of paleo-
58 P.O. item
60 Place for a star
64 Girl in a gown
66 "Misty" composer Garner
67 "___ the Magician" (old radio series)
68 More chilling
71 Table scrap
72 Sundial hour
74 Gustav Klimt's "Portrait of ___ Bloch-Bauer I"
76 Start of Idaho's motto
77 Woody's partner
79 Sets upon
82 Kinetoscope inventor
83 Mrs. Doonesbury, in the comics
86 "___ life!"
87 Fair-minded
89 Modern and technologically advanced
91 Pricey
93 Smart
94 Lush fabrics
95 ___-tzu

by Jim Page

96 Deerstalker fold-down
97 "Boston Legal" Emmy winner
100 Memory trace
104 Oversee
105 1980s major-league slugger Tony
106 Accomplishes perfectly, as a dismount
107 Lot of time
109 Fort ___, Fla.
110 Synthetic gem
111 Film extras, for short
115 Page, for one
116 Conductor ___-Pekka Salonen
117 Old Ford
118 East End abode
120 Fish eggs
121 Pentateuch book: Abbr

ACROSS

1 Trick-taking card game
5 Yemeni port famous as a source of coffee
10 Former Connecticut governor Ella
16 Take in
21 Swenson of "Benson"
22 Saw
23 Comparatively flush
24 "No men allowed" area
25 Ambiguous headline about a man charged with killing his attacker?
29 Mystic
30 Level of care
31 Connected, in a way
32 Bright-eyed
35 Santa ___
36 Earth Day subj.
38 Retired boomer
39 Ambiguous headline about a protest?
48 Gone by
49 Parcel
50 Company with the slogan "born from jets"
51 Field protector
52 Sandwich rank
54 Take ___ breath
56 Hang over
59 "What ___?"
63 Ambiguous headline about school closings?
69 Oil-rich ruler
70 Dutch painter Jan
71 Hair-raiser
72 Fall setting
73 Was contrite
76 Break
78 Field stars
80 Early hrs.

81 Ambiguous headline about a California drug bust?
87 Rocky peak
88 One with a thick skin
89 ". . . ___ saw Elba"
90 Actress Sedgwick
91 JFK-to-TLV option
93 Peter and Paul, but not Mary
95 Sugar cube holder
98 Rating of a program blocked by a V-chip
101 Ambiguous headline about a vagrancy statistic?
106 Moonshine
107 Progress smoothly
108 Broom ___ (comics witch)
109 "___ & Stitch," 2002 animated film
111 Encouraging sounds
114 Cozy corner
117 Country singer Carter
119 McKellen of "The Lord of the Rings"
120 Ambiguous headline about attorneys' pro bono work?
125 Do-do connector
127 Jump in the rink
128 "___ of Destruction," 1965 protest song
129 Actor Morales
130 Words said with raised arm and glass
133 Word for word
138 Huge
142 Ambiguous headline about a stolen Stradivarius?
146 Kind of chin
147 Vast
148 Heavy metal bar

149 Like the rim of an eyecup
150 Earthenware pots
151 Kind of valve
152 Wild guesses
153 It's not held when it's used

DOWN

1 Sets (on)
2 In the ___
3 It'll douse a fuego
4 Frequent congestion site
5 "Welcome" offerer
6 Kitchen gadget company
7 Big name in credit cards
8 Blast maker
9 "The Bonesetter's Daughter" author
10 1983 U.S. invasion site
11 Narrow inlets
12 Dramatic opening
13 Quake
14 One of New York's Finger Lakes
15 E-mail address ender
16 Place for a guard, in soccer
17 Shaker formula
18 Word with scam or sketch
19 Means of control
20 Irish patriot hanged in 1803
26 Close
27 Elaine ___ ("Seinfeld" role)
28 One end of the Moscow Canal
33 Longtime staple of daytime TV
34 Popular air freshener
37 Dated
39 West of Hollywood
40 Playing marble
41 Composer Ned

42 Their service is impeccable
43 Mushroom cloud creator, briefly
44 Columbo portrayer
45 Duo in a typical symphony
46 Exhort
47 Sudden increase on a graph
53 Scottish estate owner
55 Prefix with dactyl
57 Muppet who lives in a trash can
58 Mazda model
60 "Myra Breckinridge" novelist
61 Abnormal plant swelling
62 Info that may be phished: Abbr.
64 Trounce
65 "Still Me" autobiographer Christopher
66 Some magazine ads
67 Schlock
68 In need of a washer, perhaps
74 Head of costume design
75 Lush
77 Palm readers?
79 Gaiety
81 Manuscript sheet
82 Muse with a wreath of myrtle and roses
83 Makes unwanted overtures?
84 Jazz pianist Chick
85 Breeze
86 Maritime
87 High-___
92 Sock fiber
94 Definitely no arm-twister
96 Father Sarducci of old "S.N.L."
97 Fifth-century pope

by Seth A. Abel

99 11th-century year
100 Company with a "spokesduck"
102 Newsman Bernard
103 "The Time Machine" race
104 "Do ___?"
105 Grannies
110 It's next to nothing
112 "Grand" hotel

113 Reason for a 98-Across
115 Not neat
116 N.F.L. running back Barlow
118 Rhett Butler's last words
120 Choo-choo name
121 Trust
122 Most cunning

123 Hip locale
124 MTV's owner
125 Transmission repair franchise
126 Silver quarters?
131 Film brand
132 Numismatists' goals
134 Author Janowitz
135 Composer Satie

136 It might get the brush-off
137 Home stretches?
139 Joe
140 Anthem starter
141 Move, in Realtor lingo
143 Poli ___
144 High ball?
145 "___ true"

ACROSS

1 Lhasa ___
5 Breathing tube
12 Old cracker brand
16 Back on board
19 Pfizer product used before brushing the teeth
20 Tony winner Mike
21 Reason to shout "Eureka!"
22 Language along the Mekong River
23 Play about tenderizing meat with one's toes?
26 Beast with a bugling call
27 Patronize, as a hotel
28 "Let's Make a Deal" choice
29 Red spot on the skin
31 Drama about a butcher who sells deer meat?
37 ___ de Cologne
38 Honoree's spot
39 Gullets
40 Musical play set at McDonald's?
49 Dangerous place to pass a car
50 Pole, e.g.
51 Even
52 Actress Barbara Bel ___
54 In love
55 Blast
56 Windsor princess
58 Muppets' creator
59 Musical drama that tells the tale of a sausage casing?

61 Hat trick component
63 Ring holder
64 Musical drama about a man eating soup?
72 Mulling spice
78 Many baseball card stats
79 What you may call it
80 Business with net gains?
81 Tighten, say, as strings
82 1962 hit film whose climax is on Crab Key island
83 Conveys
84 Place in the pecking order
85 Play about a guy ordering beef from Dublin?
88 Martini & Rossi offering
89 Little fellow
90 Despite this
91 Play about swine intestines that are semidivine?
101 Miner's major problem
102 White sheet
103 Person who has something going on?
105 Allen Ginsberg's "Plutonian ___"
106 Play about meat that's good to eat anytime?
112 Elbow-bender
113 Brand name with an accent on its last letter
114 Character in many a joke
115 B.A. or M.A. offerer

116 Retired number of Dodger Tommy Lasorda
117 Goblet part
118 Juvenal work
119 Pageantry

DOWN

1 "Be on the lookout" messages, briefly
2 Oliver of "The West Wing"
3 "The Terminator" heroine
4 Common daisy
5 U.S. bond market purchase
6 Kia subcompact
7 Stage entertainment
8 N.L. and A.L. city
9 Passport maker
10 Mr. ___, scheming vicar in "Emma"
11 Take ___ at
12 Stylin'
13 Swearing-in phrase
14 Deity credited with inventing the lyre
15 Like Hoosier cabinets
16 Composer Scarlatti
17 Popular quarry for British hunters
18 Arcade game inserts
24 Relations: Abbr.
25 Worn away
30 Meant to attract
32 Possessed girl in "The Exorcist"
33 Town largely destroyed by the Battle of Normandy
34 "Ben-___"
35 Quite a ways

36 Using
40 Radio host John
41 "Dialogues Concerning Natural Religion" author
42 The Isle of Man's Port ___
43 Nonhuman co-hosts of TV's "Mystery Science Theater 3000"
44 Incumbent on
45 Attack once more
46 Sky light
47 Palette globs
48 Trapper's prize
49 Does a certain dog trick
52 Sickly-looking
53 Slovenly abode
55 Thermometer's terminus
56 Get stuck
57 Drink suffix
59 Fistfuls, say
60 Phaser setting
62 Missing broadcast channel
64 Scorecard heading
65 Dwarf
66 Compared with
67 Symbol of hardness
68 Talk, talk, talk: Var.
69 Memo header
70 Steinway & ___ (piano maker)
71 What, to Watteau
73 Five-Year Plan implementer, for short
74 "The Cosby Show" kid
75 Badlands landform
76 Bow-wielding deity
77 "Peer ___"

by Patrick Berry

80 Diets drastically
82 Go from endangered to extinct
83 Slapstick missiles
85 First name in Objectivism
86 Bibliophile's love: Abbr.
87 Grain susceptible to ergot
88 Buttonhole
89 W.W. I helmet, informally
92 Inventive sorts?
93 Line at the dentist's office?
94 Main line
95 Sprung
96 Some mantel pieces
97 Mens ___
98 Get fuel
99 University of Maine's home
100 Shade of blue
104 Get back to
107 Gray
108 Closemouthed
109 Hula dancer's accessory
110 Common pg. size
111 "Didn't I tell you?"

ACROSS

1 Key of Beethoven's "Für Elise"
7 Some trigonometric ratios
14 Sarcastic comment of sympathy
20 "Dr. Strangelove," e.g.
21 Parsnip, e.g.
22 Bewitched
23 Charles Schwab?
25 Service group
26 Cows
27 Vehicle on 30-Across
29 "This means business" look
30 See 27-Across
31 Annie Oakley?
34 Title girl in a 1962 Roy Orbison hit
37 ___ voce (quietly)
40 Others, to Pedro
41 Assimilate
44 Southwest chips-and-chili snacks
46 Viking landing site
50 Leonardo da Vinci?
52 Like one end of a battery terminal
54 "We the Living" author Rand
55 Equine
56 It has five pillars
60 Saffron's mom on "Ab Fab"
61 "My dear lady"
62 Place that's all abuzz
63 Sordid
64 Sigmund Freud?
69 Tiger Woods?
71 Rectify
72 Dish eaten with chopsticks
74 "___ would seem"
75 George Bush or Dick Cheney, once
76 Continental boundary
77 Easter Island is a province of it
79 It needs refining
82 Author/journalist Fallaci
84 Benjamin Franklin?
87 Illustrations: Abbr.
88 Cutting humor
92 "Lord Jim" star, 1965
93 Disney subsidiary
94 Gleans
96 Contemptuous expression
97 Bill Gates?
102 Seed cover
105 Cartoon mermaid
106 Construction company
107 Just make out
112 Bedtime for junior, maybe
114 Babe Ruth?
117 Country singer West
118 Nutty
119 Stranded by winter weather, perhaps
120 Initial stages
121 Sees about
122 Zeus' domain, in myth

DOWN

1 Second: Abbr.
2 SAT section
3 "Like ___ not . . ."
4 Court encouragement
5 Like Mork of "Mork & Mindy"
6 Front of a manuscript leaf
7 Smith who won the 1972 Wimbledon
8 Stirrup sites
9 Cruncher of nos.
10 Pendulum's path
11 Wrong
12 Skater's leap
13 Overlapping fugue motifs
14 See or call
15 Where hens sit
16 Grad school grillings
17 Starts in on
18 "Idomeneo," e.g.
19 Ursine : bear :: lutrine : ___
24 Chops
28 Awful
31 Mix up
32 Tout's offering
33 Pioneer org.
34 Eastern title
35 Silent auction site
36 Part of N.A.A.C.P.: Abbr.
38 Wastes
39 TV dinner holder
42 Set after melting
43 Panoramic
45 Legendary Gaelic poet
46 Classic flivver
47 Something to bid
48 Billboard chart category
49 Leaves rolling in the aisles
51 Faux gold
53 Agnostic
57 Ontario or Supérieur
58 "Chances ___"
59 Common muscle protein
61 Pokémon and the Beatles, once
62 Nutritionist Davis
64 ___ the dinosaur (extinction)
65 Japanese porcelain
66 1983 Woody Allen mockumentary
67 Backing
68 The Monkees' "___ Believer"
70 Shakespearean compilation
73 San ___, Argentina
77 Pet plant
78 Web address lead-in
79 Radio letter between Nan and Peter
80 Three strikes and you're out, e.g.
81 Hungarian spa town
83 "This won't hurt ___"
85 Tony-winning actress Verdon
86 "Leave It to Beaver" catchphrase
89 Skater's leap
90 Welsh cheese dish
91 Army outfit
93 Sermon site
95 Cutty ___ (clipper ship)
97 "No prob!"
98 Rigel's constellation
99 Breath fresheners
100 Quarterback Rodney
101 ___ Quinn, formerly of "S.N.L."

by Kelsey Blakley

13

ACROSS

1 Cause for a massage
5 K.G.B. predecessor
9 Crookspeak
14 Blog comments
19 Crony
20 Look
21 Risibility
22 Poet who wrote "Immature poets imitate; mature poets steal"
23 Tax relief, e.g.
26 Churchillian trademark
27 Chapter
28 Lies
29 Subject of a Boito opera
31 "Down ___" (Janis Joplin song)
32 Be too tight
34 Doc's wife in "Come Back, Little Sheba"
35 Timeline breaks
37 December laughs
38 "___ the morning!"
39 Mary Shelley subtitle, with "The"
44 Moved purposefully
46 Windsurfers' mecca
47 Using one's shirtsleeve as a napkin, e.g.
48 Big letter
52 Free, in a way
55 "Fish Magic" and "Twittering Machine"
56 Fig. in TV's "Third Watch"
58 TV star who directed the 1999 documentary "Barenaked in America"
61 Thingumbob
63 Consume piggishly
64 Piggy
65 Lhasa ___
69 "The End of the Affair" author, 1951
71 Miracle-___
72 "___ Crazy" (1977 Paul Davis hit)
74 Car body strengtheners
76 Answers, for short
77 Sot spot
79 Stately old dance
82 Father of Henry II
83 Fall event, usually
87 Doc bloc: Abbr.
88 Palatable
91 Live in the past?
92 World's biggest city built on continuous permafrost
94 Priority system
96 Short notes
98 Branch of Islam
101 Matter of W.W. II secrecy
107 Mindful of
108 Special ___
109 Rank and file
110 Dudley Do-Right's love
111 Permanently
112 CAT scan units
114 Cheese ___
116 Transverse rafter-joining timber
118 Reading and others: Abbr.
119 Comment made while crossing the fingers
121 Serigraph
124 Skyscraper
125 Batch of Brownies
126 Back then, back when
127 Bleu hue
128 ___ cards (ESP testers)
129 They're the pits
130 Short ways to go?
131 "The Mysterious Island" captain

DOWN

1 Countenances
2 Early racer
3 Contortionist
4 Ottoman, e.g.: Abbr.
5 Jump over
6 "Just a ___" (Marlene Dietrich's last film)
7 1914 Booth Tarkington novel
8 Disentangle
9 "Under the Pink" singer Tori
10 Circular edge
11 Put on a happy face
12 Lake that James Fenimore Cooper called Glimmerglass
13 First sign
14 Lifter's rippler
15 Salmagundi
16 Words of endorsement
17 Robert Burns poem
18 Italicizes, e.g.
24 Burning issue
25 Give up on détente
30 Barrel org.
33 It's for the birds
36 Stir up
39 Broad terrace with a steep side
40 World's smallest island nation
41 Castigatory
42 Fully ready
43 Flag raiser
45 Côte d'Or's capital
49 Chinese philosopher Chuang-___
50 Nonmechanized weapon
51 Boeing worker: Abbr.
53 European Union member since 2004
54 Car that "beats the gassers and the rail jobs" in a 1964 hit
56 Adam and Eve, at a diner
57 "Harlequin's Carnival" painter
59 Initial sounds of a relief effort?
60 Good name for a minimalist?
62 Handel oratorio
66 Russian literary award established in 1881
67 Glass bottom
68 Where the Storting sits
70 energystar.gov grp.
73 Slightly tainted
75 Bridge supports
78 Alternative to the euro: Abbr.
80 Pianist Rubinstein
81 Hair-raising cry
84 Mystery award
85 Kurt denial?
86 Sign of neglect

by Bob Klahn

88 Swiss resort with the Cresta Run
89 Ally of the Cheyenne
90 Gets to commit
93 Capital of Valais canton
95 Where Huxley taught Orwell

97 Kind of barrier
99 It sticks to the ribs
100 The whale in "Pinocchio"
102 New wrinkles
103 Reach for the stars
104 Vocal opponent

105 Second-highest mountain in the lower 48 states
106 Q player in "Die Another Day"
111 Devilkin
113 Admiral who went down with the Scharnhorst

115 ___-eyed
116 Recipe measures: Abbr.
117 Social workers
120 Muff
122 Sent sprawling
123 Turned yellow, maybe

ACROSS

1 Smears
7 Fells
11 Looks for help
15 1954 sci-fi movie with an exclamation point in its title
19 Arctic wear
20 "Il mio tesoro," e.g.
21 1980s fad item
22 Blood: Prefix
23 Yosemite Sam's cursing of Bugs Bunny's food?
25 That's a lot to do
27 Then preceder
28 Explanation for why some pillows do weird things?
30 Domingo, e.g.
31 Wash (out)
33 Photo lab abbr.
34 "Stupid," in Spanish(!)
35 Armpit, to a doctor
37 Oscar winner Helen
39 Psychiatrist's scheduling
41 Theological schools: Abbr.
43 Part of baking powder
46 Letters from Atlanta
47 Basic food choice?
55 Noontime service
56 Handi-Wrap alternative
57 Flavor tasted in some wine
58 Frees
62 [Knock], in poker
64 Mile-high world capital
66 Be the 4 in a 5-4 decision
67 Natl. Safe Toys and Gifts Mo.
68 Short-term worker who causes utter disaster?
73 Jackie's "O"
74 They're beside sides
76 Boat propeller
77 Singer K. T. ___
79 Walnut and others
80 Kind of tape
83 "Livin' on ___ time" (lyric in a #1 Don Williams country hit)
85 Lineman's datum
86 Jazz-loving young entomologist?
90 Bon ___
93 Imp
94 Slew
95 Precipitately
98 Artificial, in a way
102 Has-been
106 Puffball seed
107 Draft pick?
109 Puts up
111 ___ nuevo
112 Meal for the Three Little Pigs?
116 Lola, e.g., in "Damn Yankees"
117 Intrinsically
118 Work on analytical psychology?
121 Czech composer Janácek
122 Stretched out
123 Sports Illustrated 1998 co-Sportsman of the Year
124 Brown shade
125 Sea eagle
126 Abbr. at the bottom of a business letter
127 Too-too
128 "Ready to go?"

DOWN

1 Too-too
2 Stuck
3 Stuntwork?
4 As a result
5 Varnish ingredient
6 Some Jamaican music
7 Early casino proprietor
8 Beethoven's Third
9 Occult
10 N. Dak. neighbor
11 Do something about
12 Cover for a grandmother
13 Hot spot
14 Put (away)
15 "___ Company"
16 Pleasure-filled
17 Boston college
18 "Gilligan's Island" castaway
24 Way to go: Abbr.
26 ___ law
29 Car famous for its 1950s tailfins
31 Ran
32 "Falcon Crest" co-star
36 Measurers of logical reasoning, for short
38 Ballpark fig.
39 "How ya doin'?"
40 Designer Pucci
42 Winds
44 Narc's agcy.
45 Bug
47 "P.S. I Love You" and "Revolution," e.g.
48 "Be saved!"
49 Bet to win and place
50 "Darn it all!"
51 Naïf
52 Coin word
53 ___ girl
54 Floors
59 Experimental underwater habitat
60 "Lucia di Lammermoor" baritone
61 Like Limburger cheese
63 Position that's an anagram, appropriately, of "notes"
65 Providers of cuts
66 Water seeker
69 Announcer's call after three strikes
70 Numerical prefix
71 Dance seen on TV's "Hullabaloo"
72 Hello ___, shop frequently seen on Letterman
75 Tease
78 Certain NCO's
80 1953 Wimbledon winner Seixas
81 Small chuckle
82 Ran through, as a card
84 Rearward, at sea
87 College sr.'s test
88 1980's "Double Fantasy" collaborator
89 They're encountered in "close encounters"

by Tony Orbach and Patrick Blindauer

90 Lose in one's drawers
91 Not oral
92 James who wrote "Rule, Britannia"
96 Melodic
97 "Note to ___ . . ."
99 Portuguese Mister
100 Swiss-American composer Bloch
101 Record keeper?
103 They do dos
104 Chant
105 Ogle
107 Stuffy spot
108 Rhone's capital
110 French wine classification
113 Site of Beinecke Library
114 Digitize, maybe
115 "___ girl!"
116 Biblical brother
119 Intelligence grp.
120 Poet/musician ___ Scott-Heron

ACROSS

1 Dogs named for a region of Japan
7 Wrapped up
12 Jazz great Malone
16 Symbol for density
19 Dramatist Ibsen
20 Mrs. Gorbachev
21 Start a pot going
22 Ref. work with online subscriptions
23 Wall Street worker
26 Clavell's "___-Pan"
27 Sort of
28 Select
29 Party's nominees
31 Wasps' home
32 Catch in the West
34 Stretch out
38 Terre's counterpart
39 Broadway's "The Producers," e.g.
43 Some acids
47 Like wicker furniture
48 "The Matrix" lead role
49 Carpet choice
50 They might come back to haunt you
53 Blu-ray players, e.g.
54 Does dictation, maybe
55 Short pans
56 Island in the Aegean
57 Great Society agcy.
58 Game played with a ½- to ¾-inch ball
60 Kind of approval
61 One of the Trumps
64 Sotheby's domain
65 Alternative title for this puzzle
69 Elevs.
71 Put over high heat
73 High degree
74 Car that won the 1939 and '40 Indy 500
76 Might
77 Head honcho
78 Yemen's capital
80 Polynesian carvings
81 More than enjoyed
84 Appetizers served with sauce
87 Prosperousness
88 Subj. of many conspiracy theories
89 Symbol on a 6 key
90 "You sure got that right!"
91 It might go in a tank
94 Put one by
95 Political prisoner, e.g.
96 One way to be taken
98 Speaking spot
102 Language from which lemon and julep come
103 In ___ rush
106 Like beaches
108 Singer DiFranco
109 Elizabeth Dole once led it
114 Word with pack or pick
115 Israir alternative
116 Tempter
117 Pick of the litter
118 The, abroad
119 10-year prison sentence, in gang slang
120 ___ coil
121 Time out?

DOWN

1 Play co-authored by Mark Twain
2 City ENE of Brattleboro
3 Tawantinsuyu dwellers
4 Money you can't touch?
5 Frigid finish?
6 Like some hot dogs
7 Indians known as the Cat People
8 Refusal, in Renfrew
9 Coupon offerings
10 Mess of pottage buyer
11 Frontier name, for short
12 ___ Kan pet food
13 "___ takers?"
14 Some linemen: Abbr.
15 "C'mon!"
16 Gradually substitute
17 One way to argue
18 Comics canine
24 Early 1900s ruler
25 1960s British P.M. ___ Douglas-Home
30 Send up or put down
33 Overhead
35 Brings in
36 Plaza de toros sounds
37 It's below grade one: Abbr.
38 Cheese place
40 Finalize, with "up"
41 1966 Broadway hit with the song "My Cup Runneth Over"
42 "O.K."
43 Broadcast worker's union
44 Coolidge, Cleveland and Andrew Johnson, once
45 Ascribe
46 "O Sanctissima," e.g.
47 Not free
51 Strummed an old string instrument
52 Engine sound
53 Stinging jellyfish
57 Sheep's genus
59 "___ Say," 1939 #1 Artie Shaw hit
60 Co. with a Mercury logo
61 10-Down's father
62 Casual dress
63 Historic role played by Jack Palance and Anthony Quinn
66 Phone button
67 Superior
68 "___ Rappaport"
70 Playground taunt
72 Charms
75 Yemen's capital
77 Rub the wrong way
78 Some farm machinery
79 Sharp
81 "How cute!"

by Eric Berlin

82 Afternoon event
83 Cafes
84 Priory of ___, group in "The Da Vinci Code"
85 "Whoo-ee!"
86 Starts

88 Letters before a colon, on TV
92 Burst in on
93 Mar, in a way
94 Prefix with phobia
97 Prudential competitor
98 Steak ___

99 Parisian priests
100 "___ My Heart in Monterey" (1927 hit)
101 Perfect Sleeper maker
102 Wash out
104 ___ Helens

105 Gaston's girlfriend
107 Sixth-century year
110 Film director Roth
111 Actress Grier
112 Ginger ___
113 First word of Dante's "Inferno"

ACROSS

1 Suction devices
11 Pepper-upper
20 Knocked out
21 Many an Alessandro Scarlatti work
22 Cause of some baseball errors?
23 Texas ballplayer?
24 Modern organizer, for short
25 Castaway's call
26 Supported
27 Schmo
28 Just watched
30 Times of day, in classifieds
32 Kobe Bryant, e.g.
36 Bewhiskered fish lover
37 Where "Aida" premiered
39 Plane's N.Y.C. destination, maybe
40 "I see," kiddingly
41 Soldier's fare, briefly
42 1988 Best Picture, with the repeated line "I'm an excellent driver"
44 1980s Geena Davis sitcom
46 "The Race __" (1965 hit)
48 Dweller along the Danube
50 Hägar creator Browne
51 More decayed
53 Hamburger's article
54 Gold standards
56 Gland: Prefix
58 Going according to plan
60 Crystal __
61 Mrs., in Peru
62 Suffix with pamphlet
64 In myth, her tears created the morning dew
65 Nelson Rockefeller was its gov.
66 Commoners
69 Classic Abbott and Costello bit
72 "__ precaution . . ."
75 Round Table title
76 Shot spot
78 Unenthusiastic reviews
79 Beginning drawing class
82 "No way, no how!"
85 Turn
87 Cold-shoulders
89 "Blondie" tyke
90 Place for some bling-bling
92 Venusians, e.g.
94 Formula for "S"
95 Iron alternative
96 Lid irritation
97 Makes war
100 Sound from the rafters
101 Painter's subject
103 Suffix with morph-
104 Glassware ovens
105 "If you __ . . ."
107 Pin holder
109 Some police officers: Abbr.
110 Beat badly
111 Sample
112 "Get out of here!"
113 Shade of blue
115 Florida senator Martinez
116 Diamond border?
121 Complaint about a baseball playing area?
125 Longish stories
126 It can be a relief
127 Haunts
128 Not yet ready to be deposited

DOWN

1 W.W. I military grp.
2 Racecar-generated air current
3 Temporary residence
4 White Rabbit's cry
5 Purge
6 On tenterhooks
7 South Seas staple
8 1970s N.F.L.'er Armstrong
9 Sales __
10 '60s radical grp.
11 W.W. I French fighter plane
12 Thrice, in prescriptions
13 Get to
14 Actress Gibbs
15 Scream for the Dream Team
16 More protracted
17 Neighbor of Bol.
18 Never, to Nietzsche
19 Pothole patch
21 Unlocks, in verse
26 Peerless
29 "It's c-c-c-cold!"
30 Point
31 Part of a certain scorecard
32 Mystery writer Marsh
33 Lack of adornment
34 Hand out
35 Andy Hardy player, in 1930s–'40s film
36 Trans-Siberian Railroad city
37 LI doubled
38 Turkey heads can be found here
39 A hallucinogen
43 Show stoppers
45 Movie droid
47 Takes home
49 Precede the cleanup spot
52 MGM co-founder
55 "__ Eyes," 1969 Guess Who hit
57 Figures
59 "Piece of cake!"
61 Streaked
63 Perlman of "Cheers"
67 Web creations
68 So it follows that
70 Worrywart's words
71 New in theaters
72 Some
73 "Later"
74 British mail
77 Object of tornado destruction
80 Dash holders
81 Failed, as a pass
83 Awesome beauties
84 "I'm listening"
86 "John Brown's Body" poet
87 Atlanta-to-Miami dir.
88 Plant with dark purple berries

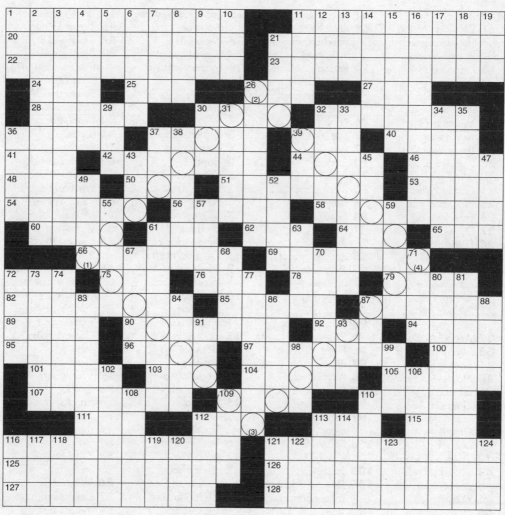

by Nancy Salomon and Bill Zais

(1) Third (2) Second (3) Home (4) First

ACROSS

1 Comfort
7 They're tapped in the woods
13 Cape Cod course
20 Transfer
21 Daddy Warbucks's henchman
22 Lowly digs
23 Remake about a red, white, and blue libido?
25 Now and then
26 Forklike
27 Dowel
28 Patriots' grp.
29 Rice-A-___
30 Boxer Marciano's given name
32 Remake about impiety during a storm?
37 Acapulco article
38 In position for a back massage
40 No dessert for dieters
41 Game co. that originated Dungeons & Dragons
42 Rhein residence
44 Pound sound
45 ___ soit qui mal y pense
46 ___ good turn
48 Ristorante suffix
51 Remake about a strip club?
55 Seepage collectors
57 Accept another tour of duty
58 Coll. hoops competition
59 Liberty
61 Time immemorial
64 Rib
66 It's cut and dried
67 To ___ (exactly)
68 Remake about a lecherous instructor?
74 Rodrigo ___ de Vivar (El Cid)
75 Diamond great Hodges
76 "Evil Woman" grp.
77 Pop singer Brickell
78 Claim
82 Stock page letters
84 Enter
87 Hold in the gym
88 Remake about a TV station/F.C.C. controversy?
93 Web address ending
94 What precedes 93-Across
96 Flight stats.
97 P
98 A lot of volume?
99 Union partner: Abbr.
101 Like a twice-used cigar
103 Following closely?
105 Fresh
106 Remake about a holy person's slip?
110 These, to Tomás
112 Wits' bits
113 Quick
114 Yale Bowl player
115 Seminal mainframe
117 Figures of speech?
119 Remake about a ribald watchman?
124 Pamper
125 Difficult
126 San ___ (Western mountains)
127 Represses
128 Night flight
129 Least interesting

DOWN

1 Part of R.S.V.P.
2 Tulsa sch.
3 It's not worth pursuing
4 Caper
5 Like some laundries
6 Feminine suffix
7 '70s sitcom producer
8 Actor Brian of "Juarez," 1939
9 President ousted in a 1955 coup
10 Buttered someone up big-time
11 PC key
12 Hot spot
13 Made
14 Come out of one's shell
15 Old Polo Grounds headliner
16 Fans' sounds
17 Japanese "thank you very much"
18 1983 Nicholas Gage book
19 Sticky stuff
24 Gather in a condensed layer
28 Tiny tunneler
30 Essen's basin
31 Transmitting
33 Just for laughs
34 Canonical hour
35 Lucky ones?
36 Much commerce nowadays
39 Arctic explorer John
43 Tight spots
45 Signal to start
47 Observed
49 "When hell freezes over!"
50 "Gotcha"
52 Familiar with
53 Many a Punjabi
54 Swinging London district
56 Rent
60 Olympic track great Johnson, familiarly
62 1998 Winter Olympics site
63 Clubs, e.g.
65 It won't run if it's fast
68 Floored, in a way?
69 Sense the unreal
70 Smooth
71 Trudges
72 Cadet's org.
73 Communicate silently
74 Great ___
79 Beckett's no-show
80 Toothbrush handle?
81 "This is on the level"
83 Wrist bones
85 "Whatever you want"
86 Where Hercules slew a lion
89 Where a whodunit is solved
90 Like gleaming shoes
91 Load
92 Leaves in stitches
95 Stumbles over
100 Marching together
102 Ballpark fig.
103 Zoo section
104 Counter creator
106 Logical Mr.
107 Atmospheres

by Elayne Cantor and Nancy Salomon

108 Cuban national hero
109 "Seascape" playwright
111 Yemeni neighbor
116 "___ Blue"
118 Scrubs sites, for short
119 Rocky top

120 Realm of Otto I: Abbr.
121 Slingshot's shape
122 Children's author/illustrator Asquith
123 What to spring to when springing ahead: Abbr.

ACROSS

1 Ancient Greece's Seven ___
6 Wrinkled melon
12 "Well, yeah!"
15 Doctrine
18 Team for which 1970 N.B.A. M.V.P. Willis Reed played
20 "Sense and Sensibility" sister
21 Axis, of a sort
23 Dire proof-of-purchase slip?
25 Annual celebration for a Catholic
26 Three-way joint
27 Complete circuit
28 What Dr. Frankenstein tried to do?
30 Not merely smoldering
32 ___ vivant
34 Jackie's second
35 Rep. of S. ___
36 Bored kayaker's movements?
43 Planned
44 Founder of General Electric
45 ___ Glue-All
49 Haughty mannerisms
50 Chilled garnish
52 Cut off
54 Battle of Hastings participant
55 Atlanta's ___ Center
56 Much-needed windfall?
60 Because of this
61 Unable to relax
62 Water bearer
63 Showing deep embarrassment
66 Water pipes
68 Less ripe
70 Old Germanic character
71 Tighten, as a corset, maybe
73 Drink in "Beowulf"
74 Like workers' salaries under a miserly boss?
79 Big prize on "The Price Is Right"
82 Portion of a flight
83 Roman sun god
84 Fleeting light
85 ___ of the Rock (Jerusalem shrine)
86 It's often put on paper
88 Missouri city
90 Actress Hayek
91 Hogwarts?
96 Nickname preceder
99 Theater sign
100 Just fine
101 Crown insets
102 Sharply focused Warsaw residents?
107 "Hellboy" star Perlman
108 Erwin of 1950s TV
111 One who's expected to deliver?
112 Clairvoyants' charges?
117 She plotted to kill Clytemnestra
118 Rugged mountain chain
119 All your work may go into it
120 H, to Hellenes
121 Datum sought by identity thieves: Abbr.
122 Rocky's girl
123 Writes a Dear John letter

DOWN

1 "Monty Python" segment
2 Queen Elizabeth's daughter
3 Care
4 Prefix with -cide
5 It takes up many chairs
6 Fortune subj.
7 Puppet show?
8 Grauman of Grauman's Chinese Theater
9 Consecrates
10 Big help
11 Shaw's "___ and the Man"
12 "The Good Shepherd" director, 2006
13 Dissimilar
14 Web programmer's medium
15 Sepoy Rebellion site
16 Wizard's prop
17 Gangster Lansky
19 Wolf (down)
22 Common sushi ingredient
24 Three-sided blade
29 Pitch
31 Cod pieces?
32 Shroud
33 In abeyance
36 Computer that originally came in "flavors"
37 Ja's opposite
38 Offering at a government auction
39 "Sayonara!"
40 Some government bonds
41 "Anything ___" (Woody Allen film)
42 Blotto
46 One who's done stretches?
47 Energize
48 Elvis impersonator's expression
50 Sweater material
51 Cream tea go-with
53 Significant degree?
56 Org. that requires schedules
57 Musical pitches
58 "I am the ___" (Beatles lyric)
59 Lease again
60 Retired professors
63 Like new bills
64 Make altogether
65 Atahualpa's people
66 Basque novelist Pío
67 Endangered wildcat
69 Fill up on
72 Aix-___-Bains
75 Poetic country name
76 White house
77 Creep furtively
78 "S.N.L." alum Fey
79 Structure finished during Titus' reign
80 Magazine's contents
81 Authentic
85 "The Witches" author
87 Potential Emmy nominees

by Patrick Berry

89 Egyptian coin
90 Medically examined via machine
92 Book printer's no-no
93 Talk sweetly
94 "Tank Girl" actress Petty
95 Something that helps you follow the game?
96 Singer Mann
97 Showed obeisance
98 Befogged
103 Exit-the-program button
104 Lice-to-be
105 "I'm Not ___," 1975 #1 country hit by Jessi Colter
106 Geraint's wife, in Arthurian legend
109 Per diem worker
110 A Swiss Army knife has lots of them
113 William Tell's birthplace
114 401(k) alternative
115 Like camel's hair
116 Home of the Seminoles: Abbr.

WORST PICKUP LINES

ACROSS

1 Ginger's friend on "Gilligan's Island"
8 Comic Kilborn and others
14 Lie on the beach
19 So-called "miracle plant"
21 Bag handler
22 Egyptian crosses
23 "Pardon me, are you from the Caribbean? Because . . ."
25 Catcher in the World Series' only perfect game
26 Humorist George
27 Better
28 Compass dir.
29 Hemingway's "___ Time"
30 "I know it's not my business, but if you were a laser . . ."
38 Coarse
39 Collins of '70s funk
40 Look (around)
42 First name in aviation
44 Middle mark
46 Letter-ending abbr.
47 Pres. Jefferson
48 "Say, is it hot in here . . . ?"
52 Key over Control
53 Free throw's path
54 Actor Cage, informally
55 Hip-shaking dance
59 ___ mind
60 N.B.A. coach George ___
62 Loser to R.M.N. in '68

64 Nobelist, e.g.
66 "Sorry to bother you, but do you work for NASA? Because . . ."
72 Dinosaur National Monument site
73 Dummkopf
74 Scottish refusals
76 Well-put
79 Rich with humor
80 Application datum: Abbr.
82 Suicide squeeze result, for short
83 Two-time losing Republican presidential candidate
85 "Excuse me, I seem to have lost my phone number . . . ?"
91 Press
92 Orioles' org.
95 Chop
96 Lemonade + ___ = Arnold Palmer
97 Doggie sounds
98 Title teen in a 1990s sitcom
101 NPR's ___ Simon
102 "I don't mean to pry, but are you from Nashville? Because . . ."
108 Conductor's aid
109 When Can. has Thanksgiving
110 Évian, e.g.
111 Sgt. maj., e.g.
113 Instruction for casual dress
114 "Even though we've never met, I'm sure your last name is Campbell. That's because . . ."
120 Make better

121 Den, often
122 It gets a licking
123 Catfish Row resident
124 Bridgewater of jazz
125 Like talkers at a movie

DOWN

1 Goya subject
2 Henry James's "The Portrait of ___"
3 Amorist
4 One voting for
5 Bird: Prefix
6 IBM competitor
7 "Piece" org.
8 Inched
9 ___ hall
10 Glandular prefix
11 Daredevil's retort
12 Montreal daily
13 Mole, e.g.
14 Peres's predecessor
15 About 11%
16 City that won the first N.F.L. championship, 1920
17 Doesn't get bothered by
18 Dweller in the Peterhof
20 Eager
24 Victim of Bart Simpson's prank calls
31 Doesn't let go to waste
32 Hero's place
33 Lure
34 Key of Bruckner's Symphony No. 7: Abbr.
35 "You must ___"
36 Publisher of All Hands magazine: Abbr.

37 Home of Roosevelt I.
41 Spanish pronoun
42 Host
43 Prefix with dot
44 CBS debut of 10/6/2000
45 Plus more: Abbr.
48 The A's, on scoreboards
49 O.K.
50 One ___ (kids' game)
51 "Never gonna happen"
52 Japanese who won the 1974 Nobel Peace Prize
56 Afghan airline
57 British tax
58 Orders to plow horses
61 Filmdom's Jean-___ Godard
62 Prefix with pad
63 Knee-slapper
64 Band with the 1999 hit "Summer Girls"
65 Coastal bird
67 ___-poly
68 Bathroom powder
69 Concert halls
70 Lash of westerns
71 Raymond's wife on "Everybody Loves Raymond"
75 Yucatán yeses
76 1998 Sarah McLachlan hit
77 Recipient of the first gold single awarded by the R.I.A.A.
78 Easy putt, say
80 ___-string
81 Any ship
84 Guaranteeing
86 Indian bread

by David Levinson Wilk

87 #2, informally
88 H.S. course
89 Creature of legend
90 Slugger Mel et al.
92 Woman of la maison: Abbr.
93 Good deal
94 Serve well
99 Safe
100 Dragster's ride
101 Baffle
103 Like marshes
104 "I wanna try!"
105 Starchy food
106 Son of Cain
107 ___ des Beaux-Arts
108 Go postal
112 Did too much, in a way
114 From Jan. 1 till now
115 Help wanted abbr.
116 Jan. and Feb.
117 Radar reading: Abbr.
118 Big Ten sch.
119 Ones "over there"

TH-TH-TH-THAT'S ALL FOLKS!

ACROSS

1 Basis for the first commercially successful video game
9 Just folks?
16 Mugger?
19 They may have smiles and frowns
21 Athlete's slump
22 Grosse-___, Québec
23 Somebody else's soaking dentures?
25 Tour stop
26 Outstanding
27 Aviation pioneer Eugene
28 Palm Beach County city, for short
29 One who might stand in front of a map
31 Prefix with sphere
33 Life stories
36 Yellowish brown
37 Ghost in a battery?
41 Experimental figures
42 Wing: Prefix
44 Their mascot is Handsome Dan
45 Was wistful
47 Thataway
48 Comedian Jay
49 Thin opening
50 Vegetarian's credo
52 Prefix with metric
53 Actress Barbara
54 Whence the phrase "Brevity is the soul of wit"
58 Love, in Livorno
61 Former pol. div.

62 Avoid being captured by guitarist Richards?
64 1986 Indy 500 winner
65 Neighbor of a Pole
67 Fluttering sound
68 Deity featured on California's state seal
69 Fed-up cry
70 Baby twins?
74 Bar fig.
75 Some NCO's
76 Isolate
77 Possessive on Chinese menus
78 One of the "Magnificent Seven"
79 Skywalker portrayer
81 Circle
82 Middles: Abbr.
83 One of the Bushes
85 Ballade endings
88 In a jiffy
89 Joyous sounds
90 Org. with the motto "The power to make it better"
92 Sherlock at the Space Needle?
95 Drub
97 "Unh-unh"
98 Repeated sounds in "Hey Jude"
102 Poet Omar
105 "Can that be true?"
106 PC linkup
107 ___ cit.
108 Magazine with a fold-in
109 Billionaire's last dollar?

114 "What Is ___?" (Tolstoy essay)
115 "Gather Together in My Name" writer
116 Get set
117 ___ degree
118 Start of a trip in a bathysphere
119 Made blue

DOWN

1 Remains undecided
2 Poker player's declaration
3 Observant one
4 Classic muscle car
5 Batter's material
6 Nocturnal feline
7 Too inquisitive
8 Vitamin supplements store
9 Farm animal, in kidspeak
10 Tabloid fodder
11 In the back
12 "The Eyes of ___" (public TV science show)
13 Bug spray ingredient
14 Cracker spread
15 Nirvana attainer
16 Good eating and clean living?
17 Not recognizable by
18 "You've Got Mail" co-star
20 Change, as a manuscript, in Britain
24 Quinces, e.g.
30 Heel

32 Great server
33 Character actor Alfred
34 Thor Heyerdahl craft
35 Official seal
38 Spiral: Prefix
39 Egyptian god of wisdom
40 Something that's turned up
42 Some residents, by census classification
43 Very detailed scope?
46 Shortages
48 Wife, colloquially
49 Its cap. is Regina
51 Asian nurse
53 Comment made with a shrug
54 Garden output
55 "A View to ___"
56 Ruckus
57 One of TV's Munsters
59 Highly opinionated sorts
60 Lifts up
63 Spitting sound
66 "La Dolce ___"
68 Above
70 Go (into)
71 Borrowed
72 "Becket" star
73 Route from Me. to Fla.
80 Connections
81 Gets bounced by
82 "Call Me Irresponsible" lyricist
83 Actor Hugh of "X-Men"
84 First woman to earn the Distinguished Flying Cross

by Brendan Emmett Quigley

86 "Am __ believe this?"
87 Apostle known as "the Zealot"
88 Line of text?
89 Done
91 Reward
93 Left hurriedly
94 Not impressed

96 "Oops!"
99 Detective Pinkerton
100 Dark time in Italy
101 Suffered
103 Rook's spot on a chessboard

104 Board events: Abbr.
106 Fictional princess
110 P.I.
111 World Cup chant
112 Time sheet abbr.
113 Put away

21 WINGING IT

ACROSS
1 "Downtown" singer Clark
7 Wheat __
11 Kohada, on a sushi menu
15 Ernst & Young employees, for short
19 Up
20 Kind of speculation
21 "__ fan tutte"
22 Actress Wood of "Diamonds Are Forever"
23 Nurse Florence sells adventures?
27 Crackerjack
28 French silk
29 Manual reader
30 Coca-Cola Co. drinks
31 Actor Steve repeats what geezers say?
35 T or F: Abbr.
36 "__ Wolf," Michael J. Fox film
37 Annual event celebrated outdoors
41 Croak
44 Hideaways
45 Smutch
47 Kansas county seat on the Neosho River
48 Bow site
49 Static
51 Designer Geoffrey
52 Hot flash
53 Ratiocinative
55 Play opener
56 Overate, with "out"
57 Lawyer Atticus avoids crazies?
62 "Anything __?"
63 __ fatuus

64 Word game popularized by James Thurber
65 Fund-raising letter, e.g.
69 Architect Christopher gobbles banisters?
72 Picks up
76 Cabinet member: Abbr.
77 Futile
78 Some military helicopters, familiarly
79 Cuts out
81 Plantation inventory
83 1970s–'80s supermodel Carangi
84 Smart __
85 Acceleration
86 Siberian
87 Sound
88 Conversed
90 "Hold your horses!"
91 Early 10th-century year
93 Famed magician cheats chumps?
100 "Stop equivocating!"
103 Prefix with 94-Down
104 Go-__
105 Rapa __ (Easter Island)
106 Disney's Captain Jack dupes church leaders?
110 A, in Austria
111 "Swell!"
112 "Monster" actor, 2003
113 Runs off (with)
114 Some stereos
115 Troubadour's inspiration

116 Indian titles of respect
117 Title hero of a classic western

DOWN
1 __ Games
2 Longtime "All My Children" role
3 Go-getter
4 Show to a seat, briefly
5 Admits
6 Particles in electrolysis
7 Gourmand
8 Food packaging abbr.
9 Charms
10 "Les Misérables" star, 1998
11 Lasting marks
12 "Lord, __ long?" Isaiah
13 Personal offer to help
14 Strip
15 School souvenir
16 __ zoologique (French zoo)
17 "Lonely Boy" singer/writer
18 Guff
24 Chill in the air
25 Worked (up)
26 Actor Jared
32 Select
33 Payment in Monopoly
34 Lord Byron biblical drama
38 Snoop __
39 How a ship may be turned
40 It may be behind a picket fence
41 Jamestown colonist
42 Bubbling

43 Some campaign expenses
44 40 days and 40 nights event
45 Turn unpleasant
46 Food writer Ruth
49 Freud's ego
50 Bottoms
51 Abbr. on top of some e-mails
52 Sue Grafton's "__ for Alibi"
54 Word before maker or breaker
55 How a rose by any other name would smell, according to Shakespeare
56 "Happy Days" boy
58 "The Situation Room" airer
59 Rejects, with "off"
60 Hootchy-__
61 Warren Commission subject
65 Familiar
66 Feudal lord
67 __ Janis, star of Broadway's "Puzzles of 1925"
68 Tea-growing area of the Himalayas
69 Gen. Clark, informally
70 Window boxes, for short?
71 Abbr. in an apt. ad
72 Bygone monarch
73 Faulkner femme fatale __ Varner
74 Straits
75 Graceful trees
79 Copyist
80 Norse deity of mischief

by Caroline Leong

81 Musical credit
82 Ones with the motto "North to the Future"
85 Without exception
86 Voter, e.g.
87 Household member, for short
89 Australia's Northern ___: Abbr.
90 ___ apart
91 Like some tires
92 Capable of getting around, biologically
94 Voyagers: Suffix
95 Faith: Abbr.
96 Kind of exam
97 Not fitting
98 Mathematician who introduced the function symbol f(x)
99 Wuss
100 River in W.W. I fighting
101 Sweeping
102 Mideast capital
107 Fed. auditor
108 ___ de coeur
109 Rejections

22 LIGHTHEADED

ACROSS

1 Illustrious
8 She wrote "Under the Sign of Saturn"
14 Body of precepts
19 Dow product
20 Country whose leader has competed in five Winter Olympics
21 Part of U.R.I.
22 Tarot reading, crystals, spiritualism, etc.
24 Arrive
25 Jack who played a sawmill worker in "Twin Peaks"
26 Mourn audibly
27 "___ yellow ribbon . . ."
29 U.S.N. noncoms
30 Wheel on a spur
33 Traditional English festival
36 Caladryl : itch :: Bengay : ___
40 Partner of music
42 Charlotte who played Mrs. Garrett on TV
43 Gaits out of the gate
44 Little John's weapon in Robin Hood legend
47 You are: Sp.
48 Does some file transfers
49 Break-even enterprise
51 Basic way up a slope
55 Comparable to a fiddle
56 Bootlicker
59 You might play something by it
61 A current flows into it

62 ___-deucy (game with dice)
64 Brooke Shields movie, with "The"
67 Bit of a snicker
68 Alma mater for Carol Burnett and Jim Morrison: Abbr.
70 Keyboard instruments
72 Some contraband
73 Fish that migrates from seawater to freshwater and back
74 Playmate of Piglet
75 Its roar is worse than its bite
77 It may be waved at the Olympics
79 Learning level
81 Language suffix
82 Overdone
84 One of the Spice Girls and namesakes
87 Northernmost borough of London
89 Well-planned
91 Elongated marine fish
93 Biathlon needs
94 Dinner bun
97 Exempli gratia, e.g.
99 Abbr. on Rockies skeds
101 "Pride and Prejudice" beau
102 Root canal, in dentist-speak
103 Hair removal site
106 Composer Franz
108 Seed cover
109 Mrs. Chaplin
110 Egg
112 "South Pacific" role

117 Nabisco's ___ wafers
119 1987 Kubrick film
123 Longtime Chicago mayor
124 Capital of France's Aube department
125 "Ta-ta"
126 Show awe, in a way
127 Fix firmly
128 Like a paradise

DOWN

1 Attorney William after whom a stadium is named
2 Given the ax?
3 Apple on a teacher's desk?
4 Neighbor of Chad
5 Sculpting medium
6 Sen. John Kerry served there
7 Sullen looks
8 Bob Hoskins's role in "Hook"
9 Zip
10 Salem-to-Portland dir.
11 Spiritual path in Hinduism
12 Off the injured list
13 Start of a referral
14 Work unit
15 Chaim Potok novel
16 Family-style Asian dish
17 See red, talk a blue streak, etc.
18 Perfume, in a way
19 Where Bernard Shaw was an anchor for 21 yrs.
23 African grassland
28 Space City baseballer
31 Had a bill, still
32 Most base
34 Pound sounds

35 Boring tool
36 Greenish-blue
37 Tarot suit
38 Proverbial portion
39 Beethoven's Third
41 Carpentry byproduct
45 London gallery
46 Alice of "Hollywood Cavalcade"
47 What "[sic]" may signify
50 Paradise
52 Ralph Kramden catchphrase on old TV . . . and a hint to this puzzle's theme
53 Ancient theaters
54 Dandelion or goldenrod, e.g.
57 They're blown in the winds
58 Nelson ___, author of "The Man With the Golden Arm"
60 Old Greek market
63 Singer Sumac
65 Tied surgically
66 Santana's "___ Como Va"
68 Press
69 Base of some ethanol
71 Opinion pieces
73 Always: It.
75 Quickly check (on)
76 Certain girder
78 Trapper's prize
80 Hiram Walker, for one
83 Parasite
85 "Should ___ acquaintance be forgot . . ."
86 French town on the Vire

by Cathy Millhauser

88 Jive, e.g.
90 Outer: Prefix
92 Singer with the double-platinum album "The Memory of Trees"
95 French greeting
96 Burn at the end?
97 Dogie catcher
98 Underarm
99 Garden fertilizer
100 Zigzag, in a way
103 Airport screening equipment
104 Centaur's head?
105 The "Claudius" in Tiberius Claudius Nero
107 Page-turners are good ones
111 Life ___
113 Mid 12th century date
114 Swedish retail giant
115 Province NW of Madrid
116 W.W. II arena
118 "___, captain!"
120 Alkali in cleansers
121 Response to a funny text
122 Procter and Gamble detergent

ALTERNATE JOB TITLES

ACROSS

1 Trace
5 Cheap
11 Gobble (down)
16 Shepherd's charge
19 1930s film canine
20 Faith, Hope or Charity
21 Land on the Yellow Sea
22 Radio knob: Abbr.
23 Suffix with phosphor
24 Bicycle mechanic?
26 Goddess whom Homer called "rosy-fingered"
27 Music genre
28 Dimwit's brain size
29 Have control of
30 Actress Beulah
32 Obstetrician?
39 Paw
41 Woman, to a waiter
42 Belts a line drive
43 Bits
44 About 10% of New Zealanders
46 "Cats" monogram
47 Econ. indicator
49 Getaway driver?
54 Sailing
55 Hardened
56 Had control of
57 Chinese port also called Xiamen
58 Likelier to win a baby contest
59 Lost traction
61 It's often masked
62 Spade portrayer
63 Dry cleaner?
68 Announcement inside the front door
70 Wrinkled, maybe
71 Site of many tie-ups
72 Slick
73 Took advantage of
74 1990s pact
77 Bond yield: Abbr.
80 Der ___ Fritz (Friedrich the Great)
81 Usher?
85 Came together
86 Tai ___
88 Lodge with a mud roof
89 Defunct women's magazine
90 Early progress
93 Prefix with phobia
94 Minuscule
95 Urologist?
99 Like wine barrels
100 Tre + tre
101 Something that's picked
102 Hitchhike
105 Humans and apes, e.g.
106 Electrical inspector?
112 Security procedure
113 Brian of the original Roxy Music
114 Accident cause
115 One with a flag
116 "___ you not"
117 Colo. Springs-to-Santa Fe direction
118 Rodeo tie
119 Halloween bagful
120 Wall St. initials

DOWN

1 Stray
2 Analogy part
3 Not yet done
4 Prepare for camp, say
5 Tube plug
6 Closer to its prime
7 Loud, as a crowd
8 Corp. shares
9 Peach or plum
10 "I do" preceder
11 Orients a certain way
12 Tree
13 MGM motto start
14 Automotive pioneer's initials
15 Support group?
16 Venus, e.g.
17 Furniture cover
18 Old comic actress ___ Janis
25 Work with feet
31 Western Indian
33 Shindig
34 Not hold back
35 Prepared, as pears
36 Parade stopper
37 ___ Gritty Dirt Band
38 Festoons a tree with bathroom rolls, briefly
39 Stored computer images, for short
40 Goal of a tryout
44 "All in the Family" spinoff
45 U.S./Eur. link
48 I or II, e.g.
50 Tired
51 MoMA display
52 Love figure
53 Swed. neighbor
54 Boring article
58 Blast furnace fuel
59 None-too-subtle encouragement
60 Lawn additive
61 80-Across, in English
62 Pipe type
63 "You're asking me?"
64 Purse filler
65 Kind of arch
66 Mother of Castor and Pollux
67 Sign up for an offering
68 Vidi, translated
69 Teams in the West
73 Practical
74 Some Dodges
75 Trade talk
76 R.D.A. label requirer
77 Warning to a puzzle doer
78 Film ___
79 Part of a low straight
82 Friend's addressee, maybe
83 Q.E.D. part
84 Doesn't do just an outline of
86 Pulpit's locale
87 In
91 1965 #1 hit "___ of Destruction"
92 Hustling places
93 1983 Super Bowl designation

by Patrick Merrell

94 Host holders
95 Dawdlers
96 Prefix with transmission
97 Home to over a billion
98 1962 Jackie Gleason movie
103 Roaster's spot
104 "The NeverEnding Story" writer
107 U.K. foe
108 Monopoly props.
109 It can make molehills out of mountains
110 Bump
111 Shoshonean

ACROSS

1 Satirist Mort
5 Company store exchange
10 La ___, Calif.
15 1960s–'70s Pontiacs
19 Plant with spiny-edged leaves
20 Pass over
21 Civil War side, with "the"
22 Go on and on
23 Part of an M.D.'s sched.
24 Reason to call the exterminator?
26 Fencing piece
27 Extend a college athlete's eligibility
29 90-Down college town
30 Former Michigan/Indiana tribe
32 Actress Massey
33 Car in a Beach Boys song
34 Ski trail
35 They may be taken in an emergency
37 Combine
38 Pavements
41 Buccaneer's locale
42 Haberdashery robberies?
45 Stuffy-sounding
46 Blood classification system
47 Handled
49 Dealer's foe
50 Zap
51 "___ Lisa Smile" (2003 film)
53 Clean fish?
56 Criticize severely
57 Footwork?
59 Revolting ones
60 Away
63 Popular rejoinders
64 Tolerate
66 F.B.I. operative
67 Hair ointment
70 Singer India.___
71 Problem
75 South American tuber
76 Directive to a masseur at a Jewish spa?
80 It's pushed in Kensington Gardens
81 "Shane" star
83 Card
84 Rig owners
86 "Dee-lish!"
87 Latin name for ancient Troy
89 Limited, as some 1960s military service?
91 Accord
93 Like many beachgoers
95 "Daniel Boone" actor
96 Ammonia derivatives
97 Barbaric
98 Elite
100 Injured
101 Unoriginal argument
103 103-Down appendage
104 Accumulates
107 Have ___ for
108 Swindle at Ben & Jerry's?
111 Very
112 Judges' seat
113 Bridge expert
114 "___ Got a Friend"
115 Colleague of Kent
116 Leader's name that's etymologically related to "chess"
117 Accord maker
118 Allied
119 Latin 101 word

DOWN

1 German/French river
2 Peak near Neuchâtel
3 Jewel at a '50s dance?
4 Revealed
5 European finches
6 Noted Barton
7 "Hud" director
8 ___ Amin
9 90-Down tribe
10 Case worker?
11 Standing
12 10th–12th century dynasty
13 Article in El Diario
14 Weak
15 Rather, to some?
16 Pint of water, say?
17 R.E.M.'s "The ___ Love"
18 Rel. figures
25 One hawking
28 Parts of el día
31 "No man ___ island"
33 All together, musically
34 Washington city on the Columbia
35 Approval sign
36 Something to avoid
37 Kind of pack
38 Cougars or Bobcats, slangily
39 "___ Whoopee!" (1920s hit)
40 Was out
42 Considers, as testimony
43 "The Lady ___"
44 "I'll think about it"
48 Job antecedent
52 John/Rice musical
54 The Little Mermaid
55 Hurt
58 I.R.S. agent: Abbr.
61 Scolding word to a dog
62 Hike
64 About 1% of the Earth's atmosphere
65 Life of a region
66 Infected
67 Greek city-state
68 City west of Daytona Beach
69 Like an angry Mao Zedong?
70 In ___ (stuck)
71 ___ Angels
72 Crocodile tears?
73 Like some cuisine
74 TV prizes
77 An archangel
78 Sentencing times
79 I.Q. test pioneer
82 Western enterprise that goes bankrupt?
85 Belgian city or province
88 Art Spiegelman best seller

by Alan Arbesfeld

90 See 29-Across or 9-Down
92 Long Island town
94 University in Bethlehem
96 Made reparations
98 Curving

99 Actress Luft
100 Kettle's place
101 Barbecue fare
102 Greenland base for many polar expeditions

103 See 103-Across
104 Gulf war missile
105 Annapolis inst.
106 Pound, e.g.
109 Bill's partner
110 Reply of mock aggrievement

GOOD NEWS/BAD NEWS

ACROSS

1 Nixon's law alma mater
5 Jinx in reverse
10 Artist Chagall
14 Fit
18 Convenient apartment
19 Plantain lily
20 Flea market find
21 Target
22 Good for a wage earner, bad for a tightrope walker
25 Tree in a Christmas carol
26 Tsk about
27 Well in hand
28 1958 #1 song
30 Bit of effrontery
31 Withdraw
33 Tantrum thrower, maybe
34 Eric Clapton's "Layla" alias
35 Lander at Ben Gurion
37 Mark for life
39 Good for a wish maker, bad for a Hollywood agent
43 Tame brew
45 Sets up
47 Bounces
48 "Sex and the City" shower
49 Some party members, for short
51 N.Y.S.E. debut
52 Social reformer Jacob
53 Verve
54 Good for an attorney, bad for a Spandex model
58 Alpaca and cashmere
59 Singer's filler
62 Staff leader
63 "The possession of fools": Herodotus
64 It's done in the form of an S or a Z
65 Endorser, sometimes
67 Common classroom sight
68 Toiletry
69 Less-than-Ruthian hits
70 Separator
71 Monk's garb
72 1960s White House pooch
73 Reins in
74 Good for a magazine writer, bad for a couch potato
77 Aware of
78 Ward of "Once and Again"
79 Prof.'s helpers
80 Small amounts
83 Org. for 1- and 101-Across
84 BMW rival
85 Like some colors
88 "Our Gang" girl
90 Good for a doctoral student, bad for a crime suspect
93 Prayer start
95 Suffix on era names
96 Clarinet paraphernalia
97 Scraps
99 News source
101 Thos. Jefferson's school
102 Mysterious
104 Quick-witted
106 Dumped
108 Music from the Miracles, e.g.
109 Good for a returning traveler, bad for a bridge player
112 Shadow
113 Some beans
114 Show protectiveness
115 "Beg pardon . . ."
116 Chichi
117 Protomatter of the universe
118 Wrangles
119 Fabricated

DOWN

1 Drew aimlessly
2 Bared
3 Stay (with)
4 Benjamin Disraeli, e.g.
5 Kind of line
6 Advantage in hockey
7 Venom source
8 Ways: Abbr.
9 Like lions
10 Joint
11 Not give ___ (not care)
12 Ipanema locale
13 Brings together
14 Snacks for Dorothy on the Yellow Brick Road
15 Good for a scientist, bad for a roofer
16 Cordelia's father
17 Brontë heroine
20 Atelier item
23 42-Down, to Pierre
24 Fleet
29 Some Web site owners: Abbr.
32 Duty
34 Whistler's tune?
36 Many a roast
38 Seized vehicle
40 "Mule Train" singer, 1949
41 Chisholm Trail stop
42 Chanticleer
44 Medical tool
46 Sonnet component
50 Alluvia
52 Fair attraction
53 Rock singer in social causes
55 Ample shoe width
56 Hoard
57 Symbol on an old quarter
58 1971 hit movie based on the novel "Ratman's Notebooks"
59 Experimental attire?
60 Temporarily out of the office
61 Good for a mail carrier, bad for an electrician
64 Did yard work
66 Gray wolf
67 Gershon of film
68 I or II N.T. book
70 Baseball honcho
71 "Strangers and Brothers" novelist
74 Turns over
75 Spinnaker
76 Porfirio ___, president of Mexico, 1884–1911
78 By surprise
81 Ruckus
82 Like almonds in many recipes

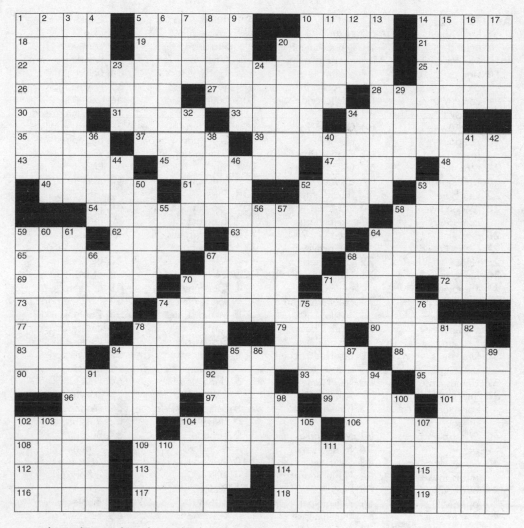

by Arlan and Linda Bushman

84 Port on a
gulf of the
same name
85 Wheel maker
86 Give a hint
87 Bowl figure
89 Halls of
learning
91 "For sure?"

92 Pre-Bill Hillary
94 Salon devices
98 They're often
heaved
100 End-of-sentence
abbr.
102 Fictional
terrier
103 Din

104 "Don't look ___!"
105 Sporty car
feature
107 Soup or
sandwich
ingredient
110 Shale extract
111 Things laid
by a gallina

CHICKEN LITTLE

ACROSS

1 Kid's name
6 Behind
10 Montana tribe
14 Half of a classic comedy duo
19 Ready to be drawn
20 __ point (never)
21 Monster-sighting spot
22 Car bars
23 "Moon River" composer
25 Bite site?
27 Daring deed
28 Fleece
30 Staggered
31 Threatening sign
32 Looks to the future
33 Shoot a ray
34 Dragster's pride
37 Comes close
38 Important constituent of igneous rocks
42 "Casablanca" actor
43 "Casablanca" music maker
44 Blockbuster offering
45 Pint in a pub
46 "Gotcha"
47 The Joker and Batman, e.g.
49 Bounce
50 Allegiance
51 Mario __ of the N.B.A.
52 Medical research grp.
53 One who says "one club," e.g.
55 Carmaker Maserati
57 Not very
60 Nixon impeachment hearings chairman
61 No-cal drink
62 Hitchcockian
63 Loose
64 Chip off the old block
66 Got together
67 Point in a space shuttle's trip
70 Provides provender
71 Area of 1940s mil. activity
72 Pair at sea
73 Skater of cinema
74 Mediterranean capital
75 "That'll be the day!"
79 Boxing's Oscar __ Hoya
80 "My Name Is Asher __" (Chaim Potok novel)
81 Manhandles
84 Studies late
85 Sends up
86 Plasterboards
88 Needle
89 Hair holder, sometimes
90 "Walk __" (1964 Warwick hit)
91 St.-Germain's river
92 Windshield option
93 Jacket materials
95 Applause
96 Very fat cats
99 Spray with bouquet
101 Author who covered the Spanish-American War for New York newspapers
104 Court site, with "The"
105 Linen hue
106 Cry made with a head-slap
107 Mass communication?
108 Stink
109 Slip through the cracks
110 Silent signals
111 Bolt to bond

DOWN

1 "Suzanne" songwriter
2 Memo starter
3 Ferry river
4 Scout warmer
5 Like a certain birthstone
6 Understood
7 Feuding
8 Setting for TV's "Newhart"
9 Fictional reporter
10 Wins big, with "up"
11 Ranges
12 10, in a way: Abbr.
13 Spun
14 Gets by
15 Ones with homes away from home
16 Der __ (Adenauer)
17 In-basket stamp: Abbr.
18 Visibly shaken
24 Reporter's asset
26 Writer Zora __ Hurston
29 Off-the-wall play
32 Farmyard female
34 Select
35 Private reply
36 Covetous
37 "I'm impressed!"
38 Questionable
39 Big bother
40 Kind of wrench
41 Back in
43 Rap sheet listing
44 Like some threats
47 Takes in or lets out
48 Not one of the majors
49 Escorted
51 Perfume part
53 Cantankerous
54 Innocents, e.g.
56 Gutter site
57 Conversion targets
58 Fabulous storyteller
59 Monopoly grp.
63 Russian range
64 Burn
65 "I'm outta here"
66 Cries like a baby
68 "Duino Elegies" poet
69 It's good at raising dough
72 "For the life __ . . ."
76 Isolate during the winter
77 Junior's junior
78 Postpaid encl.
79 Kind of candidate
81 Spindle for a grinding wheel
82 "Seascape" playwright

by Harvey Estes and Nancy Salomon

83 Novel banned in the U.S. until 1933
85 Lord Peter Wimsey accessory
87 Very sorry
88 Shred
89 Rock cruster
91 Sex researcher Hite
92 Evidence of sloppiness
93 Gulf of ___ (Joseph Conrad story setting)
94 Push
96 Watch
97 Alliance acronym
98 Salon sound
99 Sounds of understanding
100 Therefore
102 Howe'er
103 Toronto-to-Ottawa dir.

ACROSS

1 Base for food glazes
6 Waste
11 They're unstressed
17 Company perk
20 Air supplier
21 Appropriate for Halloween
22 Some ducks
23 Decline
24 Nathan and others
25 1980s computer
26 Art fan, perhaps
27 Web address start
28 Cow's favorite movie of 1983?
31 Aquarium fish
32 Guanabara Bay locale
33 Expression of gratitude, briefly
34 Internet market
35 Tropical pitcher plants and such
37 What Fred Astaire danced with
40 ___, Optimo, Maximo (Benedictine motto)
41 Start of a doo-wop phrase
44 Run out
45 Imagined
48 On the Board
50 Point of writing
51 Cat's favorite movie of 2000?
55 Like one battery terminal
59 A boost
60 Part of a dash
61 Attorney Belli
63 Sherpa
64 One-spot
68 Level
70 Not level
72 Haydn string composition

73 "___ It a Pity" (1970 song)
75 Foam toy brand
77 ___ de toilette
78 "It's ___ real!"
79 Snake's favorite movie of 1981?
87 Frenziedly
88 Oh-Wah-___ (game like mancala)
89 A transmitter
90 Game Gear company
91 The Beatles' Madonna, e.g.
92 Nebraska's Cornhusker, e.g.
96 Linesman, maybe?
98 Ancient Italian
102 Sheik's flock
104 Ark contents
106 Measure
108 1936 Cong. measure
109 "___ Rhapsody" (1996 biopic)
111 Frog's favorite movie of 1944?
116 Bolt from the blue?
117 116-Across and others
118 View from Vesuvius
119 Sister of Eva
122 Green-lights
123 Schnook
125 More harsh
129 Desiring
131 Superman's mother
132 President's inits.
133 PC application suffix
134 Hamlet and Gertrude
135 Crow's favorite movie of 1955?
142 Tall runners
143 Romeo and Juliet's home
144 Ante
145 "I swear!"
146 Cartoon art

147 Only now and then
148 Where salts go
149 Grand ___
150 Organ repair sites: Abbr.
151 Title city of a Forsyth thriller
152 Make catty remarks
153 They're tender

DOWN

1 Whiz's musical key?
2 Kennedy colleague
3 Many a boot
4 "Yeah, right!"
5 It's tender
6 Term of affection
7 Sound studio work
8 At first: Abbr.
9 Said "ah"
10 Life saver
11 Native soldier, in old India
12 "See ya!"
13 Modern viewer's choice
14 "___ madly for Adlai" (1952 campaign slogan)
15 Turned up
16 An ID
17 Kitty teaser
18 The Three Stooges had many
19 Rest
23 Sheep's favorite movie of 1991?
29 It's a knockout
30 "Little Red Book" ideology
31 Meting
36 Princess on the small screen
38 Big inits. in check processing
39 French vineyard
41 Popular Russian vodka, familiarly
42 Actor Villechaize

43 One may be secret
46 Curators' degs.
47 Modern music genre
49 Mark consisting of a series of dots
51 Kind of team
52 Step on it
53 19th-century samurai home
54 Perry White, e.g.
56 Worse
57 Cutting down, after "on"
58 Actress Téa
62 Larry of the Black Arts Theater, and others
65 Bee's favorite movie of 1983?
66 Clock std.
67 Colossal, to Coleridge
69 Actor with a mohawk
71 Some ranchers
74 "My ___"
76 Loan overseer: Abbr.
79 Judaism : kosher :: Islam : ___
80 Fine Japanese porcelain
81 They're found in fountains
82 "Decide already!"
83 ___ date: Abbr.
84 Fast sound: Var.
85 Early afternoon time
86 Tour grp.
93 Chiseler
94 Spring locale
95 "What's ___?"
97 Trillion: Prefix
99 N.Y.C. line
100 Name preceder
101 Corn order
103 Equilibrium
105 Lack equilibrium

by Roy Leban

ACROSS

1 Begin
9 Drum set
16 "Howdy"
20 Carefully study
21 Firedog
22 King Harald's father
23 Chef's comment at the poker game
25 Swiss miss, maybe: Abbr.
26 Actor Arnold
27 ___ good example
28 Stuck during winter
30 Talk show host Hannity and others
33 Pardon
36 Announcement at Penn Sta.
37 Brief rule
38 Laundry worker's comment at the poker game
41 At first, say
43 Film director often seen at New York Knick games
46 1970s Irish P.M. Cosgrave
48 Noted index, with "the"
49 Medal winners
50 Bridge site
53 "Oz" airer
54 Yardsticks: Abbr.
57 Broadway producer's comment at the poker game
61 Football Hall-of-Famer Long
62 "Lord, is ___?"
63 Au courant
64 Indian turnover
65 French possessive
66 Detective, essentially
67 Dodges
71 IV amounts
72 Portion of the iris
74 So as
76 Jackie's #2
77 Reeves of "Speed"
78 Lifer's comment at the poker game
83 Character in Trollope's "Phineas Finn"
84 Well-rehearsed
85 Number after a period: Abbr.
86 One of the Ramones
87 Vegas opener
89 Strong team
91 Life jackets
93 They take big steps
96 Car seller's comment at the poker game
100 Old TV talk show host Kupcinet
101 Speech fillers
103 Ariel and others
104 Took off
108 Loses hearing
111 "I say!" sayer
112 Spring time in Paris
113 Canceled
114 Tennis pro's comment at the poker game
121 Each
122 Landlocked Asian
123 Logician
124 Marine carriers in W.W. II
125 On one extreme
126 Experienced dizziness

DOWN

1 Sticks in the barbecue
2 A hard row ___
3 Kitchen magnet?
4 Word on the street
5 Nail site
6 Prefix with duct
7 Elite group, with "the"
8 Dog's catch, perhaps
9 Body work
10 50/50
11 Year in an Amerigo Vespucci voyage
12 Circle constants
13 Some Dadaist works
14 Who lives forever
15 Wholly
16 Kind of cooking
17 Artist's comment at the poker game
18 Bush and Clinton, once
19 Pay back
24 Den
29 Source of magic dust
31 Canon competitor
32 Piece of music
33 Michigan in Chicago: Abbr.
34 Tenn. footballer
35 Nobelist Root
39 Ancient land of France
40 Soft touches
42 Beloved
43 Asian mushroom
44 Metal craftsman
45 Farmer's comment at the poker game
47 Tommy ___, Olympic skiing gold medalist
50 Jubilation
51 Buzz in space
52 Key letter
55 Circumspect
56 Coasts
58 Carnival's promise
59 Cologne conjunction
60 Walking
61 Suffers from
64 Baked dessert
66 Certain strain
68 Blows it
69 Sun Valley locale: Abbr.
70 O.T. book
73 Center of Miami
75 Super Bowl side: Abbr.
78 Bus. page news
79 Start of something big
80 Twos in the news
81 Post in a flight
82 Fortune 500 company based in Moline, Ill.
88 Fastener
90 Vowelless number
91 Coaches
92 Walkman batteries
93 Wave, e.g.
94 Some peacekeepers
95 Girl with blue eyes and a ponytail, in a 1962 #1 hit
97 Start of a writ
98 Off-course

by Randolph Ross

99 Finish off
102 Subject of the biography subtitled "Visionary Who Dared"
105 Range name
106 Conseco Fieldhouse player
107 Ranks
109 Payoffs
110 Lava ___
115 Simpson case judge
116 Wine aperitif
117 Green brew
118 It's not right to say on a farm
119 Pothook shape
120 Turn bad

NAMES, NAMES, NAMES

ACROSS

1 Like the names at 33-, 51-, 61-, 73-, 93-, 101- and 120-Across
10 First alert, often
14 Put on a spit
20 Welcome abroad
21 "That's ___!" (angry retort)
22 "The Music Man" woman
23 Like many driveways
24 A security
25 Stat
26 Dole (out)
27 Further condition to 1-Across
29 1929 Literature Nobelist
30 "Mon ___!"
32 Substitute in the kitchen
33 Author and longtime professor of writing at Princeton
39 Hunters' needs: Abbr.
43 Inventeur's need
44 ___ Awards (annual prizes for African-American achievement)
45 Fruits de ___
46 Bob Dylan song "___ for You"
47 Supplied
48 Boatload
49 Final bid
50 Carol starter
51 Actress whose great-grandfather was a British P.M.
55 Tastiness
58 Soccer star Hamm

59 See 96-Across
60 Bauxite, e.g.
61 Three-time French Open champion
69 "Delta of Venus" author
70 Four CD's
71 Part of a rainbow
72 "___ Gold" (1997 film)
73 1988 and 1992 Olympic track gold medalist
81 Not yet shaped
82 Little hopper
83 Razor-billed birds
84 "This Old House" address
87 "That's ___" (cautionary Roy Orbison song)
88 Since, informally
89 Bar offering
91 Suffix with pluto-
92 Stock market overseer: Abbr.
93 Six-time U.S. Open winner
96 With 59-Across, a knock
99 Stone made of silicon and oxygen
100 They move shells
101 "Slaves of New York" actress
107 Standard deviation symbol
109 Knight from Atlanta
110 President Taft's alma mater
111 Stretches
115 Most basic
116 Annoyer
117 Opposite of chic
118 Minuscule

119 Oil of ___
120 He developed the "Three Principles of the People"

DOWN

1 TV schedule abbr.
2 Greetings
3 Shown again
4 Better
5 Daughter of Poseidon who was the ancestor of a prophetic clan
6 Educational grant named for a senator
7 Pot foundation
8 St.-Honoré, in Paris
9 Spread, as hay
10 Shakespearean haunter
11 Former Expos manager
12 Girl in a Beatles song
13 Stem-to-stern item
14 Drive
15 W.W. I battle locale
16 Woods, e.g.
17 Aretha Franklin's "___ No Way"
18 Wood strip
19 1961 space chimp
27 Wriggling
28 ___ Rios, Ecuador
29 Calculator button
30 Go under
31 Kind of chamber
33 Peter Pan rival
34 Theater turn-off?
35 Busy as ___

36 With all agreeing, after "to"
37 Musical John
38 Bogus
40 Awaiting
41 Circle
42 Pioneer products
46 Moscow's home: Abbr.
48 Spanish muralist
49 Stole
50 Curtain-rising time
51 Doll
52 Grp. pledged to "do no harm"
53 Storage place
54 Dallas hoopster
55 Western Hemisphere city founded in 1521
56 Writer Huffington
57 Mexico's Villa and others
62 Comic superheroes
63 Part of speech: Abbr.
64 Nix
65 Ben-
66 Cry on opening a tax bill
67 Hints
68 Nog ingredient, maybe
74 N.H.L. Hall-of-Famer who played for Montreal
75 W.W. II battle site, for short
76 "___ Hit Parade"
77 Many a part in "The Pianist"
78 Stand
79 Essen's river
80 Sketch
84 Divides fairly
85 Seattle Slew and others

by Derrick Niederman

ACROSS
1 Submit
7 Latin-American import
13 Wines from Spain
20 Grand Canyon sights
21 More elegant
22 Where the Tombigbee flows
23 Why is Y like a romance novel?
25 Au __
26 Raiding party?: Abbr.
27 Baby's first word, maybe
28 What may be raised at celebrations
29 Word to a dog
30 Counter offer?
31 Lamb specialty
33 What's C and easy, too?
37 Rest
38 Stains
39 Belts
40 Bow shape
41 Place
43 Something to be cured
46 Some are personal
47 Fund-raising grps.
48 Crosswalk user, for short
49 Many members of 47-Across
52 Unmelodic sounds
54 Dove, e.g.
55 P.D. alert
57 School dept.
58 What describes both screams and napoleons?
62 Far from florid
64 Oklahoma native
65 Biblical judge
66 Deli freebie
67 Hospital staffer: Var.
69 Cover over
71 Winner of 81 P.G.A. Tour victories
73 Appliance rating
74 Attributed
75 Quechua speaker
76 Writer LeShan
77 "Mr. Dieingly __" (1966 Critters hit)
78 Ping-Pong skills
79 How does "no" describe some baseball caps?
83 Wing
84 Cause of many a blowup
85 Top-drawer
86 "Gotcha"
87 Ship's hdg.
88 Already, in Italy
90 Some are deadly
91 Cash drawer compartment: Abbr.
93 Hero's award: Abbr.
95 Many an Olympian
97 Bass __
98 __ Ste. Marie
100 Fundamentals
104 Long time
105 What Stephen King title is suggested by the letter F?
108 Honolulu's __ Stadium
109 Study
110 Far out
111 Pisa's river
112 Lord's Prayer start
114 Berlioz's "__ Troyens"
115 All together
118 What science fiction movie do taxes and amine bring to mind?
121 "The flower of my heart," in old song
122 Reddish brown
123 Like Eeyore, in "Winnie-the-Pooh"
124 Fort __ (Oregon Trail stop)
125 Presses, folds and stretches
126 __ beef

DOWN
1 Remained
2 Precious
3 Hockey area
4 Directional ending
5 Tricky
6 Old "Happy motoring!" sloganeer
7 Profit-and-loss calculator: Abbr.
8 Junkie
9 Features
10 Florida governor before Bush
11 "How's that again?"
12 Suffix with secret
13 Nuts
14 "Woe is me!"
15 Bodybuilder's target
16 Father of, in Arabic
17 How would you describe both seraphs and unintelligible talk?
18 __ Island, Fla.
19 Like many nuts
24 Short flights
29 Jam
32 Pompeii killer
34 "__ Teenage Frankenstein," 1957 film
35 Disastrous
36 A gift, for short
42 Little girl's plaything
44 O.K.'s
45 Oscar-winner Matlin
47 Relative of the cod
49 Many New Zealanders
50 Tackle
51 What teen hangout is named by the letters PP?
53 Creep
54 Court cry
56 Losers to the 49ers in Super Bowl XXIII
59 Residents, e.g.: Abbr.
60 "__ Rainbow" (1947 musical)
61 Pearl hunters
62 Travelers' aids
63 Tease
68 Goofed
70 Em, e.g.
72 Thomas Bailey Aldrich story "Marjorie __"
80 Caught but good
81 Jolly Roger feature
82 Supermarket area
89 Woof
90 What nobody doesn't like
91 Old boxer called the Ambling Alp
92 Coached

by Nancy Nicholson Joline

94 Low-___
95 Kind of nerve or tire
96 It's listed in minutes
98 He said "I exist because I think"
99 Trampled
101 Crooner Michael
102 "Say ___!"
103 Dissed, in a way
106 Farsi speaker
107 Picker-upper
108 ___-Detoo ("Star Wars" droid)
113 Iwo Jima Memorial honorees: Abbr.
116 Ending with plug
117 One of the Cratchits
118 "Don't ___!"
119 Clattery trains
120 Itinerary abbr.

LEAP DAY

ACROSS

1 Darkness
6 Pack carrier
11 Application datum: Abbr.
14 Background of Vladimir Putin, for short
17 Route indicator
18 Traveler's woe
19 Island strings
20 Anti-inflammatory agent
21 Striped animal
22 "The Witches of Eastwick" author
23 A full course?
25 Queens contest
27 Daughter of Hyperion
29 Strike, essentially
30 Thesis basis
31 Big inits. in news and culture
32 Four fluid ounces
33 Food company with a sun in its logo
34 Cigarette pkgs.
36 Empire State Building decor
38 Put in
42 Shack topper
45 Sinatra scat syllable
46 Black bird
47 Express views
48 Pry
49 Take off
52 Open, in a way
54 Writing
55 1968 Oscar-winning musical
56 Has trouble with words
57 Smell, e.g.
58 Cuts using a box
59 Long period
60 "It's you __"

61 Upright at sea
64 Ed.'s in-box filler
66 It's hard, to swallow
70 Just above average
74 "Enough already!"
76 Red-faced
77 Hangout
78 Spot for Roosevelt
79 Apt
80 Parenthetical passage
81 Blows
82 Nus to us
84 Co. in a 2000 telecommunications merger
85 Ripen
87 South Seas monarchy
88 "Frankenstein" props
90 Kiln
91 1991 Gerardo hit "__ Suave"
93 Fall's end
94 VJ's employer
95 "Dang!"
99 Chicken go-with
102 Term. info
103 Minor minder
105 Sights
107 1966 Mary Martin musical
110 Deadly virus
111 Blender sound
112 Reagan military inits.
113 Run with gates
114 Less seen
115 Calendar col.
116 Sinuous sea dweller
117 Administers, with "out"
118 It's a secret

DOWN

1 Biblical woman from Bethlehem
2 Troubled (by)
3 Worry for a wearer of high heels
4 Takes a quickie vacation, say
5 Bud holder
6 Molokai resident
7 Co. name end
8 2001 biopic
9 Achieve significant progress
10 Long-known
11 Challenge, legally
12 Not read something completely
13 Rio __, part of the Venezuela/Colombia boundary
14 Swiss abstract painting
15 Takes a turn
16 Like a shepherd's staff
18 Has ever-changing loyalties
20 Seek a lawyer's license
24 Sink a putt
26 Monumental year?
28 Source of spills on hills
32 Channel
35 Lightweight helmet, in India
36 Come out of denial
37 Civil rights, e.g.
39 Snake, for one
40 Vast, in verse

41 Like osmium, more than any other known element
42 48 in a cup: Abbr.
43 As to
44 Twelve
50 "The Whiffenpoof Song" singer
51 Drs.' workplaces
53 Cafeteria worker's hairdo
61 Annoys
62 St. Teresa's birthplace
63 Medical supply
64 16th-century start
65 Gregg method user
66 Old White House nickname
67 Like chrome hubcaps
68 Garage jobs
69 Precitizenship course: Abbr.
70 Utter breakdown
71 Physics Nobelist Alvarez
72 Reverse
73 Kind of cell
75 Has at
83 Fem. in una casa
86 Hot rock
89 Oil used in church rites
92 Quit
94 PC software
96 The Eagles of college sports
97 Nat and Natalie
98 Target competitor
99 Pkg. no.
100 Aiea locale

by Patrick Merrell

101 Dust Bowl victim
104 Frobe who played Goldfinger
106 "Thanks a ___!"
108 Husk site
109 Suffix with infant

ACROSS

1 Clown's supply
5 Tore
9 Border
13 Comedian's supply
18 Part of F.D.R.: Abbr.
19 "Your ___"
20 Sewed up
21 Root of government
22 Pest-removal word?
24 Scott Turow book
25 Molasses cookie
27 Practice area, of a kind
30 Sound for Old MacDonald
31 Lansing-to-Flint dir.
32 Safari sight
33 R & B/jazz singer James
34 One abroad
35 Still-life subject
36 Hipsters
38 Gum predecessor
41 Tanning lotion abbr.
44 Found a new tenant for
46 Richie's dad, to the Fonz
47 Extremely easy shot
51 Applied, as a patch
53 Come to
56 George Sand, for one
57 Worth
58 "The wicked flee when ___ pursueth": Proverbs
60 Give out
62 Augur
63 During the knight-time?
65 Inn crowd
66 "Human Concretion" sculptor
67 Stiff, hot drink
71 President Madison: Abbr.
73 Drive off
76 How some papers are presented
77 Item for a Mexican pot?
78 Only insects that can turn their heads to look behind them
80 In ___ (unborn)
81 Some shirts
82 Climber's spike
83 Acts frugally
85 Tea source
88 Stall call
89 Black civil rights org. since 1912
90 Well-wisher's word
91 Col. in a profit-and-loss statement
92 "Nashville" actress
97 Narc's find
99 Certain rainwear
102 Much-used
103 Dept. of Labor division
104 Not too swift
107 With 112-Down, a pale shade
108 1930s comics girl
109 One of six, usually
113 Winter Olympics event
116 Madre's baby
117 ___-toothed
118 One who pulls strings
119 Triple-edged sword
120 They may be put on pedestals
121 Keyboardist Hess
122 Give rise to
123 Origin
124 Jr.'s exam
125 Stratagem

DOWN

1 Puff
2 Provoke
3 Circumference
4 Interference
5 Alert subject
6 "Turandot" tenor
7 Conquest of 5/29/53
8 Erase
9 Military communications expert
10 Here, in Le Havre
11 Condemned publicly
12 Trim
13 Ding-a-ling
14 Two-time U.S. Open winner
15 Strength
16 Clan chief of old Scotland
17 Extremely
23 Source of many calls
26 Sufficient, in verse
28 Written down
29 In-flight P.A. announcement
35 Prolonged separations
37 Pavement caution
39 Trouble
40 Yawning
41 1928 movie subtitled "The King of the Beasts"
42 Doom
43 Subject of numerous '70s lawsuits
45 Lassitude
48 Lamb chops accompanier
49 Chief who negotiated peace with the Pilgrims
50 Language ending
52 Never, in Nuremberg
53 Oriental nurse
54 "O Babylon!" playwright Derek
55 Actor Bruce
59 Some E.R. cases
61 Chop ___
63 Cries of disgust
64 Gardner and others
68 Vein pursuits
69 Partner of away
70 Flying group
72 1960 Everly Brothers hit
74 They have big bills
75 One of an old threesome
77 Person in a race
78 AWOL pursuers
79 Fire hose water source
80 Open
81 Granules
84 Like Brahms's Piano Trio No. 1
86 Perfect
87 Hotel force
90 Some Olympians
93 Capacity
94 Runs off (with)
95 Sun Devils' sch.
96 "Don't be discouraged"

by Rich Norris

ACROSS

1 Actress Valli of "The Third Man"
6 New York, e.g.
13 Feeling
18 Noisy bed-partner
19 Smallest of HOMES
20 Wedding march skipper
21 Start of a verse
24 Kind of witness
25 Fam. member
26 Certifies
27 Nasty biter
28 "Give the dog __"
30 Fellows
31 Relishes
35 Prepared to propose, perhaps
36 Brit. W.W. II heroes
37 "__ Want for Christmas"
41 Ooze
42 Tops
43 Antitoxins
44 Not bare
45 Part 2 of the verse
51 Directional suffix
52 Pulitzer-winning writer Sheehan
53 Hose woes
54 11th-century cathedral city
55 Punish, in a way, as a student
57 Florence's __ Palace
58 Baker's supply
59 Storehouse
62 South African antelopes
65 Put through a furnace

68 "The Violent Land" author
70 "__ Dance" (Grieg favorite)
74 Hut
75 Give a mighty blow
76 Composer __ Carlo Menotti
77 Doña __, "The Violent Land" lady
78 Part 3 of the verse
83 Edge of a rampart
84 Tolkien tree-men
85 Pike
86 Garlands
87 Regarding
88 "Yay!"
89 Prepare, in a way
91 Jinx
93 Like Falstaff
94 Praying figure
95 Apiece
96 Former "S.N.L." comic
100 Bump's place
101 Portended
106 End of the verse
110 To Shakespeare he was "high in all the people's hearts"
111 Smashed
112 Bear up under
113 Jardin zoologique inhabitants
114 False names
115 __-Prayer

DOWN

1 Pilaster
2 Like Lucy Locket's pocket
3 "Dies __"
4 Florida beach name
5 Actor George of "Disraeli"

6 Sully
7 H.S. class
8 Olympics entrant: Abbr.
9 Pound a beat
10 Get fixed
11 Rob
12 French pronoun
13 Coagulates
14 __ Sound, Fla.
15 Work
16 Leftovers
17 W.C.T.U. members
18 Actor Alastair
20 "Anything for You" singer Gloria
22 Sound at the door
23 George of "Route 66"
28 Part of A.D.
29 [Out of my way!]
31 __ Park
32 1940s–'60s world leader
33 Informal wear
34 Go (for)
35 Schroeder's predecessor as chancellor
36 Jackson known as "Mr. October"
37 Most sore
38 Fine fleece
39 Lollygags
40 Phrase of explanation
42 Top of a platter
43 Scythe handle
46 In a sluggish way
47 Department store department
48 Fraternity letter
49 Musical vamp
50 Whatever
56 Site of a 1943 Allied victory

57 Academy head
60 Super Bowl III hero
61 Awry
63 Puppeteer Bil
64 __ even keel
65 Queen's land
66 Chess log
67 Flip, in a way
69 Easy chair site
71 Flattened
72 W.W. II beachhead
73 Word
75 A.L.'er until 1960
76 Trans-Pacific stopping point
79 Celestial beings
80 Flatten
81 Binge
82 Worldwide workers' grp.
89 Blue __
90 Scrappy fellow?
91 Like shoes
92 Nicholas III's family name
93 Zero in (on)
94 "Sunset Boulevard" actress Nancy
95 Experienced
96 Soft drink Mr. __
97 Regarding
98 Porn
99 Biological suffix
101 Academic types
102 "__ pinch of salt . . ."
103 Frenchman
104 It begins "In the first year of Cyrus . . ."
105 Not a grade to be proud of
107 Call __ day
108 Rita Hayworth's Khan
109 Relig. school

by Frances Hansen

SOUNDS OF THE PAST

ACROSS

1 Clog kin
6 Come clean
12 Diner bottle
18 Harangue
19 Carol opening
20 Property receiver
22 Cook on the screen
23 "Three's Company" co-star
24 Harder to plow, perhaps
25 Finish last in a renting contest?
27 Luster on display?
29 This side of
30 Plunge suddenly
32 Thirst quenchers
33 Genealogy word
34 Deseeders
35 Spider-Man creator Lee
36 Have relevance
38 Fools
40 Top gun
41 A nephew of Donald's
42 Beat
43 Commodities exchange area
44 1899 warrior
45 Dodge
46 Breastwork
50 Took wing
53 Panel of tiresome people?
56 Manchurian border river
57 Collegiate starter
58 Seeger of song
59 Witch's place
60 Team number
61 Put away
62 Brand of sauce
63 One of the wealthy
64 Jackson 5 member
65 Bough
66 Sound off
68 Mane area
69 Chairperson?
70 Abu Dhabi bigwig
71 Ship perfume?
73 Many chords
74 Rally
76 Bob in the Olympics
77 "The Grapes of Wrath" name
78 Alliance for Progress grp.
79 Sound of a step
81 Rein in
82 It ends in Oct.
85 U.S. Open champ, 1985–87
88 Roger Rabbit et al.
89 Suffers
90 Builder's choice
91 Profitable extraction
92 Sectional
93 Recipe verb
95 Orbital point
96 Bridge-support combine?
100 Payoffs to chart makers?
102 Nominal
103 Self-important sort
105 Fit for farming
106 Another
107 Undivided
108 Stirred up
109 Searches blindly
110 Become whole again
111 Two of Henry's six

DOWN

1 Containing element #34
2 Daughter of Minos
3 Chorus section
4 Significant person?
5 Shade of blue
6 Remote
7 Inventor of the stock ticker
8 Scrap
9 J.F.K. arrival, once
10 Western tribe
11 As the case may be
12 1974 Oscar winner
13 Bitter drug
14 Castilian kinsmen
15 Genesis son
16 Workers' protectors
17 Little fellow
18 Source of caviar
21 Sea flock
26 $C_4H_8O_2$, e.g.
28 Groundless
31 VCR button
35 Sought damages
37 Annapolis frosh
38 Go public with
39 Remain sober?
41 Groundbreaking person
42 Like Galahad
43 Sky pilot
44 Group of beer drinkers?
45 On the portly side
46 Put to the test
47 Ornamental film
48 On a high
49 After-class aides
50 St. Louis Browns Hall-of-Famer
51 In installments
52 Kind of clock
53 Get one's feet wet
54 Present
55 Go with the flow
58 Origami supply
62 Tournament flora
67 City in the Ruhr
68 Can't do without
69 Grumbler
72 Phylum subdivision
73 Rocky peaks
75 Batman after Michael
77 Dixie drink
79 Hot and sour soup ingredient
80 Oven pan
81 Stronghold
82 Put out of commission
83 Represses
84 No longer green
85 Numbers game
86 Astray
87 Like "it"
88 Australia's ___ Strait
89 Sky lights
90 Turn badly?
92 It may be blank
94 Longhorn's rival
95 Soil sci.
97 Japanese sport
98 Hardly haute cuisine
99 Point at the dinner table?
101 ___-kiri
104 Nonacademic degree

by Richard Silvestri

35

CONDENSED BOOKS

ACROSS

1 You can get a grip on it
5 Thunder sound
9 Jitterbug, e.g.
15 Uttered with contempt
19 Filmmaker Wertmuller
20 Mediterranean city known anciently as Ptolemaïs
21 Joe Orton play "Entertaining Mr. ___"
22 Ready, to Shakespeare
23 Medical suffix
24 Feature of some skirts
25 Memoirs of a psychology lab maze builder?
27 Libido
28 Implied
30 Famed aviator
31 Book about gold medalists who dump their spouses?
36 Imitative behavior
37 Quirk
38 Author of "The Female Eunuch"
39 It gave out nos.
40 Television plugs
43 Tale of a frightening encounter with a lion?
51 Testifiers
53 Take in
54 Light-feather filler?
55 Waugh or Guinness
56 Indigo-yielding shrubs
60 Like most fine wines
63 Perennial trouble spot
66 Running a few minutes behind
69 Makeup items
70 Study on anthropoid regimentation?
73 Literally, "way of the gods"
76 "Don't ___ anything!"
77 Twin sister of Apollo
81 Tapioca sources
83 Yellowish brown
85 Individual
86 The Braves: Abbr.
87 Tropical Asian palm
90 Eight-time Orange Bowl champs
93 Story of a Fed. narcotics inspectors' raid on a sauna?
99 Neighbor of Isr.
100 Takes too much
101 When repeated, a 1963 hit
102 Morse code click
104 Mirror ___
107 Confessions of a drag queen?
113 Prying
116 Muscat resident
117 Bird shelter
118 Basic training manual for Marines?
122 Have ___ for
123 Burden
124 Smell ___
125 Least wild
126 "Soap" family name
127 Portend
128 Bill's opponents
129 Compact
130 Cartoonist Drake
131 Harness-racing legend ___ Hanover

DOWN

1 Kind of light
2 Rocket fuel ingredient, for short
3 Florentine: spinach :: lyonnaise : ___
4 Multicolored dog
5 Bit of this and that
6 Razzle-dazzle
7 "If I Were ___ Man"
8 "This isn't worth arguing about!"
9 Brit. award
10 Politician Landon
11 Jean Paul, e.g.
12 Kind of terrier
13 Noun-making suffix
14 College in Portland, Ore.
15 Gap between neurons
16 Military chaplain
17 Tanks and such
18 Wee
26 Disconcert
29 Drive-___
32 It's good to have these about you
33 Fabric name suffix
34 Bonds
35 Big oil supplier
39 First-rate
40 One of TV's Cartwrights
41 Place for a hero
42 Flew
44 A Muse
45 Bank acct. datum
46 Kind of chip
47 Rap's Dr. ___
48 Meter reading
49 Junkie
50 Physics units
52 Vast amounts
57 Breeds, so to speak
58 Parts of a code
59 Solidly built
61 Fluff
62 Activist Davis
64 Records
65 Neighbors of Ukrainians
67 Soprano in "Louise"
68 Misrepresent
71 Like warehouse goods
72 Like a child's drawing of the sun
73 "Get out!"
74 "Hell ___ no fury . . ."
75 Welcome sight after a shipwreck
78 Bryologist's study
79 Blackened
80 Blacken, in a way
82 "Men ___ From Mars . . ."
84 Anchorage-to-Fairbanks dir.
88 Waveless
89 In good time
91 Sheets and pillowcases
92 Air alternative
94 Request on some invitations
95 Gland: Prefix
96 Batman and Robin, e.g.

by Marjorie Richter

97 Anti-Nazi leader of W.W. II
98 Stay-at-homes
103 Holder of the highest career batting average in baseball history
104 Alpaca tender
105 Fate, in Greek myth
106 Analyze
107 "This ___ of those things . . ."
108 Bother
109 Santa ___
110 Ten or higher
111 Chopin piece
112 Put back
114 In the past, in the past
115 Duel souvenir
119 Mens ___ (criminal intent)
120 S.F. setting
121 Hog's home

ACROSS

1 Classic soft drink
5 Exaggerate
11 L.I.R.R. stops
15 Illustrator Silverstein
19 Wharton grad, maybe
20 ". . . upon receipt ___"
21 First name in mysteries
22 Mata ___
23 Part of the Musketeers' cry
26 Neighbor of Britannia
27 Prefix with sphere
28 1956 Charlton Heston role
29 Expressed
30 Rip off
32 Buffalo
34 Kind of bobsled
36 "See ya!"
37 Troubled capital
41 "'Neath the ___" (Wellesley school song)
42 Refined
44 Sandwich filler
47 Third party label: Abbr.
50 Big blaze
54 1998 Wimbledon winner Novotna
55 Flap, so to speak
56 Stir up
57 Capital built around Kyongbok Palace
58 Less covered
59 Positive
61 Four-time Super Bowl-winning coach

62 1973 Rolling Stones #1 hit
63 Classic whodunit
69 More than brighten
70 Hebrew letters
71 Annoys
72 Places for plants
73 Acidic prefix
75 "Beat it!"
76 "Didn't I tell you?"
77 Lighthouse locale
78 Game requiring no equipment
82 What a mess
83 KFC order
84 Ultimate challenge
85 Judy Garland's real surname
86 Like some cows
87 Suffix with techno-
91 Partner's part, maybe
97 "On the Beach" novelist
98 Starts over
99 Hercules fell in love with her
100 London's ___ Road Studios
104 Make
105 Leaning against
106 It began in 1337
110 Twice tres
111 Farm complaint
112 Second of two
113 ___ point (makes sense)
114 Crosses, e.g.
115 Languishes
116 Deprecatory reactions
117 Saw

DOWN

1 Most fresh
2 Betting option
3 Baseball announcer's phrase
4 I, abroad
5 Cry of horror
6 Side dishes: Abbr.
7 1910s–'30s Harper's Bazaar designer
8 Old-time cars
9 Family head
10 Compensate for
11 Part of a letter
12 Traffic
13 Washday brand
14 Identical
15 Polishes
16 Part of some palaces
17 "Steppenwolf" wife
18 Shade of white
24 "The Bottle ___" (Stevenson tale)
25 Klutz
31 Norse god of discord
33 Like some Fr. nouns
34 Back stabber
35 Guffaw
37 Wisconsin city or its college
38 Climatology subject
39 Type spec.
40 Judaism, e.g.: Abbr.
43 "Bad Boys" actor, 1983
44 1930 tariff act co-sponsor
45 Not playing with ___ deck
46 City ESE of Calais

47 Gulfweed
48 Long odds
49 Expressions of love
50 One of the Fates
51 Don Quixote, e.g.
52 As a rule
53 Signs a lease with
54 Girl with a gun, in an Aerosmith song
58 Some people are stuck with them
60 Lord, say
64 Old town on the Hudson River
65 "Two Treatises on Government" writer
66 Cato's clarification
67 Arrival phrase
68 Prepared to hang
74 ___ a time
75 One righting a wrong, perhaps
78 Tries to get by leaping
79 Meridian
80 Shopper's favorite
81 Longing
83 Joke target
85 Rock variety
86 Fishhook attachments
88 Fashion show locale
89 Lounging
90 Foursome
91 Get
92 Richards of tennis fame
93 TV/film actor Mackenzie ___

by Matt Gaffney

94 Smiling
95 Dies, with "out"
96 Hunter's quarry
97 Arab League member: Abbr.
100 Starting stake
101 Data amount
102 Iuborg, e.g.
103 Canal sites
107 Latin metropolis
108 Golfer Woosnam
109 Thal vessel

ACROSS

1 Superman's father
6 Assess
11 Pang
16 Small ammo
19 ". . . in __ tree"
20 Absorb the cost, in slang
21 Actor __ S. Ngor
22 Certain investment, for short
23 Her car broke down
26 Short, for short
27 Horses
28 Hardly flighty
29 Supply
31 Mystical character
32 "__ Girl Like You Loved a Boy Like Me" (old song)
34 Sketch-based TV show, briefly
35 Deep-six
37 Mystic
38 "Whew!"
39 "__ Mio"
41 Amtrak stops: Abbr.
42 He's exploring new terrain
47 Nationality indicator
51 Sweet-sounding Horne
52 Mandela's org.
53 Fizzles out
55 Licks
56 Cats
58 Spiral shell
59 Paper deliverers have them: Abbr.
60 Blink rapidly
61 Time keeper, at times
62 Uses mouthwash
64 Codgers' replies
65 He has mood swings
69 The Everlys' "When Will __ Loved"
70 Helps with
72 Latin foot
73 Choice words
74 Nightmare
75 Certain sing-along
76 Genetic research aid, often
79 Branch of Islam
80 In the past, in the past
81 "Chuang-tzu" principle
82 Intensity
83 "Stay!"
84 He's gotten carried away
88 Tater
90 Soprano Lehmann
91 Practice
92 Goya subject
96 Yenta's quality
98 "Sleepy Time __" (1925 song)
101 Speech with a lesson: Abbr.
102 Drafts, maybe
103 Value
104 Unveiling cries
106 Beethoven contemporary
108 __ Z
109 He's always asleep by midnight
113 Rag
114 Modern cartoon genre
115 Actor Jonathan of "Brazil"
116 Four-time Masters champion, to fans
117 Babe's abode
118 Challenges for college srs.
119 Strained
120 Inspirations

DOWN

1 Comics
2 Unclear
3 Get in sync again
4 Not so strenuous
5 Scientology guru __ Hubbard
6 Makes a lot of progress
7 What to say to a doctor
8 Sporty trucks, for short
9 Basic ideas
10 Patriot Allen
11 Cousin of plop
12 "Alfie" lyricist David
13 Purge
14 Ballroom dance
15 Everglades bird
16 He has a lawyer
17 Londoner, e.g.
18 They fix locks
24 Longtime Playboy artist LeRoy
25 __ Olay
30 Entry
33 Low socks
35 Long __
36 A util.
40 Gambled
42 Classic sports cars
43 The deep
44 Prov. on Hudson Bay
45 What science fiction writers do
46 Trim
47 Made a muff
48 "Let's wait"
49 She likes having children around
50 "__ De-Lovely"
54 "Whole" thing
56 Barbara, to friends
57 Charged item
58 Cornfield sounds
60 "Hopalong Cassidy" actor
62 Fit for a King?
63 Prefix with comic
65 African language group
66 Displace
67 Tiny bit, in France
68 Globs
71 Much sought-after author
74 Jollies
76 Admits nothing?
77 Three times, in prescriptions
78 Groovy
79 Golf course purchase, maybe
81 W.B.A. outcomes
83 Timber trouble
85 Author Samuel
86 '70s detective series
87 Sent smoke signals, maybe
88 Some sportswear, slangily
89 Tacky note
92 Capital of Lesotho
93 The Coneheads, e.g.
94 Actress Garth
95 Sotto voce remarks
97 Gurkha's home
99 Embrace

by Nelson Hardy

100 1944
Preminger film
104 Very, in Vichy
105 Where Achilles
was bathed
107 Ersatz
110 __ Maria
111 Ambulance V.I.P.
112 More than pass

ACROSS

1 Make itinerary changes
6 Strip on the Mediterranean
10 Former Gov. Bush of Florida
13 One of about 2,400,000 in the United States
18 Isn't just given
19 Was in the hole
20 Instrument, in jazz lingo
21 More than whimper
22 Medical resident of '60s TV
24 Rapa ___ (Easter Island)
25 Fruitlessly
26 Café Américain visitor
27 "Later!"
28 Computer ___
30 Run at the curb
31 Honey
32 Vaulters' landing places
33 Charge with a new responsibility
35 Stoolies, at times
37 Make a denial
41 Antiquity, in antiquity
43 What's more
44 Millionths of a meter
45 She played Julie in "Julie," 1956
46 Ploy
48 Suffuses
49 Put on a pedestal
51 Serves
52 Ploy
53 Abuses the throne
54 "La vita nuova" writer
55 Kind of engineer
56 It's a cover-up
57 Some nouns: Abbr.
58 Kelly McGillis's debut film, 1983
62 Diagnostic proc.
65 Furies
66 E-mail option
67 Author Sinclair
72 Service stations?
74 Burlesqued
75 Hanging loose
76 Marauds
77 Emmy-winning Tyson
79 Camp activity
80 "Uncle Vanya" role
81 Muslim generals
82 Natural neckwear
83 Flattens
84 #1 hit of 1956
88 Deli hanger
90 Stay dry
91 Fool
92 They may be split
95 Be visibly elated
98 Deadly nerve gas
99 Leader in Israel
100 Bust ___ (laugh uproariously)
101 Household pest
103 Pierce-Arrow contemporary
104 Heroics
106 Vortexes
107 Uris protagonist
108 "___ Mable" (W.W. I best seller)
109 Some kind of a nut
110 Nonrecyclables
111 It may make you see things
112 Corset part
113 Didn't hit the snooze button

DOWN

1 Made over
2 "Harlem Nocturne" composer Hagen
3 #1 hit for the Chordettes
4 Capital since 1923
5 ___ particle
6 Father of modern rocketry
7 Looks for
8 There are two per hundred
9 Fruity drinks
10 Novel published under the alias Currer Bell
11 Growing population areas
12 American University locale
13 Primogeniture beneficiary
14 Mahalia Jackson autobiography
15 "___ no idea!"
16 Drudgery
17 Grind, maybe
21 Flight engineers?
23 Speaks elegiacally
29 ". . . ___ quit!" (ultimatum)
33 Paul Newman's directorial debut
34 Biblical witch's home
36 Padded envelope
37 Attends as a visitor, with "on"
38 Voice lesson topic
39 S and M
40 Sugar suffixes
41 "By gar!"
42 Hot stuff
44 Purple dyes
47 Touch
48 Buyoffs
49 Big name in vegetables
50 "Of course!"
53 Torpedo, In British slang
55 Baseball's Flood and others
56 Holds off
59 Democracy since 1937
60 Lift
61 Fur resembling beaver
62 ___ Park, Calif.
63 Ark's first disembarker
64 Anticipatory exclamation
68 L'Enfant Plaza designer
69 Reprimand
70 City founded by Harald III
71 Loch ___
72 Seven up, e.g.
73 "It's ___!"
75 Long Island university
77 Jeweler Pierre and family
78 Horned lizard, e.g.
82 Hagfish relative
85 Worsts
86 LAX letters
87 Get one's head together?
88 Environmentalists' magazine
89 Piddling
91 December forecast

by Robert H. Wolfe

93 Gussies (up)
94 That's a wrap!
95 Deepened
96 Helen's mother
97 They may be
against you
99 Goes on
102 Part of a name
105 Magic org.

ACROSS

1 Disagreeable sort
5 Smeltery waste
9 "Shank," in prison lingo
13 Eritrea's capital
19 Colosseo site
20 Word with rush or credit
21 Rock's Mötley __
22 Conked
23 Valhalla V.I.P.
24 Functioning in all respects
25 Heckle
26 Not at sea
27 Break a tie in a shocking way?
31 Came after
32 1995 earthquake site
33 Occupational suffix
34 News org. founded in 1958
37 Kind of pit
40 Not adhere to promises
43 Land of poetry
44 Shocking 1980 movie sequel?
50 Plant shoot: Var.
51 Rig
52 Tom Sawyer's younger half brother
53 Trump's line
54 Bygone Dodges
56 Boxer-turned-actor Tony
59 __ Ivory Wayans
61 Ready for publication
63 Ward of "The Fugitive"
65 Vein yields
66 Suffix with meth-
69 Mark the beginning of Lent in a shocking way?
74 Part of CBS: Abbr.
75 Corporate giant named for a mythological character
76 Certain column
77 Restroom wall, often
78 Stomachache reliever, familiarly
80 One on the dark side
83 Ending for most odds
84 Cry at an awards ceremony
87 Clobber
89 Jack of old oaters
91 "No returns"
92 Shocking 1966 song lyric?
97 Foreign title
98 Star in Aquila
99 '60s–'70s Italian P.M.
100 Prov. east of New Brunswick
101 Apr. addressee
103 Speaker of note
105 Lovelace's "To __, From Prison"
110 Shocking bank offerings?
116 Old photos
118 Bring into resonance
119 Moonfish
120 Country road features
121 Bit of regret
122 Tennis score
123 Baseballer Martinez
124 End of a fitting phrase
125 Sluggish
126 Schismatic group
127 College major, slangily
128 Towel stitching

DOWN

1 "Time in a Bottle" singer
2 Monster of a 1956 film
3 Screwed up
4 Swahili's language group
5 Iran, once, and others
6 Piercing place
7 Burns title starter
8 Classicist's field
9 Journalists, jocularly
10 Fishermen's spears
11 Autobahn cruiser
12 "It's __ real!"
13 Heavenward
14 Title for Wences
15 Spree spot
16 White key
17 TV pooch
18 Say further
28 Part of any Verdi composition
29 Heart
30 Sideshow performer
35 Early Brit
36 Black
38 Floored it
39 Blood: Prefix
41 Composer Satie
42 One of the judges in Judges
43 Longtime Israeli ambassador to Washington
44 Opportune
45 Civics, e.g.
46 Pioneer computer
47 Dentist's request
48 Country singer Tubb
49 Deems proper
50 One "C" in C.C.C.
55 Panoramic photos
57 Energy
58 Oriental incense
60 Prior to
62 Chinese discipline
64 Visitor to Siam
66 Melodic pieces
67 Au pair: Var.
68 Beats by a hair
70 Cousin of calypso
71 Like some teas
72 Prefix with -plasty
73 "Half __ is better . . ."
78 Second in order
79 Make a break for it
81 Styptic pencil stuff
82 Defense acronym
84 It's a deal
85 Beep
86 Land on the Red Sea
88 Like some relationships
90 Unusually long
93 Land under Down Under: Abbr.
94 Blowhole
95 Ripened cheese
96 Hang loose
101 Spin doctor's concern
102 Up
104 Whopped, old-style
106 Holy scroll
107 __ couture
108 Cry from within
109 Fools

by Fred Piscop

111 Buck's mate
112 Educ. helpers
113 "How ___!"
114 Big story
115 Prefix meaning
    "one-billionth"
116 N.L. cap
    monogram
117 Merino mother

ACROSS

1 ___-Ashbury (hippie district)
7 Native Israelis
13 Hunted
20 Like some sports
21 R-rated
22 Not carried, as a burden
23 Giza resident falsifies travel documents?
26 Sci-fi author Lester ___ Rey
27 Fashion
28 Ragtime dance
29 Garbo's "The Mysterious Lady" co-star
30 Blazing
32 Some platters
34 Spring addressee, for short
35 Fellow fears following strict code of conduct?
44 Sandwiches for dessert
45 Earlier form of a word
46 Mouth part
47 "Slither" star
48 Amigo
50 "Reflections on Ice-Breaking" poet
52 Composer Schoenberg
56 History of short-lived indiscretion made public?
61 Certain grace
62 Not 82-Down
63 ___ Tunas, Cuba
64 Comment from the fold
65 Wagner's father-in-law
68 Discovery
70 Decision
72 Jezebel
74 Astonish
75 Wrigley field?
76 Fullest, slangily
77 English Channel feeder
79 Rising star's insecurity eased by weight loss?
87 Imbue with spiritual awareness
88 German coal-producing region
89 Friction reducer
90 Hanks role
92 Some are green
94 Coca-Cola brand
97 Hitchcockian
98 Emcee will never be forgotten?
102 "Hurrah!"
104 Composition of some sheets
105 Number next to a plus sign
106 Drill
109 Where "Otello" premiered
113 Contemporary of Duchamp
114 First private engineering school in the U.S.
117 Hubris alienates devoted comrades?
121 Late riser
122 Like some glances
123 Old Blood and Guts
124 Make an officer
125 Overseas hunt
126 Simon Legree

DOWN

1 Made tracks
2 Seraph of Sèvres
3 Charming scene
4 Elephant group?
5 Open military conflicts
6 Battlefield sorting
7 Application datum: Abbr.
8 If everything goes wrong
9 Hash house
10 Barely done
11 Woodstock gear
12 Part of S.S.S.: Abbr.
13 One with a line
14 Little or young follower
15 Israel's first U.N. delegate
16 Bar staple
17 With 98-Down, Oedipus and Willy Loman
18 Key word
19 Has to do (with)
24 Auel heroine
25 Kruger National Park terrain
31 Designer Simpson
33 Summer ermines
35 Amerind shoe
36 Bahraini, e.g.
37 Imminent
38 German war admiral Karl
39 "___ impressed"
40 It's half the faun
41 P.D. employee
42 Joyful dance
43 Sidi ___, Morocco
48 U.S.M.C. one-striper
49 Clever
51 Campus building
53 Shelley's eyes
54 Pastoral expanses
55 "Saving Private Ryan" re-enactment
57 Have a date
58 Syndicate head
59 Cabinet part, briefly
60 Antipasto ingredient
65 Stevedore
66 Cry after a coin flip
67 Witnesses
69 Sitters' headaches
70 Kind of wheel
71 Let go
72 Toots
73 Newly made
75 Ristorante desserts
76 Folkways
78 Montagne's opposite
80 The Wizard's unveiler
81 Emerald and ruby
82 Not 62-Across
83 "The Alienist" author
84 Explorer Amundsen
85 Timothy Leary, to some
86 Desert dignitary
91 Capital of Poland?
93 Shut off
95 1964 Manfred Mann hit
96 Body
97 Contract tactic
98 See 17-Down
99 Medallion meat
100 Best part
101 Transported
102 Old manuscript marks

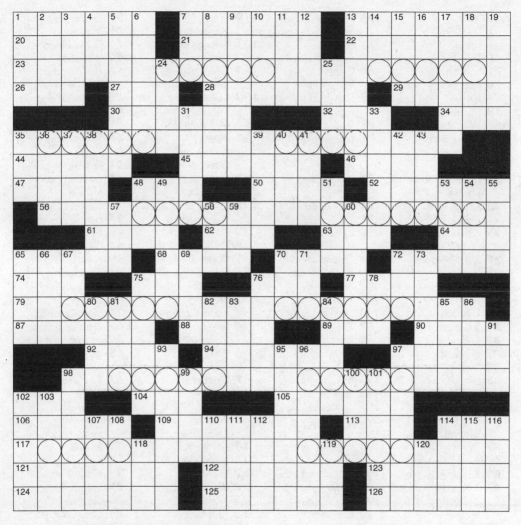

by Robert Malinow

ACROSS

1 Distiller's grain
5 Thus far
11 Scratch
14 Friars Club emcees
18 "Commander," in Arabic
19 Loose dresses
20 Starbuck's skipper
22 Legal memo phrase
23 Arafat and Rabin, for two
25 Offspring of 11-Down
27 "Dr. Zhivago" locale
28 Early afternoon time
30 Overturn
31 Least trained
33 Roman war goddess
34 Marker
35 High roller's pocketful
36 G. & S.'s Lord High Everything ___
37 Done for
40 It's a knockout
42 Singer Patti
43 Richard Wagner's second wife
44 Cybersearch result
45 They're full of dates
46 Quads' sites
50 Big force in politics
53 Part of A.P.R.: Abbr.
55 Gallic honeys
56 Islet
58 Baby Ruth ingredient
60 Ben Franklin proposal: Abbr.
63 Bathtub murder victim
64 Green Party V.I.P.
66 They help maintain balance
68 Sign
71 Beer-drinking consequence, maybe
73 Woolgatherer's state
74 Pugnacious
76 "How ___?" (question to a diner)
78 Champion with a two-handed backhand
79 "Get it?"
80 Honey
82 Xi preceders
84 Crisp breads
85 "Don't ___!"
86 "___ Gold" (Fonda film)
88 Comtes, comtesses, etc.
90 Opening with dexterity
93 ___-Bo (exercise system)
94 It's for the birds
96 Exigency
97 Like scofflaws
99 Canadian peninsula
100 Crowd
104 Blue Eagle org.
105 Where change is made
106 Girasol, e.g.
108 Visit through primal therapy
110 Lithos
112 Relief pictures?
115 Carp
116 "I Puritani," for one
119 London flea market site
121 George and George W., e.g.
122 Fido's dinner, maybe
123 Melodic
124 Der ___ (Adenauer)
125 Peter's "A Shot in the Dark" co-star
126 Ball girls?
127 Vacillate
128 ___ up to (approached)

DOWN

1 Organic farmer's need
2 Unprincipled
3 Protection for the maligned
4 Town in County Kerry
5 Pit stuff
6 Prefix with resin
7 Naturalist Fossey
8 Prewar
9 Pass on the sauce
10 Big Bertha's birthplace
11 Principal in a well-publicized breakup
12 "Eureka!"
13 Toothed wheel
14 Takes the cake
15 Kind of protest
16 Cat in "Cats"
17 Withdraws
21 Major's successor
24 Initials at sea
26 Disposed
29 Dundee denial
32 W.B.A. stats
34 Mitterrand's successor
38 "Wait ___!"
39 Galileo, for one
41 Marvel Comics hero
42 Warrant
43 They need a good whipping
46 Name on a can
47 Charlotte ___, Virgin Islands
48 Fata morgana
49 "Shalom!"
51 Film material
52 Pressing needs?
53 Man in la famille
54 How a pun may be phrased
57 Pound sound
59 Maid's introduction?
60 Grounds for divorce, in some states
61 Brats' looks
62 African scourge
65 Be a water witch
67 City near Seattle
69 Effluvium
70 Modern forensic tool
72 Passive principle
75 Kind of officer
77 Former Barbary State
81 Gen. Robt. ___
83 It's available in bars
85 Back
87 ___ Hill (Oyster Bay, N.Y., landmark)
89 Joel Chandler Harris title
90 Poe miss
91 "Carnival" composer/lyricist
92 Allen Ginsberg, e.g.

by Nancy Nicholson Joline

93 "Peter Pan" role
95 TV colleague for Mary
97 Dempsey foe
98 Vet
100 Early TV clown
101 Rue de ___
102 Handle props?

103 Put down one's hand
105 Low
107 Half the "Monday, Monday" band
109 Author of "Il nome della rosa"

111 Smart-alecky
113 Platte River tribe
114 1998 N.L. M.V.P.
117 66, e.g.: Abbr.
118 Biblical rebuker
120 Roar

42 "C" CHANGE

ACROSS

1 Game equipment
7 Part of the Northland peninsula
13 Puzzled
20 Open, in a way
21 Indiana University campus site
22 In a disastrous way
23 Health-conscious fish?
25 Harmonize (with)
26 Bow
27 Spain's last King Ferdinand
28 [Oh, well]
30 Pier group work
31 European coin
35 Roof problem
37 Attack on a fort, maybe
38 Etcher's window work?
41 Clinton Cabinet member William
43 Kind of market
44 Trickster
45 Staple of Southern cuisine
46 Madly in love
50 Take for a while
51 Inspiration
52 Bank security
53 Lump of clay, say
54 See 79-Across
55 Information repository
58 Comment from a scolded person
60 100 dinars
61 Unhappy spectator
62 Ring around the collar?

63 Canada's ___ Bay
64 V-formation group
67 Op. ___
68 Told to shape up
71 Poker Flat chronicler
72 "Gulliver's Travels" feature
74 Keats was one
75 Rat-___
76 See 77-Down
78 Tree with tanning bark
79 With 54-Across, furnace emission
82 Eastern royal
83 Fixes, in a way
84 Fish hook
86 Half of an '80s TV duo
88 Smooth (out)
89 "A Loss of Roses" playwright
90 ___ tree
91 Most like Chianti, say
93 Relish
95 Hole in hosiery?
97 Do car wheels
100 Circle overhead
102 It's south of ancient Shiloh
103 Lord in love with Lady Clare, in Tennyson
105 Plug
107 Ring around the collar?
108 Dead on target
112 Backbreaking
114 Friendly sentry?
118 Outlaw
119 Traps, as an Arctic ship
120 Business practice
121 Breaks away
122 Cuddle up
123 Wee

DOWN

1 Lousy
2 Sit ___
3 Cubemaster Rubik
4 Like a defense contractor's contract
5 Kind of beetle
6 Eastern European
7 Activity for sunglass wearers
8 Earned
9 Part of a hosp. record
10 Kind of life
11 Replies to a newsgroup
12 Scandinavian land, to natives
13 64-Across's locale: Abbr.
14 Unbelievable
15 Loose
16 Activity for a crooked politician?
17 Any Platters platter
18 Armrest?
19 "Riders to the Sea" writer
24 Part of the Old Testament
29 Poor links play, as they might say in England?
32 Building inspector's topic
33 Troy, in poetry
34 Legs, slangily
36 It has a line through it
38 Is repentant
39 D-Day beach
40 Really severe economizing?
42 Be undecided

43 Apalachee Bay locale: Abbr.
45 Russian saint
47 Important guest group
48 Flip out
49 More fit
51 Butter at breakfast?
56 "Le Coq ___"
57 Maxwell competitor
59 Ally McBeal, e.g.: Abbr.
61 Mechanical device for baseball practice?
62 Spot for a cursor, maybe
63 Kitchen appliance
64 Emmy-winning Lewis
65 Persian Gulf land
66 Heavens: Prefix
69 "That's ___ . . ."
70 Lash
73 Hillock
76 Camera diaphragm
77 With 76-Across, a game ender
78 Make ___ (mug)
79 Hopper
80 Imperfect speech
81 Up to this point
85 Like two peas in ___
87 Blood vessel securer
91 Open up
92 Perception
94 Get off
95 Informant
96 Tiger Hall-of-Famer Al
97 Ishmael's people
98 "20,000 Leagues Under the Sea" actor, 1954

by Manny Nosowsky

99 Of Nehru's land
101 Gain computer access
104 View from an oasis
106 Ball-bearing items
109 Reservoir filler
110 Garden decorations
111 On pins and needles
113 Vietnam War opposer: Abbr.
115 N.Y.C. clock setting
116 Up to, informally
117 Bestow on, to Burns

ACROSS

1 [I am shocked!]
5 Nogales nosh
11 More than impair
18 Completed
19 Popular salad ingredient
21 They help catch criminals
22 A fact-finding civil court judge __
24 Completed
25 Settles on, in a way
26 Hockey Hall-of-Famer Francis
28 Appeared
29 Active starter?
30 An improvising jazz musician __
35 Beeswax
37 Compass heading
38 With 44-Across, a veteran
39 Spots
42 Gala
44 See 38-Across
45 Corner
49 Directive
51 A helpful bridal shop clerk __
55 It may be forfeited
56 Silicon Valley giant
59 Writer Rand
60 Delayed
61 Piz Bernina group
62 Small amount
63 Traffic signal, at times
65 "Valley of the Dolls" girl
66 A hard-working coal miner __

71 Doone of fiction
73 Word with steak or search
74 Bruce nicknamed "The Little Dragon"
75 Noted sprinter
78 Ring of color
80 French article
81 __ prayer
83 Was behind
84 A bottom line-oriented executive __
87 Split part
89 Rum's partner
90 Last word of "Angela's Ashes"
91 Not so nice
94 __ Kippur
95 Turned on
96 Dickensian complaint
98 Convictions
100 A thorough insurance adjuster __
106 Like many Iranis
110 Witch
111 Ancient gathering place
112 Like some stables of myth
113 Supposes to be
116 A diligent police detective __
120 Exactly 3 hours for a marathon, e.g.
121 1997 film hit
122 Web destination
123 Bands of athletes?
124 End of an O'Neill title
125 Horse race

DOWN

1 Messenger
2 Spanish tourist town
3 Modern high school class, informally
4 Slangy forecaster's word
5 Smidgens
6 The Altar constellation
7 Big bloom
8 Turkish pooh-bah
9 Winter Olympian
10 Gold and silver, e.g.
11 Jailbird
12 Track part
13 With you
14 Wing: Prefix
15 Decorative loop
16 Where security is discussed
17 Old laborers
20 "It's __ of the times"
21 Stand for the deceased
23 Bad postures
27 Kind of partner
30 Like a heap
31 Expert finish
32 Ghost
33 Boat with a high bow
34 Not be careful with a bucket
36 In arrears
39 "Fernando" singers
40 "It's a __!"
41 "The Tempest" event
43 Zilch
44 Wide-ranging display
45 Big fund-raiser

46 Takes off, cowboy-style
47 Month after Ab
48 Sports award
50 Where Hamlet cogitated
52 One greeted on a ranch
53 Harp's cousin
54 Start of a boast
57 Actions at auctions
58 Chocolate treats
63 Nasty biter
64 Bounced checks, hangnails, etc.
67 Rumor
68 Aphrodite's lover
69 Appleton locale: Abbr.
70 Navy worker
71 Secular
72 "Yes __?"
76 City on the Truckee
77 Product encased in red wax
79 Kind of kitchen
81 Whistle-blowing spot: Abbr.
82 1-Down and others: Abbr.
85 Plops down
86 Timid
88 Double-dealing
92 It may be hit by a driver
93 The elected
95 Worse than tricks
96 Order to a dog
97 On high
99 Most discerning
100 Wedding band, perhaps
101 Word in the Boy Scout Law

by David J. Kahn

102 One of a kind?
103 Put ___ to
104 Like some coins
105 Finlandia House architect
107 Show again
108 "___ say . . ."
109 Atlas feature

112 "Moses" novelist, 1951
114 Fiver
115 Mantra sounds
117 Flee
118 Together
119 1999 Pulitzer Prize-winning play

ACROSS

1 Rule-breaker
4 Certain residue
8 Sumer, nowadays
12 Broker's advice
18 Gist
20 Star impersonator?
22 Such that one might
23 Gag order?
24 1973 Rolling Stones #1 hit
25 Winston Cup org.
26 British exam taken at the end of secondary school
27 Postal order?
30 Mentions
31 Word-word link
32 Registering, as a dial
33 Exclusive
34 Atlanta-based cable channel
35 Ward of "The Fugitive"
36 They're found in veins
38 Writer ___ Louise Huxtable
40 Religious order?
48 Noblemen
49 Imperfection
50 "Keystone Kops" producer
51 Pecking order?
54 Washington and Shore
56 Detachable container
57 Got off
58 Indian Ocean swimmer
61 Reef lurkers
63 Bank
67 One year in a trunk
68 Becomes intertwined
70 Cookie with a crunch
71 Sly look
72 Fly, e.g.
73 Threatening words
75 Expensive trim
76 Stroked item
78 Small military vessel
80 Restraining order?
82 Gravedigger
86 Red-brown
87 New England catch
89 Batting order?
94 Eternally, in poetry
95 Courtroom entry
96 Kingdom on old Asian maps
97 Word to a doctor
99 Stout, freshwater fish
102 Money in the music business?
105 "Foucault's Pendulum" author
106 Odd-numbered page
108 Shipping order?
111 Fake ID holders
112 Collected
113 In conclusion: Fr.
114 Rush order?
116 God depicted holding a crook
117 Rephrase
118 Part of a tennis court
119 ___ Fitzgerald
120 Periods
121 Chinese money
122 Warner Bros. collectible

DOWN

1 It's striking
2 Batch of solicitations, maybe
3 Lab tube
4 Bona ___
5 Darling
6 Basketball's ___ Alcindor
7 They may be uncovered on a street
8 Tolstoy's ___ Ilyich
9 Sunders
10 Hidden motive
11 Direct order?
12 "___ She Lovely"
13 Whose ark?
14 Explorer ___ Núñez de Balboa
15 Heat up
16 Eyeballed
17 Split
19 Campbell of "Party of Five"
21 Lincoln's Secretary of State
28 Bazaar merchant, maybe
29 Short pieces
31 Believe
35 Tiniest bit
37 Gets (through)
39 Food for a doodlebug
41 Audience research focus
42 Wool cap
43 1970s–'80s TV family name
44 Nonworking order?
45 Golden yrs. cache
46 ___-Cat
47 Constellation near Cassiopeia
51 Patriarch of the Flying Wallendas
52 Tennis's Nastase
53 Kind of curve
54 New World order?
55 Pas ___ (dance solo)
59 Western Amerind
60 Recover from a run
62 Whirled records?
64 Part of the U.S./Canada border
65 Kay of "Physical Evidence"
66 Team need
69 Daughter of Mnemosyne
72 Before the opening, say
74 Either Zimbalist
77 Youngest March sister
79 Accept
81 Sack
82 1950s G.O.P. name
83 Uncalled-for
84 Like some decorations
85 Held the top spot
87 Stays with
88 ___ Phraya (Asian river)
90 Jidda's locale
91 Tiny fraction of a min.
92 Terse
93 G.I. John?
98 Overnight spot
100 Single-named singer
101 Suffer defeat, slangily
103 Gather
104 Minneapolis suburb

by Patrick Berry

106 Gain succulence
107 Carbon compound
108 Since
109 Twiggy digs
110 Runs out
111 Arizona city
115 Cross shape

ACROSS

1 Stadium walkways
6 Actress Blanchett of "Elizabeth"
10 Something to talk about
15 Postponement
19 Suffix with sect
20 Woody's role in "Annie Hall"
21 Kansas City college
22 It may be hard to get out of
23 ___, Insurance Salesman
25 ___, Funeral Director
27 Remedy
28 Party wear, maybe
30 "Sabrina" star Julia
31 Cadbury Schweppes brand
32 Winter woes
33 Farmers' association
34 Five-time Derby winner
37 Western Pacific republic
38 Dirt expert
42 Big blow
43 ___, International Mediator
46 End of many e-mail addresses
47 A mean Amin
48 Noted Howard
49 Words before distance or discount
50 Dentist's request
52 Schism
54 ___, Travel Agent
58 Boozed (up)
59 Unending
61 Trade
62 Make over
63 Got the message
64 They come after quarters
65 Center of Miami
66 Matriarch
68 Order in the court
69 Some pipes
72 Indian queens
73 ___, Children's Entertainer
75 It's tall when exaggerated
76 R.P.I. grads
77 "Gee whiz!"
78 Torch lighter at the 1996 Olympics
79 Excess
80 Big diamond
81 ___, Charity Organizer
86 Work well together
87 Long roads
90 Driving aids
91 Calls off
93 Summer colors
94 Jobs, to friends
95 Hearty cheers
96 1950s tennis star Pancho
99 Search party
100 How not to get caught
104 ___, Towel Manufacturer
106 ___, Literary Agent
108 Resembling, with "to"
109 Musical direction
110 It's breaking out
111 Item with a ladder
112 Dosage amts.
113 Fund
114 Source
115 French beans?

DOWN

1 Indian king
2 Get ___ for one's money
3 Alcoholic drink served over cracked ice
4 Coatings
5 Duke of Flatbush
6 Spiny things
7 Wings
8 Tubes
9 Socket
10 Wrapped, as for a football game
11 Tracks
12 Papal name first used in A.D. 140
13 Malicious
14 The very end
15 Seafood dish
16 Lawn mower brand
17 "I couldn't agree with you more!"
18 Play area
24 At all, in dialect
26 Life force, to Freud
29 Brio
32 Had a conscience
33 1951 Best Actress Emmy winner
34 "It's ___!"
35 Sector sides
36 ___, Suspense Writer
37 Branch
38 Intl. org. since 1948
39 ___, Shoe Salesman
40 1957 Detroit debut
41 ___ la Paix
44 British actress Holden
45 Simplifies
50 Up
51 Still there
53 Backstreet Boys fan, maybe
54 Garden needs
55 With it
56 Cap
57 Accord
58 Mystery or sci-fi
60 Puts on
62 Tyro
64 Pens, perhaps
66 Four-star
67 Russian alternative
69 Storm preceders
70 Fabulous time
71 Clockmaker Thomas and others
73 Shoots well
74 Oscar winner for "The Cider House Rules"
77 Giant hero
81 It might hold one back
82 Angel's desire
83 Match for Mars
84 Popular chocolate snack
85 Navy men
86 Light, white wine
88 180's
89 On guard
92 Bidding
94 ___ voce
95 Outbreak
96 Pre-desktop publishing photo
97 Frightful sounds
98 Understanding
99 Swimming site

by Randolph Ross

100 "There ___ excuse!"
101 Settled
102 Turn over
103 A Spanish crowd?
105 Barry who sang "1-2-3"
107 Prefix with -cide

ACROSS

1 G
5 Select, with "for"
8 Ah follower
12 Atomic pile
19 Moroccolike leather
20 Dramatic court action
22 Vital engine conduit
23 Working in a mess
24 Vain mountaineer's motto?
26 Didn't come to terms
28 Rank in the 40-Down
29 Disney V.I.P., once
30 Inactivity
32 Auxiliary
34 Like mesh
35 People who love baths?
39 Part of Q.E.D.
41 "When in ___ tell the truth": Twain
42 Soldier material?
43 Some fraternity men
44 Poke holes in
48 Like a monster
50 Wiretap victim's wish?
54 Seethe
55 Belgian river
57 U-___
58 Actor Greene
59 Düsseldorf donkey
60 Put on
61 Part of some gym exercise equipment
63 The very best
64 Problem for the Shanghai police?

67 James Michener opus
71 "Something of Value" author Robert
72 Blink of an eye
73 Abe's Mary
77 Lush material
78 "___ Ha'i"
79 Defraud
80 Switch add-on
81 Graffiti?
85 Coils
87 Rembrandt's land: Abbr.
88 High rollers?
89 Like a good bond
90 Make reparations
91 Sign seen in Times Square
93 Pirate flag in the summer sun?
98 Alexander, to friends
101 Like
103 Stop listening
104 Praline ingredient
106 Suffix with honor
107 Spoiled brat's display
111 Policy of a strict naval blockade?
115 Superman's mother
116 Spanish valentine sentiment
117 Give up
118 Grandson of Eve
119 It's far out
120 Take note of
121 Turner in Atlanta
122 Suggestive

DOWN

1 Trampled
2 ___ soit qui mal y pense (classic motto)
3 Squirrels' haunts
4 Matter of growing interest
5 Fish hawk
6 Electrician's need
7 Become attracted by
8 Some savings accts.
9 Drillmaster's syllable
10 Kind of garage
11 Nocturnal animals of the upper Congo
12 Aussie hopper, for short
13 Revolutionary Michael Collins's country
14 Pink-eyed panther, say
15 Union site
16 1960s-'70s All-Star Luis
17 Start
18 Hear again
21 Go-between
25 Decked
27 No-see-ums
31 Sony founder Morita
33 Identical
35 Big name in Web software
36 Symbols of industry
37 Pulitzer winner Alison
38 Call a halt to
40 Service for a 28-Across
43 Freudian topic
45 Civil wrong
46 Part of A.D.

47 Page
49 Victim of Hercules
50 Big brass
51 Billiards need
52 Retreat
53 Ballet bend
56 "___ lied!"
61 One may be taken to the cleaners
62 Besmirch
63 Plastic surgeons' work
64 Piggish remark
65 Zero
66 It may get in your hair
67 Novel ID
68 Farm wagon item
69 Maine, e.g., in Metz
70 Manfred von ___ (The Red Baron)
73 Dry
74 Stars with a belt
75 Clergyman/poet John
76 Medicates
78 Light wood
79 Be relevant to
82 Dripping
83 Meal starter?
84 Playing to someone's vanity, maybe
86 War-torn capital of the 1980s-'90s
92 Big 12 school
93 Judd of "Taxi"
94 Long past
95 Like O'Neill's "Bound East for Cardiff"
96 Avoid a trial, say

by Manny Nosowsky

97 Blotto
98 Hitachi competitor
99 Knock for __
100 Lay low
102 Regrettable
105 Gentlewoman
108 Zola heroine
109 Leathery sunbather
110 "No sweat"
112 ". . . __ thousand times . . ."
113 Deli choice
114 Early development

ACROSS

1 Band aid
7 "I, Robot" author
13 Tasters' testers
20 Higher ground
21 Couch, in a way
22 Beach in a 1964 hit song
23 Nice people collect them
25 It may be flared
26 In the limelight
27 "Honor Thy Father" author
28 Business graphics
30 Out of chains
32 Change a bill, say
34 Dwelling in Durango
35 Like some Riesling wines
38 Great balls of fire
39 Kimono closer
41 Sultanate citizen
42 Beat to a pulp
45 Sound system component
50 Statistician's margin for error
52 Standing rule
53 Savoie sovereign
54 Lao-___
55 Pianist Schnabel
56 Drink with a kick
58 Blotto
60 The Switchblade Kid of cinema
61 Secures under cover, with "in"
62 Big Band music
64 ___ Walton League (conservation group)
66 Skedaddles
67 Wise guy
68 Clamorous
70 Hummable, perhaps
73 Facial foundation
75 Chest-thumping
76 High-tech co., once
79 Draft choice
80 Not quite right
81 Rites of passage
84 Suggestive
86 "Absalom and Achitophel" poet
87 "The Pearl Fishers" composer
88 Service arm: Abbr.
89 Spring shower, possibly?
91 Woodstock band, 1969
93 Drop down?
96 Sink hole
97 Flimflam
99 Some approaches on the links
102 Sweets
104 ___ Lang, Superboy's girlfriend
108 Alternative fuel
109 Claim in a collectibles ad
112 Sign of a goof
113 Siberians' relatives
114 In a weakened state
115 Section of London
116 Not in any way
117 Drives back

DOWN

1 Hick
2 Word after "Ole"
3 Cream ingredient
4 Slow
5 B & B, e.g.
6 Paper worker
7 Mac maker
8 Did a smith's job
9 Place for a pupil
10 Tiger, for one
11 East of Essen
12 Evening bell
13 Long in the past?
14 Part of the Bible: Abbr.
15 Punishment unit
16 Last "course" of a spicy meal?
17 Earth, in sci-fi
18 Sends out
19 Chili topper
24 Gull
29 Hot
31 Comic strip dog
33 More than sore
35 Yielding
36 Modern farm birds
37 Whipped up
38 Toots in a restaurant
39 Common name for hydrous silica
40 Entrance
43 Entr'___
44 Book-cracking
46 Treble clef singer
47 Issue suddenly
48 Roasts, e.g.
49 White wine apéritifs
51 Adder's threat
52 Valuable plastic
56 Actress Farrow
57 Landing
58 Game-stopping call
59 Characters in fables, usually
60 Scuff
62 Low spot of land
63 Faced a new day
65 [Gotcha!]
66 Dundee citizen
67 The lightning bolt on Harry Potter's forehead, e.g.
68 Similar
69 Computer command
71 #1 spot
72 Bad trait for a politician
74 Grace's end
75 Spark for the Giants' 1951 pennant win
76 Biblical site of the temple of Dagon
77 Story connector
78 "Cómo ___?"
81 Hot off the press
82 Letter-shaped construction piece
83 Bygone car option
85 Distant settlement
86 Mid-6th-century date
90 Southern Australia explorer
92 Obedient one
93 Fibber of note
94 Kim of Rudyard Kipling's "Kim"

by Nancy Salomon and Harvey Estes

95 Kudrow and Bonet
96 Meted (out)
97 Rumor squelchers
98 Originated
100 Cage co-star in "Leaving Las Vegas"
101 Phone, slangily
103 Pins' place
105 Glorified gofer
106 Present time
107 Added stipulations
110 U.N. working-conditions agcy.
111 Wrath

ACROSS

1 Czech capital, to the Czechs
6 Take 5, clue 3
10 Private schools: Abbr.
15 Stop, in Paris
20 Mathematician with a formula named after him
21 ___ Kea
22 Harold of "Ghostbusters"
23 Distrustful
24 Take 4, clue 1
25 Hebrew fathers
26 Take 5, clue 5
27 Orgs.
28 TAKE 1
31 Risks
32 Marriage and others
33 Connery successor
34 Mother, colloquially, in Britain
35 Take 3, clue 1
39 How some pkgs. are sent
40 Lots
42 Decay constants, in physics
46 Illegal bank practices
48 Take 1, clue 1
49 Musical quality
50 TAKE 2
55 Those, in Tegucigalpa
56 Neighbor of Liech.
57 Quaint verses
58 Ancient Italic people
60 A-Team member
61 Auditor, e.g.: Abbr.
64 Hit the nose
66 Insurable item
67 Chip dip
69 Folk's Guthrie
71 Francis or Henri

72 Vietnam War Gen. Creighton
74 Sled piece
77 Pleasureful retreat
79 TAKE 3
83 Underground
84 Discrimination against the elderly
86 Hulled grain
87 Prepare for war
89 '60s Mets shortstop Chacon
90 ___ this earth
92 Burden
93 Versailles, for one
96 Suffix with absorb
97 No. of beachgoers?
99 Former Ugandan strongman
101 Award-winning Disney Broadway musical
102 Family docs
104 Clark's girl
106 TAKE 4
112 In a tizzy
114 Charlie Brown's exclamation
115 Algonquian tribe
116 Aussie marsupials
117 Treacherous ones
120 Witching hour
121 Colorful salamander
122 "Don't give up!"
123 Singer Horne and others
124 Brave one
126 "Let 'em have it!"
128 TAKE 5
135 Kitschy '50s film monster
136 Take 3, clue 3
137 Supernatural
138 Track gold medalist Rudolph
139 Build, as a monument
140 ___ que (because): Fr.

141 Recovers from a flood
142 Take 4, clue 4
143 Certain entrance exams, for short
144 Casino lure
145 Take 5, clue 4
146 Like Eric the Red

DOWN

1 Adamant ant?
2 Bride of Boaz
3 Wings
4 Thyme, e.g.
5 Recitalist Rubinstein
6 Gossiped
7 Keeler and Dee
8 Med. sch. subject
9 All-nighter, maybe
10 Athenian magistrate
11 Partnership
12 ". . . ___ old soul"
13 Sawyer or Keaton
14 Concordes
15 Crimson Tide
16 Take 4, clue 2
17 Take 3, clue 2
18 Sea eagles
19 Cobb and others
21 Sugar for beer-making
29 Legal trademark user
30 Arab chieftain: Var.
34 Work force measure
35 Shelter in TV's "Survivor"
36 Relative of -esque
37 Paris street
38 Humorist Bombeck
40 Like windows
41 Modern image makers, for short
42 Bank department
43 Take 5, clue 2
44 Suffix with liquid

45 Dewey Decimal ___: Abbr.
47 Chits
48 Lose one's blush
49 ___-night double header
51 Making a team
52 Supplants
53 South Africa's KwaZulu-___ province
54 Certain constrictor
59 Tenement locale
61 Vena ___
62 Unlikely Playboy Channel watcher
63 Take 2, clue 1
65 Murmur
66 Encourages
68 Snick-a-___ (combat with knives)
70 Hodgepodge
72 "Begone!"
73 Graduated
75 Leprechaun's land
76 Take 5, clue 1
78 ___ spumante
80 Wharton hero
81 Charged
82 Common ___
85 Victorian virtue
88 More powerful
91 March instruments
93 Elder and Younger English statesmen
94 Citrus drinks
95 Tiff
97 Picnic dish
98 Prince Charles's avocation
100 Towards the tail
101 Many miles off
103 Attention amount
105 Take 2, clue 2
107 "You ___ Beautiful"
108 Memorable dos

by Charles M. Deber

DOUBLE OR NOTHING

ACROSS

1 Michener best seller
7 Fed. loan agency
10 Nolan Ryan, once
15 Where to do some bodywork?
18 Gets the red out?
19 National League division
21 Limonite's pigment
22 Legend on the ice
23 Temporarily
24 Certain partner: Abbr.
25 They come on the 25th
26 It may be tidy
27 Ending with Juan
28 "The Carpet-Bag," in "Moby-Dick"
30 With 63-Down, a New Mexico county
31 Confectioner's goof?
35 Introduced
37 Merle Haggard, self-admittedly
38 Troubadour's tune
39 One of Thor Heyerdahl's boats
41 Snap brim, e.g.
42 Washington dingbat?
47 They're cross-shaped
48 Lixivium
49 London's Old __
50 '60s campus news

51 Forceful group?
52 Men in the hood?
54 Part of P.S.T.: Abbr.
55 Mexican sandal
59 Texas state tree
62 Street that hosts a music festival
64 Slash, for one
65 Meal for a moth
66 "Magnum, P.I." setting
67 Occasion to use the good china
69 Kisser
70 Victorian
71 Major introduction?
72 Serial novel's start
73 It gets into hot water
74 Stunt
76 X into MXX
77 Kind of propeller
79 Load line locale
80 N.F.L. coach with 347 career victories
82 Castle site?
83 Keep in a cellar, maybe
86 __ colada
87 Dress decoration?
90 With 118-Across, part of a child's schooling
92 Tech stock choice
93 You, to Yves
94 Inventor Sikorsky
95 Trips
97 Samoan simpleton?
102 Physics Nobelist Penzias

103 One with unusually fine hands?
105 Goon
106 Lighter producer
107 Outmoded copier
108 Trans __ (Asian range)
109 Like some nuts
113 Hertfordshire river
114 Calyx segment
115 Jiffs
116 Dominican's dwelling
117 Southwest extension
118 See 90-Across
119 Book before Esth.
120 Line feeder, of a sort

DOWN

1 Fido's greeting
2 __ Minor (northern constellation)
3 Spring time: Abbr.
4 Florida island
5 Doshisha University locale
6 It spans the 33-Down
7 Fossil fuel found in coastal veins
8 Aromatherapeutic additives
9 Take __ at
10 Five-star
11 Autumn arrival
12 Churchill's "__ Finest Hour"
13 It may bring on a sigh
14 Hosp. sites
15 Mediocre steamed dish?
16 Branch managers?

17 Philip II dispatched it
20 Letter drop, e.g.
29 Circular tube
30 20th-century tree painting?
31 Play in an alley
32 Not spectacular
33 Blue preceder or follower
34 Crow, e.g.
36 Reek
40 Author Rand
43 It's known for its bell ringers
44 Sports stat
45 Window alternative
46 One of the rare earths
51 Like some face powders
52 Terrorist's taboo?
53 See 84-Down
55 Uses one's 60-Down
56 Hives, medically
57 A party to a party?
58 Novelist Morante
59 Swift contemporary
60 Side flaps
61 Flashy dance?
63 See 30-Across
64 Cultural Revolution leader
67 Like some controls
68 Kepi-sporting soldier
73 Fujimori's land
75 They may be laid out
76 Easy dupes
78 Spain's Guadalquivir, e.g.
80 Stand in
81 500
83 Jason's charge
84 With 53-Down, smarts

by Dana Motley

85 Speculator's target
86 Teetotaler's order
87 See see as sea, say
88 Like a coxcomb
89 Vienna premiere of 1805
90 Pacer's place
91 Less certain
96 Snowbird's destination, perhaps
98 Recognition responses
99 Physician to Marcus Aurelius
100 Shows shock
101 Bridget Riley's genre
104 Lott's predecessor
107 Chinese menu letters
110 Besides
111 Unit of energy
112 Turn red, perhaps

ACROSS

1 Alley
5 Fashionable '70s wear
10 Duke of ___, historic Spanish general
14 Bit of cleverness
17 Solemn responses
19 Captivate
20 Kind of cloth
21 Suffix with brilliant
22 Singer-actress Janis
23 Mario Puzo best seller
24 Medical advice, often
25 IV measurements
26 A. God of war
   B. Goddess of the earth
   C. God of love
   D. Ruler of the gods
30 Most of Mauritania
31 Flu source
32 Wear and tear
33 Head, slangily
34 Designer Wang
36 Story of France
38 Big voting bloc
39 A. "Les Troyens"
   B. "Pelléas et Melisande"
   C. "La Mer"
   D. "Faust"
46 Pay stub?
47 1962 film set in Jamaica
48 Consents
49 Tao founder
50 Early Eastern mercenary
53 Boeing rival
55 Talk, talk, talk
56 Snowy ___

57 Zip
58 Olympics
60 Two-time link
63 A. Egg and matzo meal
   B. Tomatoes and cheese
   C. Corn or barley
   D. Chickpeas or beans
68 Dump
69 Dish eaten with rice
70 Britney Spears, to some
71 Part of 1,000
72 "Whew!"
73 Calls off the romance
75 Translucent quartz
76 Heartbeat quickener
80 Gen. Lee's grp.
81 Snowmobile parts
83 Judge in 1995 news
84 A. Karl Malden
   B. Robert Mitchum
   C. George C. Scott
   D. Burt Lancaster
89 Make it up to
90 Big East team
91 Where Bill met Hillary
92 Movie pooch
93 See 5-Down
94 Anaïs ___ "The Novel of the Future"
97 Friction
101 A. "Mommie Dearest"
   B. "Lonesome Dove"
   C. "Angela's Ashes"
   D. "Times to Remember"

106 Pot top
107 Mrs. Chaplin
108 Like an early-evening sky
109 "___ Crooked Trail" (1958 western)
110 Preceding, in verse
111 Singer with wings
112 Not thinking well
113 Spell
114 From, in France
115 "Sure, I'm game"
116 Staggering
117 Within: Prefix

DOWN

1 Gemstone
2 Oven maker
3 [I'd like some oats over here . . . !]
4 Chisel
5 With 93-Across, words of delight
6 Actresses Dana and Judith
7 Besmirches
8 Last question in this puzzle
9 "Rich Man, Poor Man" novelist
10 1953 A.L. M.V.P.
11 Composer Frederick
12 Customs request
13 Busy bodies
14 Disease-causing bacteria
15 Piano teacher's request, maybe
16 Mosaic piece
18 Hit the roof
19 1950s soldier, in brief
27 Like some seals
28 Awards for Asimov and Clarke

29 Put in a new medium
35 Start and end of a magician's cry
37 Emulates Regis?
38 Card game with a pool
39 "Haven't heard a word"
40 Land
41 One of Dada's daddies?
42 Indivisible
43 Very much
44 Subject of a Nash poem
45 Swung, nautically
51 ___ set
52 Problem ending?
54 Meadow sound
55 Resembling preserves
58 Certain photo
59 Faction
60 Ban locale?
61 Slice for a pizza?
62 Popular dot-com stock
64 ___ Bay, Philippines
65 Fall event
66 TV announcer Hall
67 Egg ___ yung
73 Perceive
74 Fastidious
76 County near Liverpool
77 Cause of some disturbances
78 Stern with a bow
79 For instance
80 Barely speak
82 Shudder, e.g.
84 Fished with a net

by David J. Kahn

51 SHINING EXAMPLES

ACROSS

1 Crushing blow
10 Cook, for one: Abbr.
14 Shoot for, with "to"
20 Size up again?
21 Suburb south of Paris
22 They may be in trunks
23 Blocks
24 Daytime Emmy winners
26 Stable staple
27 Columnist Thomas
28 More frosted
29 Jai alai basket
30 ___ Gailey, of "Miracle on 34th Street"
32 Car dealer's offering
35 Needy people?
37 Play analyzer
39 "___ cost you"
40 Most cloying
44 Zany
47 A heap
50 Architectural feature
51 Some bullets
53 Pool party?
55 Draft org.?
56 Stable staple
57 River from Superior to Huron
58 Curtis and others
60 Sites for some analyses
61 One of the Cyclades
62 More than miffs
63 Belief
64 Best Song of 1961
68 Everything, to a lyricist
71 Morning glories
72 Traffic directors
73 He beat Arthur at the 1972 U.S. Open
74 "To Autumn," e.g.
75 Include
76 Lively, in scores
79 Early '50s game fad
84 Chemical suffix
85 Oyster's place
87 Wyoming's Grand ___
88 Hardly exciting
89 Oil producers
92 Out of this world
94 Clinic supplies
95 All, for one
97 Recipe direction
99 Viña ___ Mar, Chile
100 Catch
102 Disestablish
104 Kind of aerobics
107 Valuable viola
110 À la Thurber
112 ___ de trois
114 "King Kong" studio
115 Cry from Ralph Kramden
117 It may be tucked in
120 For one
121 Cognate
122 Clementine, e.g.
123 Called for
124 "Et voilà!"
125 Sky streaker

DOWN

1 Auto option
2 Prevent
3 Anne Frank's hiding place
4 Even
5 Paris picnic place
6 Like some suspects
7 Core groups?
8 Computer monitor, for short
9 Peggy Lee's "___ a Tramp"
10 Mozart opera title starter
11 Appetite arouser
12 Kilt patterns
13 Prepared a manuscript
14 Desert menace
15 Phantom
16 Neurological problem
17 Some savings
18 Software installation requirement, often
19 It, in Italy
25 Evolutionist's interest
28 Tie in
31 Bing Crosby's record label
33 One of the coasts: Abbr.
34 Move in mire
36 Delivery in the field
38 Spenserian beings
41 Allen and others
42 Luther Billis of "South Pacific," e.g.
43 Assignations
44 Chain units: Abbr.
45 Know-how
46 "Bustin' Loose" star
48 Sketch
49 Bergen spoke for him
52 Onetime lottery org.
54 Poor rating
59 Hook shape
60 Muumuu go-with
63 Drifted
64 Cancer, astrologically
65 Band aide
66 Make up
67 Sign of a winner
68 Brand of hair lightener
69 Like a romantic evening, maybe
70 "Justine" star
71 Dairy Queen offerings
74 Leaves time?: Abbr.
76 Book ends?
77 English seaside resort
78 Big Mac ingredient
80 Buenos ___
81 R & B music showcase
82 "The Rum ___ Tugger" (song from "Cats")
83 Silly one
85 Children's author ___ Rabe
86 Hosp. tests
90 Was more than miffed
91 Threaten, like a dog
93 Hegelian article
96 Threesome
98 "High Sierra" star
101 1961 Heston role
103 Slow movement
105 Squeezing (out)
106 Guiding principle
107 ___ all-time high
108 Gloomy Gus
109 Force ___ (draw)
111 "Gossip" co-star Headey

by Elizabeth C. Gorski

113 Galley order
116 Showed
signs of being
in love
117 John, Paul and
George: Abbr.
118 "Told ya!"
119 ___-state

WASH YOUR STEP!

ACROSS

1 Part of a combo
5 Person carried on others' shoulders
10 Vessels seen in "Saving Private Ryan": Abbr.
14 Dent in the coastline
19 Caesar's cry
20 Prefix with centric
21 Sieben follower
22 They stand for things
23 Time pieces
24 True
25 Cloning Dolly, e.g.?
27 Jacques Cousteau's life, in a nutshell?
30 Catches on
31 Address in Calcutta
32 Caddie, often
33 Cut down
34 Wacko
36 Examines closely
38 Skip town
44 Pam of "Jackie Brown"
47 What Broadway backers may have?
49 Judah's mother
50 Outshine
53 "O curse of marriage . . ." speaker
54 Feminine suffix
55 British can
56 Essen's river
59 Discouraging words
60 Items in a recycling bin
62 Like some items at customs
66 TV character, to some adolescent boys?
72 Superb
73 Give up
74 King of Kings
78 Guy Lombardo's "___ Lonely Trail"
79 Peerless
80 Speak like Sylvester
81 Big ape
84 Without heat
87 It ends a threat
88 Canceled credit card?
91 "Contrary to popular belief . . ."
93 Bugs
94 Fanatic
95 Lambs: Lat.
97 Barbecue bar
99 Dizzy
101 Some chanters
106 Timesaver
111 How OPEC communicates?
113 "E pluribus unum," e.g.?
115 Sirs' counterparts
116 Strong draft
117 Actress Aimée
118 Mmes., in Málaga
119 ___ ease
120 Siouan tribe
121 They might be loaded
122 Where to see a Sonora sunrise
123 Discourse detour
124 Verb with thou

DOWN

1 Gripes
2 Airy rooms
3 Secret stock
4 Cold fish
5 "The House Without a Key" hero
6 Maintained
7 "Look Back in Anger" wife
8 Strength
9 Forks over the dough
10 Galloway gal
11 U.
12 Saint known as the Little Flower of Jesus
13 Prepare (oneself)
14 Part of IBM: Abbr.
15 "Me neither!"
16 King in G. & S.'s "The Gondoliers"
17 Suffix with defer
18 Sounds from a scolder
26 Least tan
28 Skillful
29 Bluenose
33 Agcy. concerned with false advertising
35 Pizza ingredient
37 Like a bobcat vis-à-vis a pussycat
39 "Pipe down!"
40 City of northern France
41 Janis's partner, in the comics
42 Star player for the Cosmos
43 Those, to Tomás
44 Salami choice
45 Fats Domino's music, for short
46 "___ the train a-comin'" (Johnny Cash song opener)
47 Prize in a popular game show, for short
48 Old land bordering Luxembourg
49 On sale
51 Like some of the Rockies
52 Flipped out
57 Diminutive suffix
58 Taxi forerunner
61 Op. ___
62 What some games are won by
63 W.W. II zone
64 Prodded
65 Comfy spot
67 The Platters' "___ Mine"
68 Like corduroy
69 Song on the Beatles' "White Album"
70 Flip
71 Oversell
74 Church nook
75 "Very funny!"
76 Loads
77 Hard knocks
79 Ham container?
82 ___-Locka, Fla.
83 Picture of Elvis on velvet, e.g.
85 English author Lofts
86 Scholar's sphere
89 Staples of rock groups
90 Crunchy sandwich
92 Turns down
95 Acid neutralizer
96 Blow up
98 Prize money
100 Calls

by Nelson Hardy

102 Cry of terror
103 "Keen!"
104 They may be involved in busts
105 Shooting game
106 One who crosses the line?
107 Tennis star Mandlikova
108 Spanish bears
109 Actress Madlyn
110 Some hwys.
111 Zaire's Mobutu ___ Seko
112 Bone: Prefix
114 Didn't bring up the rear?

ACROSS

1 Airline info
7 It may be caught in winter
13 Ice cream shop employee
20 Ron of CNBC
21 Rocker Dee Dee, Tommy, Joey or Johnny
22 With a creamy cheese sauce
23 Redbook (1848)
26 Home (in on)
27 Princess tester
28 Final bit
29 They may be B.C. or A.D.
30 Owl hangouts
32 Present prefix
33 Runner Devers and others
37 Yearbook (1949)
41 1953 Emmy-winning actress
44 Wrong
45 Prefix with cortical
46 Brown of Talk magazine
47 Beetles may be found in them
50 Never gone
54 Tap idly with the fingers
55 Guidebook (1994)
57 Nest noises
58 Rice and Robbins
59 Org. with inspectors
60 Singer Zadora
61 Place for splints
62 Meandering curve
63 Bible book (1977)
67 Area between center and right, say
70 Bean ___
71 French collagist
72 CD-___
73 Ex-Cosmos great
74 Souvenir stand item
77 Comic book (1997)
81 When some people eat lunch
82 Erich ___, author of "Emil and the Detectives"
83 "Mr. Apollinax" writer
84 "The West Wing" actor
85 Not a thing
86 Fathers and sons
88 Songs sung by candlelight
89 Law book (1866)
96 Thirst (for)
97 Bibliophile's suffix
98 Bach composition
99 Setting for many jokes
102 Visibly peeved
104 Eyesore
105 New money
106 Review book (1982)
113 Curtainlike fish snarer
114 Charge, British-style
115 Chilling words
116 Marine food fish
117 Fills in
118 Big name in antivirus software

DOWN

1 Posh
2 "___ Majesty's Secret Service"
3 False friends
4 ___ Bell
5 Rock producer Brian
6 Hong Kong harbor sight
7 Cutters
8 ___ Solo of "Star Wars"
9 London label
10 Setting for "The Practice"
11 Feral
12 Program until 1966
13 Commonsensical
14 Don't let go of
15 0-for-5 performance for Mark McGwire, e.g.
16 You can dig it
17 Foot, to Fabius
18 What N.Y./Phila. baseball games are usually played in
19 Children's character in the Hundred Acre Wood
24 ___ mortals
25 Straight
30 Cry in a crowded hall
31 Angler's gear
34 Kind of proposition, in logic
35 Noted wine valley
36 Early time
37 Some tides
38 Sufficient, old-style
39 Lady lobster
40 Super Bowl XXXIV champs
41 5 1/2-point
42 "Ghostbusters" co-star
43 Small amounts
48 Struggle
49 Politician's declaration
51 Ball bearing?
52 Vigor
53 It lands at Lod
54 Slicing request
56 Sorceress
57 Chews on
61 ___-Hawley Tariff Act of 1930
63 "O.K."
64 They may be arranged in banks
65 Greek group, for short
66 #4 on ice
67 Wish granter
68 Star in Perseus
69 Pains, so to speak
70 Field of stars?
73 Kitchen light
74 Locker room supply
75 Child's bedtime treat
76 Actor Mandel
77 Barely covered
78 Classic drink
79 Code subject
80 Tubular food
82 Cousins
85 Child watchers
87 Quiets
90 Sappho's poet friend
91 Undergarment
92 Something to sing in
93 Swimming
94 Small thing
95 Word source
99 Well-muscled
100 Response to "Am not"

by Randolph Ross

101 1953
A.L. M.V.P.
103 F.B.I. workers:
Abbr.
105 Word prefixed
by who, what
or when
106 1,000 fins
107 French goose
108 Suffix with pay
109 16 oz.
110 Indecisive end
111 Dungeons &
Dragons
game co.
112 Acapulco gold

54   BALLPLAYERS' FAVORITE

ACROSS

1 Nasty campaign?
6 Insect trap of sorts
11 Cabinet display, perhaps
17 Singles
21 Not just decorative
22 Strength
23 In a New York minute
24 "___ here"
25 . . . food?
28 Lodge
29 "___ say!"
30 Algeria's second-biggest city
31 Nonclerical
32 More than devotees
34 Year Trajan was born
36 . . . song?
40 New York City stadium name
41 Bliss
43 Important spelling feature of "iridescent"
44 Actor Armand
46 Pitcher Shawn
47 Archeological find
49 Response: Abbr.
50 Give the eye
53 Jam
56 Kindly
58 "No ___!"
59 Pizzeria order
63 . . . animals?
66 Org. with a big PAC
67 Maintained
68 Supermodel Campbell
70 Move like a scared rabbit
72 Teeny
73 Sky-chart scales
74 Inter ___
77 "Nosiree!"
78 Belligerent Olympian
79 . . . boat?

81 . . . sci-fi flick?
83 Certain resale item, informally
86 Gun
88 Stab
89 Quadruple gold medalist, 1936
90 Kind of car
92 C.E.O.'s
95 Events for which to get decked out
96 Decked out
97 Tenn. neighbor
98 . . . actor?
102 Alternatives to Merlots
104 Bruise
106 Put away
107 American Indian pony
108 Solvent
110 Court action
111 Game usually played in a ring
113 Produce
118 Home of Gallo Winery
120 Wearer of 71-Down
121 Exact
123 Color quality
124 . . . TV character?
128 Deck
129 Place for police
131 French city heavily hit in 1944
132 South Dakota, to Pierre
133 Something taken into account?: Abbr.
134 Locale for pins
135 . . . James Bond movie?
141 Follows a recipe direction
142 Like many a phone caller
143 "___ Paris"
144 Val d'___, French ski resort
145 Mosquito, e.g.
146 Stinker
147 Forty-___
148 Old

DOWN

1 Flambé
2 Emphatic letters
3 Gangland communication
4 Cockpit dial: Abbr.
5 Fiddle-de-___
6 Brawl
7 Upright
8 Critical point
9 Hiver's opposite
10 Cancel, in a way
11 Report of proceedings
12 City where the first Woolworth's opened, 1879
13 "Arabian Nights" creature
14 Sign
15 Lots
16 E-mailer's option
17 Emulated a Boy Scout
18 . . . book?
19 Overdramatize
20 Stitches
26 Scraps
27 Doesn't maintain even consistency
33 Niels Bohr. e.g.
35 Suffix with social
37 Single
38 Like horses
39 Neighbor of Bhutan
42 Hold
45 Smart ___
47 Uncompromising law
48 Pollster's quest
49 Word in a tied score
51 Division of a subdivision
52 Toot
54 Something to believe in
55 Heater
56 Louvre Pyramid designer
57 Mat material
59 One-fourth of a '60s group

60 "Well, did you ___?"
61 . . . candy?
62 Used a lever on
63 Snow creation
64 Lennon/ McCartney's "___ Loser"
65 A, as in Augsburg
69 Put ___ in one's ear
71 Clan's pride
73 N.Y.C. airport
74 "May I have your attention?"
75 Photographer's cover
76 Possibilities
80 Election news
81 Some think they're terrible
82 Scene of fierce W.W. I fighting
84 O'Neill's "A Touch of the ___"
85 Cutlass, e.g.
87 Tennessee athlete
89 John Boyd ___, 1949 Peace Nobelist
91 Check
92 Novelist Janowitz
93 Minnesota's St. ___ College
94 Beau ___
95 Sci-fi escape vehicle
96 ___ Dhabi
99 Very, to Verdi
100 Woolf's "___ of One's Own"
101 W's brother
103 Replies at sea
105 Most lamebrained
107 Time of smooth sailing
109 Summer heat-beaters
111 Checked out
112 Checks
114 Saigon celebration
115 Makes it
116 Ways to make a big splash

by Nancy Nicholson Joline

55 NOON

ACROSS

1 A little lower
5 Like some respect
8 Secondary bank
14 One whose social life is going to pieces?
19 Utopia seeker
21 Bad-mouth
22 Voice one's view
23 Sadist
24 Embodiment
25 Empire
26 "Calling America" band
27 "Autumn in New York" co-star
28 Great money-saving achievement?
30 High beams
32 To be more accurate
33 ___ citato
34 Joan of art
35 Victim of erosion
36 J.F.K. posting: Abbr.
37 Phaser setting
39 Robert Conrad courtroom drama
41 Result of a moon-landing accident?
48 Toys with runners
50 Sea into which the Amu Darya flows
51 Biblical verb
52 Black brew
53 Even
54 Bacon bit
56 Hungarian wine
57 Pulitzer-winning novel of 1925
58 Make tiny knots
59 From Yerevan: Abbr.
60 Prefix with type
61 Religious figure in a hot-rod race?
69 Go along
70 ___ apart
71 Detroit-based org.
72 Considerable
73 Having eyes, in verse
74 Drivel
76 Medieval
79 Like a 911 call: Abbr.
80 Tease
81 Final Four game
82 Stonehenge priest
84 Disappearing restrooms?
87 "The Sound of Music" name
89 Groucho, in "A Night at the Opera"
90 Take off
91 Certain attachment
92 Good sign?
94 Disdain
97 Clear
100 Nonpaying gig
103 Veterinarian's promise?
105 Italy's Val d'___
106 Hindu title
107 Simple souls
108 Kind of duty
109 Lot
111 Hold firmly
112 Temporary wheels
113 Stomach
114 Calendario marking
115 Point up
116 Port Huron Statement grp.
117 River of Flanders

DOWN

1 Mill product
2 "A Passage to India" heroine ___ Quested
3 Drumstick for Fido?
4 Considerably
5 Noted French encyclopedist
6 Not abstainers
7 To be, in Bordeaux
8 Of the arm
9 Unmask
10 Opposite of après
11 Gangster called "The Enforcer"
12 Teaching assignment
13 Sub
14 One who knows how to swing
15 At full gallop
16 College student's declaration
17 Provide
18 Legal defendant: Abbr.
20 It has a head and hops
29 Western setting
31 Prong
32 Now
35 Infection suppressants
36 Not healthy-looking
37 Something blue
38 Ring around the collar?
40 Speeders make it
41 Mann of many words
42 Come to
43 "Try ___ see"
44 Nordic wonder
45 Grind away
46 1980 Tony winner
47 Land in Ezekiel
49 Parlor piece
55 Show signs of overuse
56 In a tough spot
57 Cast forth
59 Lace tips
61 Illinois birthplace of William Jennings Bryan
62 Color-changing lizard
63 Like some vbs.
64 Actress romanced in real life by Rudolph Valentino
65 First name in daytime TV
66 "For bonny sweet ___ is all my joy": Ophelia
67 Subject of an annual festival in Holland, Mich.
68 Beldam
73 Organ stop
74 Guardian Angels wear
75 Single-named supermodel
76 In drydock?
77 Year in Claudius's reign
78 Shingle letters
81 Brandy cocktails
83 Stage part
85 "Wrap" artist
86 Hoodoo
88 Disinfectant compounds
91 Manuscript units
93 Electron collector
94 Massacred
95 Novelist Barker
96 Volunteer
97 Ornamental loop
98 "Everybody Is ___" (1970 hit)
99 Wrap (around)

by Richard Silvestri

100 Litter
101 Past perturbed
102 Floorer
103 About
104 Rembrandt contemporary
105 Ins. sellers
110 Prohibition promoter

FIGURES OF SPEECH

ACROSS

1 Eat in a hurry
5 Comet rival
11 Low spot
15 "See you"
19 Jabir al-Ahmad al-Sabah, e.g.
20 Egg container
21 Touching activity
22 Author Hunter a k a Ed McBain
23 "Give me a mudpack," e.g.
26 Director of the "Dr. Mabuse" films
27 Collectibles, so to speak
28 Fume
29 Peace offering
31 Succeeds
32 Bad blood
34 Row of pawns, e.g.
35 Broker's action
38 ___ of Japan
39 "My suitcase is better than yours," e.g.
41 A Swiss army knife has lots of them
43 Subdued
45 Wands
46 They fill holes
48 "Any bullets in this thing?," e.g.
56 Land of the eland
59 Have an effect
60 Firing squad?: Abbr.
61 Rogue
62 Cut back
63 Best-selling car in America, 1997–2000
65 "Olympic track events are thrilling," e.g.
70 Visibly astonished
72 Borrower's handouts
73 Game with a ball that no player ever touches
76 Gothic author Radcliffe
77 Paul of "Casablanca"
80 Says "please" and then some
81 "You might want to check the carburetor," e.g.
85 Roll top?
86 Fleeting feeling
87 How to get something from nothing, perhaps
90 Practiced
91 "I'll give you $100 for that buffet table," e.g.
97 Theater sound
99 Place for a plug
100 Little one
101 Says no
102 Carrier that bought Piedmont in the 1980s
104 Most strapping
106 Indicator of current trends?
107 Swamps
111 St. Patrick's home
112 "I'm making a quilt," e.g.
115 "Tess of the D'Urbervilles" cad
116 It may make a big haul
117 Optometrist's solution
118 Gathering
119 Stand in the flames
120 Dillies
121 Looney Tunes regular
122 Striped stone

DOWN

1 Tapestry thread
2 Baseball's Vizquel
3 Head hunters' targets
4 Order member
5 Difficult pills to swallow
6 Indulge, perhaps
7 Strikes out
8 Hieroglyph images
9 Spoil
10 First-aid item
11 Film director Vittorio
12 Play wrap-up
13 Papal name
14 Watercolorist ___ Liu
15 Put something on
16 Successor to the Studebaker
17 Bicycle type
18 Unwanted feeling
24 One way to sell something
25 A bird may have one
30 Toy factory equipment
32 Perceptiveness, in a manner of speaking
33 It's rarely a ratings hit
35 Swells (up)
36 He was spared by divine intervention in Genesis
37 U.S. citizen-to-be
39 The facts of life?
40 Like virtually all schools nowadays
42 Make airtight
44 Tire shop work
47 Starrett family savior
49 Vein
50 Wheel from Holland
51 Place for a Yale lock?
52 Ruining, as a deal
53 Platinum-selling 10,000 Maniacs album of the '80s
54 Athlete who wrote "My Game"
55 Thumbs down
57 Bristle
58 Italy's main broadcasting network
63 Plant with heart-shaped leaves
64 Ring of color
66 Horror film effects
67 They may be given from behind a curtain
68 ___ de plume
69 Male sheep, in Shropshire
70 Org. that aids the stranded
71 Stocky antelope
74 Transformer former
75 Compound in ale
77 Event in a forest
78 Spurred
79 Meter inserts
82 Evident wealth
83 Smooths
84 Racer blade?
88 Having only the upper part showing, as a heraldic beast

by Patrick Berry

89 Sea air
91 Best Actor title role of 1968
92 Superior in lubricity
93 Overhaul
94 Rial spenders
95 Name on a dictionary

96 Least inhibited
98 Surprise party command
100 Underhanded
102 Release
103 Macho sort
105 Recipe abbr.
107 Cuba's ___ of Youth

108 "90210" extra
109 Comparer's problem, maybe
110 River whose name means "hateful"
113 Wahine accessory
114 Shooter

ACROSS

1 Opponent of 120-Across
5 Mac
8 Den ___ (Dutch city, to the Dutch)
12 Little dipper
17 Roughly
19 Qualified
21 Tony : theater :: ___ : fashion design
23 Change a letter in 1-Across to spell . . .
26 Engage in histrionics
27 Place
28 Wife of Bath's offering
29 Away from the bow
30 Bill's co-adventurer, in the movies
31 Ninnies
33 Napoleon, for one
35 Imposture
37 Succumbs to gravity
38 Thicket
39 Eschew spontaneity
43 Dressage factors
45 Commandment pronoun
46 Change a letter in 23-Across to spell . . .
48 Those seeking junior partners?
50 Choral rendition
51 Affect
52 News office
53 Cast a line
56 The "W" of W. H. Auden
57 Rejoin rudely
58 Prefix with magnetic
60 Poet Mandelstam
62 Anteceding
63 Change a letter in 46-Across to spell . . .
66 "___ durn tootin'!"
69 "Swan Lake" piece?
70 Extreme shortage
71 Cellar, in real estate ads
75 Genesis locale
77 Secure, as a passenger
80 Nova follower
82 It's out of the mouths of babes
83 Trojan Horse, e.g.
84 Form of abstract sculpture
85 Change a letter in 63-Across to spell . . .
89 Fresno newspaper
91 Silver oak leaf wearer: Abbr.
92 Comic strip "___ & Janis"
93 Bulb
94 Place for a swing
95 "Mighty ___ a Rose"
96 Place where Gauguin painted
98 Drew Carey, e.g.
100 "When ___ door . . . ?"
102 Bit of "Big Brother" equipment
105 One of the singing Winans family
106 "Clan of the Cave Bear" author
107 His work inspired Broadway's "Nine"
110 Change a letter in 85-Across to spell . . .
114 Selena's musical style
115 Ante, in a sense
116 Birth-related
117 Connoisseur
118 Narrow margin
119 Out of reach
120 Change a letter in 110-Across to spell . . .

DOWN

1 He went for baroque
2 Sub
3 Port authorities
4 Summertime percentages
5 Canopy supports, perhaps
6 Last in seq.
7 Body work?
8 Camouflages
9 "___ ben Adhem"
10 H.S. math
11 "Hogan's Heroes" villains
12 Roast
13 Vinegar base
14 Minn. neighbor
15 Readily conscriptable
16 "Milord" chanteuse
18 Sylvester, to Tweety
20 Dieters' woes
22 Ambulance V.I.P.
24 Book before Deut.
25 Roundup aid
32 Noise from a fan
33 W.W. I soldier
34 Place where a 33-Down fought
36 La donna
38 Role for Liz
40 Starbucks order
41 Floral fragrance
42 Who should believe a liar
43 Ties up the phone
44 $H_{dos}O$
46 Not running
47 Natives call it Misr
49 "For shame!"
50 Nautilus captain
53 Pix that perplex
54 Tarzan creator's monogram
55 Walk pigeon-style
56 Most judicious
59 QB's cry
61 Honshu honorific
63 Engine problem
64 Scruff
65 ASCAP counterpart
66 One-third of a phrase meaning "etc."
67 Clinker
68 Vicomte in "The Phantom of the Opera"
71 Bay's competition, in song
72 Treats unfairly
73 Venus de ___
74 Old Chinese money
76 Iron man?
78 "Three Coins . . ." fountain
79 Mysterious character
81 Lead a square dance
84 Take care of
86 Level of command
87 Out of sorts?
88 Settled scores

by Henry Hook

89 "Here comes the judge!" utterer
90 Swelled head
94 Like saltwater taffy
97 "To give her poor dog ___"
98 Unconventional
99 Unfamiliar
101 Something to bend or lend
102 1/20 ton: Abbr.
103 Sound of a frog?
104 Goya subject
106 Dilettantes' passions
108 Telecommunications setup, for short
109 Empty
111 Hebrew letter
112 Musician Brian
113 Proteus's domain, with "the"

ACROSS

1 Track specialist
6 Steel braces with right-angle bends
11 Not reacting
16 Where a sock may go?
19 It may be pitted
20 One way to run
21 Marisa of "Slums of Beverly Hills"
22 Japanese band?
23 Inside look at a Theban king?
25 Brilliance
26 Secant's reciprocal: Abbr.
27 What some scouts seek
28 Busboy's job, sometimes?
31 Wastes
33 Like some picture frames
34 Flings
35 Tower in the water
38 Kernel's cover
41 Wharton offerings: Abbr.
43 "Yippee!," e.g.
46 "Take ___ at this!"
47 Fencing match inspection?
52 What a really outlandish claim may be?
55 Song of "Salome"
56 Kid's cry
57 Young hogs
58 Palazzo Madama locale
60 Prepare to wash, perhaps
61 Master of Bach suites
65 Precious strings
66 Spread
67 What a timid actor might do as a pirate?
71 Some people weave on them
72 Secular clergy members
73 Married Madrileña
74 Bar figures: Abbr.
75 Aquafresh alternative
76 Beat
80 A carrier has one: Abbr.
81 Cuba libre ingredient
82 Amazed exclamations from bullfight spectators?
88 Ventilation duct?
91 Monteverdi title character
92 Where piasters are currency
93 Promptness prompter
94 Loiters
97 "That's great news!"
98 Encapsulated observation
101 More than a nip
102 Mystery writer Marsh
105 Home games for the San Francisco Giants?
110 Cast
113 Novelist Radcliffe
114 Willow rod
115 Take orders from Lloyd?
118 Chinese philosopher Mo-___
119 Baby hooter
120 "This is ___ new to me!"
121 See 86-Down
122 Canal site
123 "Isabella" poet
124 Where to see an advert
125 "Steppenwolf" author

DOWN

1 Jane Smiley best seller
2 "Why should ___ you?"
3 "___ Rose" (song from "The Music Man")
4 They may be necessary
5 Drive away
6 The recent past
7 Brand of racing bikes
8 A psychic may sense it
9 Some TV's and VCR's
10 Lifting devices hung from helicopters
11 Echo
12 Not putting on any weight
13 "Little" girl in "David Copperfield"
14 Get as a result
15 World's highest large lake
16 Athletic types
17 Not just up
18 Slender traces
24 Actress Merkel and others
29 Dam builders: Abbr.
30 Bills, e.g.
32 Starter starter?
35 Rare bills
36 "Nothin' doin'"
37 Don't skip
39 Like some trauma patients
40 Marine off.
41 Connecticut city
42 Hippie gathering of a sort
44 Future presenters, in the past
45 Spots for bees
48 March event, in more ways than one
49 "The Hot Zone" topic
50 Hall-of-Fame announcer Harry
51 Steely Dan's "___ Lied"
53 Peak in Greek myth
54 Famous dying words
59 Some burial vessels
60 Ostentatious
62 Running full speed
63 "Hogan's Heroes" corporal
64 "Quién ___?" ("Who knows?")
65 Radical 1960s grp.
66 Tears
67 Singer LaBelle
68 Bury
69 Ned Land's rescuer
70 Pitcher ___ Nen
71 1814 Byron poem
75 "The Third of May" painter
77 John Major, e.g.
78 "Imperfect Sympathies" essayist
79 Time to attack
81 It has precedents
83 Large-oared craft on a ship
84 .0000001 joule
85 Military branches: Abbr.
86 With 121-Across, they're bright on Broadway
87 Often-poked pitchman
89 Carry on
90 Foils

by Karen Hodge

95 River isle
96 Bull: Prefix
98 Weaken
99 "Who's the Boss?" co-star
100 Former Screen Actors Guild president
101 February forecast, perhaps
103 The lucky ones?
104 Nostalgia stimulus
106 ". . . mercy on such ___": Kipling
107 Reader's Digest co-founder Wallace
108 Fit
109 Give a hoot
111 Food for snakes
112 Studies
116 Fashion inits.
117 Course setting: Abbr.

ACROSS

1 Acadia National Park locale
6 Mystery writer Paretsky
10 More fitting
15 Stoolie
18 Actor Davis
19 Heal, in a way
20 Like surfers paddling surfboards
21 Three-time World Cup star
22 Black box on "The Addams Family"?
24 Identify fish by sonar?
26 Wind-borne pet
27 Middle of a run?
28 Laplander
29 Track group?
30 What angry wasps might do to a room?
34 Step before spin-dry
35 "High Noon" wife __ Kane
36 Farfetched
37 Tic-tac-toe plays
39 It's trilling
43 "I've got it!"
45 O'Connor's successor as archbishop of New York
46 A lot of Polynesia
47 Checkers strategy?
55 G's
56 Trask twin in "East of Eden"
57 Give birth to
58 Durbin of '30s–'40s musicals
59 "I feel as old as yonder __": "Finnegans Wake"
60 Fancy
61 Altdorf's canton
62 #1 song hit whose title is spelled out in the lyrics
63 Do follow-up?
65 Who carried artist Holbein to the party?
68 Nickelodeon feature
69 1984 Jeff Bridges title role
71 Kind of rule
72 The heat
73 Diamond __
74 Candy brand
75 Go down
76 Org. with refunds
77 U.S. diplomat Silas
79 Group of criminals doing figure eights?
82 Dress finisher
83 Send out
84 Factor in life insurance premiums
85 Flag football teams
86 Gives a hand
90 Library section: Abbr.
93 Doo-wop song syllable
94 Marriage acquisition
95 What adds class to Chinese porcelain?
103 Big scrap
105 "The Haj" author
106 Early skipper
107 Switch add-on
108 Big KFC order?
110 Esther Williams's choice?
112 Neighbor of the Bumsteads
113 Pot builders
114 One way to go to a party
115 Oregon Trail city
116 "The Body Snatcher" author's inits.
117 Jerome Hines, notably
118 Big Apple inits.
119 Private

DOWN

1 Applesauce maker
2 Take __ (try)
3 Biblical query
4 Sturdy chiffon
5 Thoughts on paper?: Abbr.
6 Not covering much
7 About
8 Popular digital camera maker
9 Fed on
10 Outrage
11 First
12 Real eye-opener
13 Part of the U.K.
14 Catch one's breath
15 Prompt
16 King of Naples in "The Tempest"
17 Tightens (up)
21 Everyday
23 Quetzalcoatl adornment
25 Sets up
28 Spot for three men in a tub?
31 Has a lot of nerve
32 Camus's "L'__ de siège"
33 Vet
38 Vermont Sen. Bernard __, Congress's only Socialist
39 Fiberglass sports equipment
40 Sporting?
41 School buddy, maybe
42 "Nel __, dipinto . . ." (1958 lyric)
43 "Come __?"
44 Pilot
45 Stretch (out)
48 "Is Sex Necessary?" author
49 "Daktari" actor Rhodes
50 Showing
51 Exhausts
52 Priest, to Nash
53 Already existing, as a phrase
54 Snitches
56 "The Chinese Parrot" hero
60 Last line in a riddle
62 Weightlifters' lifts
64 Is vexing
66 Big bell sound
67 Fill up
70 Steps aside
75 48-Down, e.g.
77 Joltless joe
78 CPR pro
80 Pinkish yellow, e.g.
81 Globe plotter
82 "Merry Christmas" preceder
86 What one might beg to do
87 Start, in a way
88 Frightens

by Manny Nosowsky

89 Milk: Prefix
90 Pushes one's way
91 "Yea, verily"
92 Sports score notations
93 Rough-napped
96 Easter activities
97 Accord
98 1980s Schwarzenegger role
99 Subatomic particle
100 Apollo 15 astronaut James ___
101 Hubbub
102 Pyle on TV
104 Matey
109 ___ manner of speaking
110 Nine-digit ID
111 Hitter's stat

ACROSS

1 Feature of a murder mystery
7 It's often done by phone
11 Chocolate source
16 Evanesces
21 Soporific
22 Bow to
23 Hurdles to a degree?
24 Take up room
25 Classroom-supplies market report?
28 Mustang catcher
29 Family name with a checkered past?
30 Passing comments?
31 Russian figure skater Sokolova
32 Wood mill apparatus
33 Unwanted look
34 Heidi's home
35 Nike, e.g.
36 Some eBay users
37 Recipe direction
38 Teacher of Samuel
39 Not hold it in
40 Pop up
41 Cutlery market report?
45 Site for spores
48 Kind of fork
51 Rugged ridge
52 First king of Phliasia, in myth
53 Effuse
54 Film job
56 Old Polo Grounds star
57 Ruined
58 Wise guys?
59 Put out
60 Bedding market report?
65 Porter musical
66 1968 champion at Forest Hills

68 Conflict that ended at 11:00 on 11/11
69 Singer Easton
70 Like an excellent game for a pitcher
71 State bordering Veracruz
74 Parlor letters
75 Rabbi's alma mater
78 Knee-slapper
80 Actress Pia
83 Joan, e.g.: Abbr.
84 Six-footers
87 Fix, as a pipe joint
88 Fruit market report?
91 Former Portuguese colony in India
92 "___ Like You" (1967 hit)
93 "Hee Haw" humor
94 It's usually 3, 4 or 5
95 500 cars
97 500 places
98 Manipulate, as the books
99 Memento
101 Wiggle room, in a shoe
102 Computer key: Abbr.
103 Farm-stock market report?
108 Subjects for hypnotists
111 Pirate's box
112 Charley's love in "Where's Charley?"
113 Electricity source
116 Took an extra course?
118 Rafter's thrill
119 Downy

121 Explorer's quest, with "the"
122 Agave fibers
123 Preferred invitees
124 Broadcast
125 Bridge enthusiast?
126 Feat of clay?
127 Metals market report?
130 Infidel, in Islam
131 Endured
132 Sample
133 Power problem
134 Soviet subs
135 Player against Player
136 Arctic transport
137 Exercised pull?

DOWN

1 Linking verb
2 In full bloom
3 Washed off
4 Many an expectant father
5 Recipe direction
6 Sushi fare
7 Growth
8 Reeds section
9 Nothing ___
10 Eye burner
11 Distant
12 Short operatic piece
13 Street-smart
14 Utah ski resort
15 Old spy org.
16 Schoolmarm's discipline dispenser
17 Armpit
18 Nursery-supplies market report?
19 Ethyl acetate, e.g.
20 Sky lights
26 Drivel
27 Barons and earls
32 "___ Diary"
34 Pugilist poet
35 Gull

36 Comics sound
38 ___ an era
39 Isolated locales
40 Table part
41 Kit ___
42 Suggestive
43 See 57-Down
44 New Jersey city
46 Very, in music
47 Sound from a monastery, maybe
48 Stiff hair
49 County seats in Minnesota and Oklahoma
50 Electrical equipment market report?
53 League of Nations seat
55 Reason to rat
57 43-Down, to Adam
58 "The ___ Love" (Gershwin tune)
61 Expressions of disbelief
62 Window dresser of TV sitcom
63 ___ Hall
64 Actress Messing of "Will & Grace"
65 Sibling, often
67 Facilitators
72 Unit of nautical time
73 Missouri vacation destination
76 Lively intelligence
77 MO town
78 Nehi flavor
79 Protection
81 Raggedy doll
82 Look
85 Slander, e.g.
86 Scarf
88 Yokels
89 Polio scientist
90 Lion-colored

by Michael S. Maurer

93 Robert of Broadway's "My Fair Lady"
96 El ___
98 Notes of a sort
99 Artifice
100 Sly
104 Animal that's fond of 84-Across
105 Like library talkers
106 Balzac's "La Cousine ___"
107 One rushing to a hosp.
109 Land bordering Mesopotamia
110 Some field workers
113 Thingamajig
114 Claim
115 As one
116 Honshu city
117 "1876" author
118 County of Ireland
119 Whomp, old-style
120 Tipsy
121 Chatter
123 It seems like forever
124 Dark doings
125 Test choice
127 N.F.L. positions
128 Exercise target
129 Exercise pull?

ACROSS

1 Former Virginia senator
5 Small band
10 "If ___ You" (#1 Alabama song)
14 One-time rival of Hogan
19 High guy in Dubai
20 Makeup artists?
21 Place for a mass meeting?
22 Mass meeting
23 Public declarations
25 Start of a quip
27 How some things are set
28 Smarty
30 Lip
31 Compass-drawn line
32 Pleasant way to walk
33 Height
35 Quip, part 2
42 Plow pioneer
44 Screen site
45 More than intuition
46 Bulldog Days participant
47 Relative of -y
48 Primer material
49 It's heavily Hindu
51 Justice Frankfurter
53 Disney opener
56 Le Havre-to-Paris dir.
57 Cote chorus
58 Conductor Lukas ___
59 N.H.L. goalie Chris
61 Whopper
62 Quip, part 3
68 Expresses disdain, in a way
69 Take to the cleaners
70 Fail to medal
73 Sun Bowl venue
76 Visa statement abbr.
79 Longtime McDonald's chief
80 Enlists again
81 Parents
82 Scoffs at
84 Wow
86 Clinton's denom.
87 N.C. State is in it
88 Heavy hydrogen, e.g.
90 Magazine items
93 End of the quip
96 Starting from
97 "I Love a Parade" composer
98 Way home from a bar, maybe
99 Engine production
102 Hardwood sources
105 Pipsqueaks
109 Author of the quip
111 Digest
113 Cross swords
114 ___ early age
115 Water chestnut, e.g.
116 Enough, sometimes
117 Tries to stop expanding
118 ___ prize (came in first)
119 Actor Keach
120 Hot pot

DOWN

1 Scale sequence
2 ___ Air (Mideast carrier)
3 Trash collectors?
4 Side in a 1940 battle
5 Strong holds
6 Seine feeder
7 Pin cushion
8 Cookie salesgirl, perhaps
9 Legendary Irish bard
10 Throw in, as a question
11 "Funny!"
12 Tours with?
13 Takes away
14 Sign of a B'way hit
15 Feeling while reeling
16 Exile isle
17 "___ well . . ."
18 They may provide highlights
24 Neighbor of McGuire Air Force Base
26 Page of a book
29 Standard deviation symbol
32 Across, in verse
34 17th-century Spanish painter of religious scenes
35 In the time that
36 Commands
37 Les États-___
38 "Well done!"
39 Spartan queen of myth
40 "What ___?"
41 Some resorts
42 Bridges in movies
43 Nondairy spread
48 Crude dude
50 It may get under your skin
52 Famed film flop
54 "Sick!"
55 Hatchery supply
57 Innocent one
59 Football Hall-of-Famer Graham
60 Lexicographer's concern: Abbr.
61 Fugue preceder, often
63 Wagga Wagga residents
64 Varieties
65 Rev.'s delivery
66 Prefix with cortex
67 "Absolutely!"
71 Work with a pug
72 Glimpse
73 Latin 101 word
74 Poland's Walesa
75 It's set by a runner
76 ___ California
77 Lowdown
78 Louisville landmark
80 Master anew
82 Tempest in a teapot
83 Home base for un astronaute
85 Spelling?
89 Endured
90 Beats easily
91 Thousandth of a yen
92 Pleasant drives?
94 French 120-Across
95 Provides a seat for
99 Voting booth hanger-on?
100 Mata ___
101 Press
103 Japanese stringed instrument

by Elizabeth C. Gorski

ACROSS

1 San Antonio brewer, once
6 Home of El Greco
12 Broad bean
16 Catch
19 To go, to Godot
20 Departed without ceremony?
21 Mosque bigwig
22 Clamor
23 Order at a Vegas pizzeria?
25 Not absolute
27 Two Oscar winners for best acting?
28 "Star Wars" knight
29 Colorado natives
30 Gopher wood vessel
31 Suffix with prank or trick
32 Positioned, as artillery
33 Unkind comment
34 Handle the arrangements for
36 Ingredients in a Flintstones sandwich?
41 Code-breaking govt. group
42 It'll open your trap
44 1981 miniseries set in A.D. 72–73
45 Surrounded by lawn
47 Two features of interest on the sunken Titanic?
51 In medias ___
52 U.P.S. delivery
55 Reverse
56 ___ choy

57 Eisenhower's successor at NATO
61 Not right
63 "Never Cry Wolf" author Farley ___
65 Set down
67 Wisecrack
68 Kind of metal
69 Singer Washington
70 Father-to-son bequests
71 Gillette brand
72 Sax-playing Simpson
73 Draft picks?
74 Execs
75 Ice cream flavor
76 Out, socially
78 Nobel area: Abbr.
79 "Believe ___ not!"
81 Initials at sea
82 Guy Fawkes Day mo.
83 Raw materials for a feather pillow?
88 Sponge
91 Evening do
92 Troubled
95 Dashboard abbr.
96 Types of gemstones?
100 Islamic chiefs
102 Oman man
104 Observer's record
105 Actor Ken
107 New Deal program: Abbr.
108 Coupler
109 Couples
110 Theater show that follows a commercial?
114 You might be asked to keep one

116 Items in a Victoria's Secret marketing presentation?
117 Vocalist Rawls
118 ___ Minor
119 Went alone
120 Canon fodder?
121 Egyptian headdress symbol
122 Byproduct of cheesemaking
123 Seating area
124 Articles by nonstaffers

DOWN

1 Ottoman V.I.P.'s
2 Led on
3 Something you use at every turn
4 Splinter group
5 Disloyal to the state
6 Fuel car for a steam locomotive
7 Veteran
8 Miner's quest
9 Large-scale
10 It's not damaged by cutting
11 Ben Jonson wrote one to himself
12 Object of condemnation
13 Italian artist Modigliani
14 On good grounds
15 Org. with a caduceus logo
16 Fishing lure attached to a rod?
17 Hostile
18 Spoils
24 Grasshopper's teacher, in Aesop

26 Dilapidated boat
28 Red Sea port
32 Carroll creature
35 Typewriter key
37 Mil. officer's position
38 Algiers quarter: Var.
39 English racing village
40 Cooking fat
43 Have
46 Jamaican export
48 Blended
49 Who leads an anarchy?
50 Che Guevara's first name
52 Nobelist Neruda
53 At full speed
54 Things linked in the minds of '70s music fans?
58 Checks for ages, say
59 The "A" of James A. Garfield
60 Has kids
62 Jack-tar
64 Pallid
65 Floral wreath
66 Madcap
69 Part of a Web address
70 Former British money
74 Clifflike ridge
75 Claims, as the throne
77 "___ plaisir, monsieur"
78 Road to ruin
80 Eggs
84 Colorful newspaper
85 They get scoops
86 "Der Ring ___ Nibelungen"
87 ___ sleep
88 Big name in kindergarten

by Patrick Berry

89 Fit
90 Small and weak
93 Delta, for one
94 Like tires
97 Nonuniversity type
98 Like Roman senators
99 African herd animals
101 "The Nine Tailors" author
103 Big __
106 Person with a 114-Across?: Abbr.
110 Garden area
111 Reader's Digest co-founder __ Wallace
112 Familiar with
113 Sit (down)
115 Big mouth
116 Sound after a pinprick

63 UNTREATABLE CONDITIONS

ACROSS
1 Put on
6 Close relatives of a 5-Down
12 Like a dove
19 Payee, perhaps
21 Snappy item?
22 "Buck up!"
23 Builder's condition?
25 Kind of gland
26 Cite
27 Cold place
28 Coal place
29 Like some humor
30 Stab
31 Subject of TV's "Life and Legend," 1955–61
33 Psychologist Lee and others
36 Langley outfit
38 The Father of Science Fiction
39 Actress Alvarado of "Little Women"
40 Sign up
43 Jest
46 Vietnamese leader deposed in 1963
48 Schneider
50 "Between two ___, which hath the merriest eye": Shak.
52 Love
53 Study, study, study
55 Behold, to Pilate
56 Not common
57 Loudly laments
59 The good life
60 Mauna ___
61 National competitor
62 Hails
64 Ain't it the truth

67 Doze
69 Doze
70 Schoolteacher's condition?
74 Mil. honor
76 Boat that's ready to be mothballed
77 Open-sided beach shelter
78 Get ready for a big game
81 Ransack
83 Word with ground or Japanese
85 Bayes who sang "Shine On, Harvest Moon"
87 Was crooked
88 Fancies
89 Designer Rowan
91 Big gulp
92 Many a tournament
93 Kind of nut
94 This may work on your block
96 "Traffic" cop
98 Like some bookstores
99 Dined à la maison
101 Patron saint of dancers and actors
103 Action movie plot device
105 Kind of test
106 Influential set
107 Clockmaker Thomas
108 Mock, in a way
111 Blast
114 '60s muscle car
116 Decline with age
118 Got ready for a big game

120 Midwest college or its town
122 Road paver's condition?
124 Take over for
125 Indolent
126 Comfort
127 Slips by
128 Reveals
129 Actress Streep

DOWN
1 Scrub
2 Put off
3 Off the wall
4 War of 1812 port
5 Ruling
6 Prefix with terrorism
7 Not all wet?
8 Duty
9 Refuges during tornadoes
10 Tall and branching
11 It's heard in "Besame Mucho"
12 Hail ___
13 "Forget it!"
14 Driver's condition?
15 Dudgeon
16 Magician's need
17 Chinese gelatin
18 Count
20 Slow up
24 Architectural band
32 British book of genealogies
34 Floor scrubber's condition?
35 "___ when?"
37 Moon of Uranus
38 Mount ___
41 Church musician's condition?
42 Beast of burden
43 O.K.

44 Visa competitor
45 Versifier's condition?
47 Bricklayer's condition?
49 Reeves of "The Matrix"
51 Lousy food
54 Famous hostess
58 Roofer's condition?
63 Erwin of early TV
65 A. A. Milne play "Mr. ___ Passes By"
66 Queen of the Cowgirls
68 Rhea's Roman counterpart
71 Rival of 114-Across
72 Lowest of the low
73 Took it on the lam
74 Minute amount
75 LP part
79 Peter Fonda title role
80 Remain unsettled
82 Spiked
84 Liveliness
86 Accept
90 First-aid info
95 Dazed and confused
97 Vitamin C source
100 Intrinsic
102 Fracases
104 Hello or goodbye
108 Draw nigh to
109 "Love in the Ruins" author Walker ___
110 Collectible car
111 Reason for an R rating

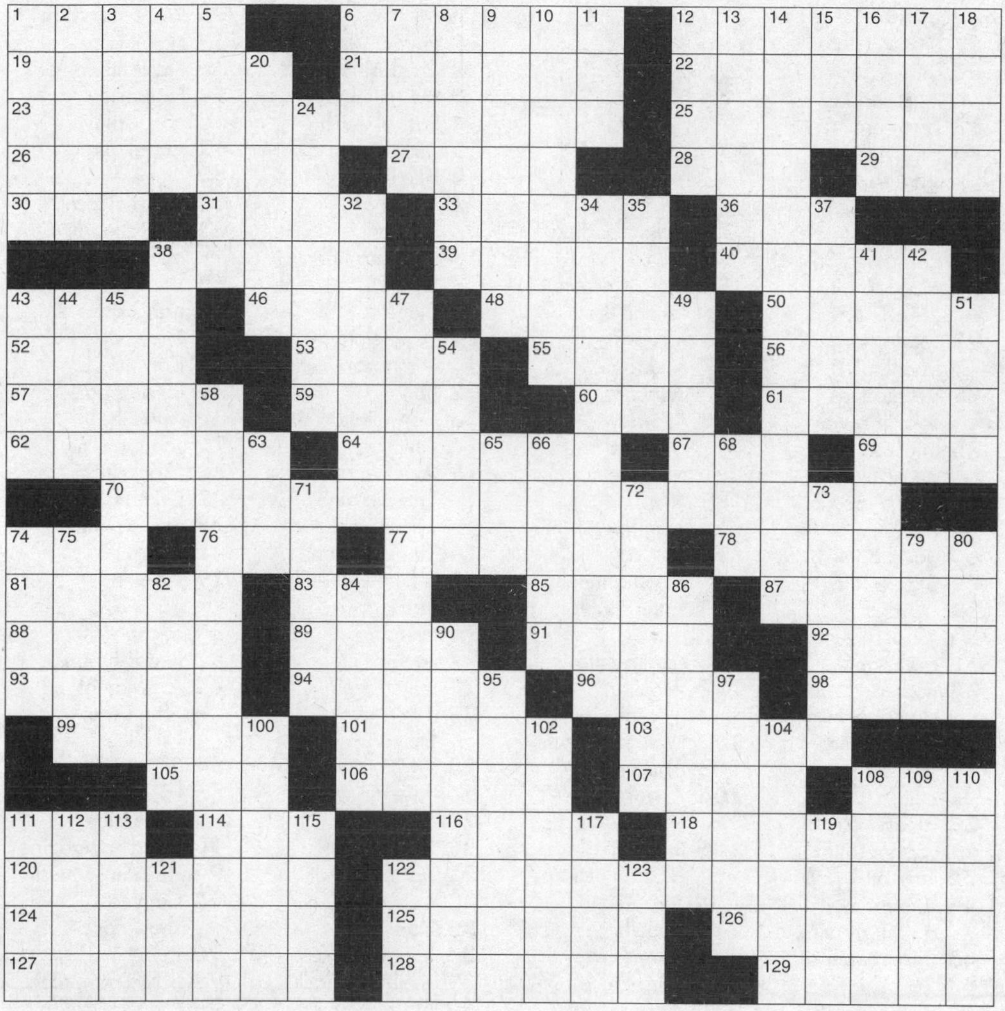

by Michael Ashley

112 The third man?
113 Actress Ward
115 Individuals
117 Bygone brand on U.S. highways
119 Leave in neutral
121 Cheat, slangily
122 Fifth of eight
123 Motherly type

64 HOMONAMES

ACROSS

1 Street on a snow-covered hill
7 Agitated
12 Farm animals
16 Highway sign abbr.
19 A Gandhi
20 Writer with the pen name Saki
21 Magician in "The Tempest"
23 Tote a narrow opening?
25 Worked the soil, in a way
26 Intervals of an octave and a second
27 Ruins a good book?
29 Start to fix?
32 __-Ball
33 Modern June birthstone
34 Popular street name
35 Onion made of a sturdy cotton fabric?
38 Noblewoman
41 Japanese dog
42 Tiny bit
44 Like many a first-grader
45 Zine reader
48 Engine
49 Some sprays
54 Hun-armed bandit?
56 Bookie?
58 Fire
60 "__ ed Euridice" (Gluck opera)
61 Carrot, e.g.
62 Stealin' from a bloodsucker?
64 One of the Challenger astronauts
68 Occupied
70 Letter abbr.
71 Satiate a ghost?
73 Friend of Françoise
75 Bradley and Epps
76 Closing act?
77 Terse crackling sound?
83 Internet novice
85 Second versions
87 Add more lubricant
88 Attorney General nominee Baird
89 NATO member: Abbr.
91 Have an evening meal
92 In the slightest degree
93 Most humid
97 Vacation by a pier?
102 Wall St. worker
103 Abu __
105 Apparatus with pedals
106 Big Apple inits.
107 Praying actions cause ennui?
110 Flugelhorn's cousin
112 Washing machine part
113 People who live next to a Y?
119 Rampages
120 Icicles' starting points
121 Turkish mountain
122 C.I.A.'s forerunner
123 Torah holders
124 Alternative nickname to Pat
125 Two-seater

DOWN

1 Photo
2 __ flash
3 Mil. chief
4 Part of A.F.B.
5 __ Mawr, Pa.
6 Like a palooka
7 Brand of light beer
8 Orchard unit
9 Blame
10 Not std.
11 "Camelot" composer
12 Ball
13 Consultation sites
14 Function
15 Azerbaijan and Ukraine, once: Abbr.
16 Puts gems on a flute player?
17 Best part
18 One of Taylor's eight
22 Tiny openings
24 1934 hit "__ Dinka Doo"
28 Grammy category
29 Kind of tea
30 Singer Bonnie
31 Sci. of insects
33 Sch. groups
35 Door part
36 Indian dress
37 Methane's lack
39 Narrow inlet
40 Eulogizes
43 Numbskulls
46 Guinness and others
47 Sodium hydroxide, to a chemist
49 Idolizes
50 "Hold On Tight" group
51 Switch heads?
52 Sabrina of "The Cosby Show"
53 Rest time: Abbr.
55 Half of seis
57 Stalactite former
59 Figures for poker players
62 Capek play
63 Not e'en once
64 Certain copy
65 Scratched-up leather straps?
66 Workers' rights grp.
67 Give out
69 Calls for
71 Potsie's pal, with "the"
72 Jaguar, e.g.
74 "Rocky III" actor
77 Crime boss
78 River to the Caspian
79 Arrive, as darkness
80 Sycophant
81 Reddish purple
82 __ May of "The Beverly Hillbillies"
84 Sound of fright
86 Fashion designer Gernreich
90 Hearst magazine
94 Helps in a heist
95 Cinema showings
96 Gob
98 Some computers
99 Branch Davidians leader
100 __ soit qui mal y pense
101 Series enders
102 Black __ cattle
104 Sire
107 Corn syrup brand
108 Zhivago's love
109 Commotion
110 Year in Sergius III's papacy
111 See-__

by Peter Gordon

114. Shostakovich's
"Babi __"
Symphony
115 Place to get a
screwdriver
116 1967 Rookie
of the Year
117 Scottish
explorer John
118 Hog haven

65 IN CROWD

ACROSS

1 Teaching device
8 View from Windsor Castle
14 ___ Bay, part of Lake Huron
20 Shrunken
21 Tasmania's capital
22 Winner of all four grand slam titles
23 Famous presidential declaration
25 Person with no pockets
26 Spots
27 Rosacea and others
28 "Cómo ___ usted?"
30 One of the 12 tribes of Israel
31 Plots
34 Start of some Spanish place names
35 Eddie Cantor's "___ Whoopee"
36 Suffix with butyl
37 Mozart's "___ fan tutte"
38 Eye-catching beachwear
42 Claims, briefly
43 In all respects
46 Talking bird of poetry
47 ___ Park, Colo.
49 "As Good As It Gets" actor
50 Barbecue item
52 Consider again
54 Deposed tyrant
55 Casual Friday casualties
56 Grind
59 Tennessee Williams, to family
62 They may get a dusting
66 Speaker accompanier, perhaps
67 ___-B (Proctor and Gamble division)
69 Dynamic opener
70 Jalopy
72 Forty-___
73 Ferment
75 Like many Hitchcock films
80 Day-___
81 Gyrates
83 Name on some Scotch bottles
84 Gone by
85 Puts one's foot down
87 Chief Ouray's tribe
88 "A Passage to India" family
92 Pitch
94 Reacts to a shock
96 Weapon on an 89-Down
98 Some campaign charges
99 "My Fair Lady" song
104 Take off
105 Ticket abbr.
106 It'll hold water
107 Person looking for a seat?
108 Half of a famous 1930s duo
109 Slant
110 "Joseph and His Brothers" novelist
111 Bobbin
113 Run (for)
114 More contrived
116 Meal enders
122 Puts up
123 Kind of fuel
124 Amusement park features
125 Easy ___
126 Unveil
127 Barely

DOWN

1 Telepathy, e.g.
2 Cable channel for film devotees
3 Olé
4 Like Mother Teresa
5 Deprives of judgment
6 What settles
7 Irish lass's name
8 1977 James Brolin thriller
9 Obtrudes
10 Fit
11 They may be full of gas
12 Poetic preposition
13 1973–74 faddist
14 "The Great ___" (1979 film)
15 Request from a thirsty Spaniard
16 Wander
17 Stock no-no
18 "The Mambo Kings" co-star
19 Watch
24 Latvian, e.g.
29 Worker with hides
31 Agt.'s cut
32 ___-see
33 John of "Viva Max!"
35 Year in the rule of Ethelred the Unready
38 Shot putter?
39 One of football's Fearsome Foursome
40 Enables a runner to score, maybe
41 Manage
44 Two pages
45 Coats
48 Foil alternative
50 Sharpen
51 "Great Expectations" hero
53 Going back to repeatedly
57 Sky over Strasbourg
58 First name in architecture
59 Big music news
60 "Yes ___?"
61 Gibson fan, say
63 Speech stumbles
64 Figures
65 Part: Abbr.
68 Charter
71 El ___, 1942 battle site
74 Circus prop
76 Pancreatic hormone
77 Dines at home
78 Number of coins in the Fontana di Trevi
79 Foul-up
82 Broadcast
86 Activity at a sorority
89 See 96-Across
90 Squirming
91 Place for runners
92 Big successes
93 Claim
95 Musician's need
97 Pee ___, Carolina river
100 "Citizen Kane" inspiration
101 Seeds
102 Kind of cut

by Nancy Nicholson Joline

103 Pooped
108 Approximately
110 Dole
111 Dance instructor's call
112 Place to see José Morelos
113 Damned

115 Food preserver
117 Quandary
118 Pick up
119 ___-European
120 French possessive
121 Daytona-to-Vero Beach dir.

WHAT THEIR TEACHERS SAID

ACROSS

1 Pachyderm of fiction
6 Byword
11 Seville snack
15 Cookbook abbr.
19 "He was my prize student"
21 "The Time Machine" people
22 Snack brand that sponsored Dale Earnhardt
23 "I used to catch him passing notes in class"
26 Pastoral setting
27 Don with a gift of gab
28 Having more hair on one's chest
29 Hospital lines
30 Cowboys make them: Abbr.
32 Loads
35 "He was a real character"
37 Overplay
39 Bank that may get in trouble?
41 Fossillike
42 Kings prophet
44 Hugo contemporary
46 Bygone Chinese ruler
50 Doing horribly
52 "She loved to do homework"
55 It's half due
56 Former Irish P.M. Cosgrave
58 Playing marble
59 Resin source
60 Firecracker's path
62 Patches up
63 Puccini's "___ Lescaut"
64 "Cities of the Interior" novelist
65 Kind of action
68 Maven
69 Sudden contraction
70 Arrested
73 1988 Olympics locale
75 Gate
80 Hero
81 Terrible shot, in hoops
83 Third son of 71-Down
84 Bartolommeo, for one
85 "Romance languages interested her"
88 Sympathize with
90 "Z" actor
91 Didn't withdraw
93 Record protector
94 Japan-based computer co.
95 St.-___, capital of Réunion
97 Acquiesce
98 "He was a fast learner"
105 A-mazed?
106 Natl. Diabetes Awareness Month
107 Downed
108 Sycophant
110 Bookstore sect.
112 Prefix with center
115 "He used to make up unbelievable tales"
120 Lhasa ___
121 Site of the smithy of Cyclops
122 "He had a very special effect on me"
123 Penury
124 Cannon of "Out to Sea"
125 Affectedly creative
126 "You're ___ talk!"

DOWN

1 Shout out
2 Burn soother
3 Key of Tchaikovsky's Piano Concerto No. 1
4 Cousin of "woof"
5 "He always asked a lot of questions"
6 Like some checkups
7 Iditarod entrant
8 Legal stds. maintainer
9 Marvel
10 Jason of the N.F.L.
11 Pop/funk singer ___ Marie
12 In ___ (quiet)
13 Put forward
14 Focused
15 From A ___
16 Loss through emigration
17 Sampras asset
18 Child's hopping game
20 One that's holding back?
24 Old World crow
25 Colorful flier
31 Evening
33 What a follicle holds
34 Spanish subjects
36 Leisureliness
37 Plenty perturbed
38 Ex-TV host ___ Stewart
40 Third of eight
43 It has a negative charge
45 Pricey
46 Not just 67-Down
47 Sale sign
48 Way to go: Abbr.
49 Initial Bond offering?
51 It comes before Friday
53 Consider officially
54 Something to take when you're tired?
57 Specialized (in)
61 Oily liquids used in dyemaking
63 "He was always looking up at the ceiling"
66 Eyes, poetically
67 Hits
69 Schleps
70 Cleared (of)
71 See 83-Across
72 Serious
73 Place for a firing
74 Follow ___ (do detective work)
76 Call
77 Show some enthusiasm
78 Herded
79 Eastern wrap
81 ___ parisienne
82 Carpenter's need
86 And others too numerous to mention
87 Someone to see before retiring?
89 Toy brand
92 Expels
96 Tight
98 Shah ___ (Taj Mahal builder)
99 Public storehouse
100 Expressed amazement

by David J. Kahn

101 Witchlike
102 Minneapolis suburb
103 Adar follower
104 Stage occupier
109 Latvia's capital
111 Addison's "How are thy Servants blest? O Lord!"
113 Marsh growth
114 Not ___ many words
116 Ground cover
117 ___ Lingus
118 Slangy "Au contraire!"
119 Bleed

ACROSS

1 Finished, as doughnuts
8 Latin step
13 Justice Ginsburg's maiden name
18 What a car may be put into
19 Expresses, maybe
21 Dress styles
23 Echo
24 Rank
25 Play the flute
26 Prison party?
28 Where golfers slam-dance?
30 Systems of rules
31 Took the cake?
32 Tony-winning actor of 1962 and 1990
33 Rebellious Turner
34 Lennon's in-laws
35 Lively circle?
37 Foes of Fortinbras, in Shakespeare
38 Ad __ per aspera (Kansas' motto)
40 Overcharge
41 Was in misery
42 Eucharistic plate
43 Bundle
46 Jewelry designer Peretti
47 Henry's sixth
48 Street of mystery
49 Protection against rustling?
53 Culmination
57 Feel empathy
59 "Here __ Again" (1987 #1 hit)
60 "Touch me with noble __": King Lear
61 Chelsea Hospital architect
62 Lover of Aphrodite
63 Diet breaker, maybe
65 Piece of evidence in a trial
66 Kerouac or Burroughs
67 Approaching
68 Drives a getaway car for, e.g.
70 Prefix with chloride
71 Actor Everett of "Citizen Kane"
73 Lollapalooza
74 Netting on all sides?
77 Methyl methacrylate, e.g.
78 __-doke
80 It might follow "one, two, three"
81 Flexible response
83 Ribbon holder
85 Rub the wrong way
87 Paranoiac's worry
88 League members
89 Sound loudly
90 Drops from above
91 Garage job
95 Old Egyptian letters
96 Where 88-Across play
97 Staccato indicator
98 It's getting carried away
99 Impertinent group?
102 Hawkeye/Hot Lips encounter?
105 Army medic
106 Patron
108 Adjacency
109 Cold explosion?
110 Goddess of sorcery
111 Promising
112 Sonny __, Duke Ellington's longtime drummer
113 Impede
114 Israel's parliament

DOWN

1 California city, informally
2 Sports Illustrated's 1984 Sportswoman of the Year
3 Not moderate
4 Best of seven, say
5 Some football plays
6 This, in Tampico
7 Exploit
8 Geologists' studies
9 Stopped lying?
10 "Do the __"
11 Short time
12 Buttercup family member
13 Surround
14 ". . . bump on __"
15 Stylish gown
16 Peace maker
17 Brush up on
20 Made noises at night
22 Heroine of Wagner's "The Flying Dutchman"
27 Intruder alert?
29 Lottery org.
32 Sweet Spanish wine
35 Clod chopper
36 Bay filler
37 Restaurant serving
38 Alpine stream
39 Nonsense involving farm bedding?
40 Game in which jacks are highest trumps
41 To boot
42 PETCO park squad
43 Look through a window, maybe
44 Claim
45 Space for a cymbalist?
46 H's position
47 Ready
48 Pipe cleaner
50 Becomes aware, with "up"
51 Not even
52 Over
54 Bring to life
55 Not so nice
56 Sign on a door
58 Crown topper
64 Mind
69 1943 Bogart film
70 Drag
72 Liepaja resident
75 Rampant
76 Supermarket section
79 Big cuffs?
82 Product of a solution
83 Cauterizing
84 St. Patrick's Day celebrant
85 Hold tight
86 Oversaw
87 Way
88 Brass section
89 Top piece

by Richard Silvestri

90 Play list?
91 Drinks to sip
92 Colt legend
93 In pairs, botanically
94 One destined for baldness?
96 Dogpatch name
97 "Paradiso" writer
98 North Sea feeder
100 Hook's mate
101 Part of a summer forecast
102 Cold cuts, e.g.
103 Former German capital
104 Black, to Blake
107 Curling surface

ACROSS

1 More than enjoyed
9 Makes a bundle
14 Whodunit awards
20 Not at all gentle
21 __ Heep
22 Graffiti artist's addition
23 Threshold
24 Legal punch?
26 Site of a dramatic 1815 escape
27 Greets
29 Letters at sea
30 "Shop __ you drop"
31 Word on a bridge card
33 Banquets
34 Ibsen doll?
36 Whom a courtier may address
37 Adventuress Nellie
38 Hand protector
40 Many a pollee
42 Out of it
45 Most pious testifier?
47 Take off
48 Suffix with pay
50 One-__ (kids' game)
51 Netscape purchaser
52 Numbers of interest: Abbr.
53 Bother
55 A little, musically
58 Low-cal drinks
62 Actor Morales
64 Dainty attire
65 Cheese made from ewe's milk
67 Burgeoned
68 Whatchamacallit?
69 Air marshal's explanation about keeping his pilots alert?
71 In good health
72 Pipe up or down?
73 Menus, in Metz
74 K rations, e.g.
75 Kind of floor
76 Not gradual
78 Armenia and Georgia, once: Abbr.
79 Perform well
80 Some disrespect
81 Potent potable
83 "Time __ a premium"
85 Like some blood types: Abbr.
86 Be in time for
87 Haggling over how high is up?
93 __ dictum
95 Signer-upper
96 Word repeated by a French Hamlet
97 Social worker?
98 ". . . __ in Kalamazoo"
99 Travel brochure listings
101 Light controller
103 Language quirk
105 San Francisco's __ Hill
106 __ Friday
107 Levels
110 No angel
112 Scofflaw student?
115 Attacked
117 Lorre's role in "Casablanca"
118 City on Ishikari Bay
119 Girl of old comics
120 Got tight
121 Put __ to (end)
122 Sharpshooters

DOWN

1 Take on
2 Like __ from the blue
3 Marinara most likely to be used?
4 Side by side
5 Double turn
6 Not very logical
7 Holder of a 101-Across
8 17th-century diarist
9 Transporter to remote areas
10 Aesthetic
11 "South Pacific" role
12 Stationery brand
13 __ mai (dim sum dish)
14 Narcissist's problem
15 British actress Diana
16 Like some holiday apparel
17 Unit by unit, in succession
18 Makes electrical improvements
19 "There's a Girl in My Soup" star, 1970
25 Host, as a party
28 Sport in which athletes crouch
32 Strong cleanser
35 Natl. Adopt-a-Dog Mo.
36 Benefit of a southern exposure
39 Three-legged ornamental table
41 Mil. plane for quick takeoffs
42 Adds on
43 Starts
44 Kind of license
45 Milliners
46 Food converter
49 First lady's namesakes
54 Waldheim was its head
56 Secretly hiding
57 Early Ping-Pong score
59 Hiker's counsel?
60 Thin and slippery
61 Janitor
63 Mr. Moto's employer
65 Rental ad abbr.
66 New York river to Lake Ontario
70 Actress O'Shea
77 Not pvt.
79 Excited
82 Dragged through the mud
84 Willy Loman, for one
86 Small two-wheeler
87 Not marbled
88 Glut
89 Like 1,001 nights
90 Oscar de la __
91 __-X
92 Writer-director Jordan
94 "__ dog!"
100 Small denominations
102 Like pumps
103 "__ Crime?" (Judy Holliday song)
104 Not shiny
106 Place

by Manny Nosowsky

108 Veneer
109 ___ the Great
   (boy detective)
111 Young 'uns
113 Honorific
   sometimes used
   uncertainly
114 Mauna ___
116 Pop

ACROSS

1 Attach, as a patch
6 How high can you go?
15 Like DNA
20 "Time in a Bottle" singer
21 Over
22 Heaps
23 Set one's sights on
24 Back-pedaled
25 Walk, slangily
26 Shoemaker Thom
27 East German secret police
28 On
30 Dash
32 Shakespearean setting
37 Jazz singer Anita
38 Kind of park
40 School mo.
41 "___ first . . ."
42 Cut
44 Up on, as the jive
48 Red army member
49 Not so stiff
51 Whisper sweet nothings
53 Pig
54 "___ Jury" (Spillane novel)
56 "M" director, 1931
57 Takes a break
61 ___ Antigua
62 Rough areas
64 Back in?
65 Number of days in Avril
67 Something bad to have on one's head
68 Big belt
70 Lady-killers
71 Overplayed
72 Chucklehead
73 Forest denizens
74 Pitch
75 Supremely spooky
77 Uneven do
79 Shake
80 Work the land
82 Cool, to the Fresh Prince
83 Farm routine
85 Hoover employee, once
86 Back, in a way
88 Nitpick
92 Symbols of office
94 Flyers' org.
96 Wrinkled
97 Allied commander of 1918
98 Buck book
102 Like Hilo, Hawaii, vis-à-vis other major American cities
105 Stud site
106 Spanish port
109 "Symphonie espagnole" composer
110 Vegas venue
111 Speaking up?
116 Hamelin musician
117 Sierra ___
118 Deep crimson
119 Kind of shooter
120 Irene ___, figure in Sherlock Holmes stories
121 Bottom land
122 Hospital work

DOWN

1 Little rascal
2 Longtime "All My Children" role
3 Sophisticated lady
4 It's heard at some ball games
5 Take home
6 Opposite of sur
7 Most qualified to serve
8 Proofs of purchase: Abbr.
9 "Dumb & Dumber" actress
10 Ian's "own"
11 Tour grp.
12 Morsel a horse'll eat
13 Golfer's concern
14 Conclude by
15 Jet Propulsion Lab site
16 Manages
17 1 or 2
18 Omit
19 Put a damper on
27 Lacking
29 HBO competitor
31 Noted debut of 10/7/82
33 Blotto
34 "Hooray!"
35 Michael Jackson's first #1 song
36 Kind of set
38 Watered down
39 Film director Nicolas
41 By and large
42 Sp. titles
43 Recommendations
45 Film with four sequels
46 Slowpokes
47 Fanatical
48 Feathered head ornament
50 Trudged
52 Storm producer?
55 Virginia, in Versailles
57 Strike back
58 Sermon ender
59 B'way posting
60 Play thing
63 Family portrait, of sorts
64 Shutout spoilers
66 German Expressionist Nolde
68 Skyscraper
69 What's what in Mexico
73 Flaw
76 One who cries foul?
77 "Leaving Las Vegas" co-star
78 Reserve
81 Shopper's annoyance
83 Corn or soybeans
84 Kind of putter
87 Noisy celebrant
89 Big pol. campaign donor
90 ___ Stern
91 ___ city
93 Imitate
95 It may result in a smash hit
97 Casbah headgear
98 One weber per square meter
99 Couldn't stand
100 Flynn of film
101 Govt. divisions
102 Dorian Gray's creator
103 Cause of an accident, maybe
104 Law school class
107 Place to stick a comb

by Harvey Estes and Nancy Salomon

108 Face-off
112 Pal of Piglet
113 ___ Darya
(Asian river)
114 Sun ___-sen
115 Suffix for
King James
116 L.A. clock
setting

ACROSS

1 TMC competitor
4 Proceeds here and there
8 It's shot
12 Small amount
16 Cache
18 Cut __
19 "Harold __" (old comic strip)
20 Rundown
21 Wasted gas
22 Vanquish
23 Foe of the Iroquois
24 One sought for advice
25 Piccolo alternatives
26 Bacon feature
27 Doodler's aid
29 Regulated, as property
31 Crackers
34 Cause of a blown engine, maybe
35 Spanish babes
36 Taste-testers' turndowns
37 See 107-Down
38 Alpine river
41 First assembly-line carmaker
43 Yom Kippur observer
45 1983 David Bowie #1 hit
47 Drink whose name is a homophone of 48-Across
48 Like some socks
50 Is rife
51 Several czars
53 Crowbar
54 Take away
55 Noted Schubert piece in F major
56 Disney design
57 Hip parts
59 Opportunity, metaphorically
60 __ Pedro
62 Munchkin
63 Refusals
64 Type widths
65 __ Clinic
66 __ Baba
69 Big inits. in trucks
70 Farrow and Hamm
71 Last thing said before dinner?
72 Masefield play "The Tragedy of __"
73 Pigeonhole
77 English town next to Banstead Downs
79 Prefix with arrange
80 Not hunched
82 Spooky
83 Relinquish, as rights
85 Posit positively
86 Hardly a quick trip
88 Foreign language topic
91 Bit of dinero
92 Urgent message
93 They can make a suer suffer
94 Git
95 Actor John
97 Start of an oath
99 Prefix with linguistics
100 Beaten down
103 Examines
106 __-jongg
108 Previously, once
109 "Plain Language From Truthful James" writer
110 Shin
111 Fast talk
112 Store selection
113 Basket material
114 "__ known . . ."
115 1944 Bing Crosby hit
116 Place for a comb
117 Kind of column
118 Word following clue 114-Across
119 Part of an inheritance?
120 Itch

DOWN

1 ←
2 Arrives jauntily
3 Like some favorites
4 Talkathon
5 Restricted __
6 Sign of an indifferent homemaker
7 O'Rourke, e.g., of "F Troop": Abbr.
8 Mushroom producers
9 Exclamation akin to "Whew!"
10 A founder of the state of Israel
11 ←
12 Indian state
13 Mars
14 Just a thought
15 Founder of Little America
16 Perry Como player
17 God of war, magic and poetry
20 ←
28 Dactylitis locale
30 Teachers' org.
32 "The Night of the Hunter" screenwriter
33 ←
37 Hosp. readouts
39 #1 position
40 Staff symbol
41 Chilled
42 True
44 Gumbo vegetables
45 Pseudologue
46 Former regulatory org.
49 __ Perot
52 ←
53 ←
58 Actor Herbert
59 Cornerback Sanders
61 Always, to Shakespeare
65 Martin and Matalin
66 ←
67 Tie-ups
68 Prelude
70 Religious title: Abbr.
73 Staying power
74 Old magazine __ Digest
75 Place to order une bière
76 Article in Die Welt
78 Name of 12 popes
79 Silent treatment?
81 Rat-a-tat
84 Cut off (from)
87 Bank-to-bank transactions: Abbr.
89 Diner sign
90 Ukr., formerly
94 Visit briefly
96 Warm and comfy
98 Made a scene?
99 Conservatory piece
101 "__ Tu" (1974 hit)

by Bill Zais

102 Capone captor
103 Ah follower
104 Place for a padlock
105 One with a rain check?
107 37-Across was its first earl
111 Spree

ACROSS

1 Stinkers
8 Desirable guests
14 Renders harmless
20 Like some algebra
21 Framework over railroad tracks
22 Phrase meaning "in order to"
23 Collins/Tarkington book about winning a game of roulette?
25 Full
26 Peter, Paul and Mary: Abbr.
27 Hoskins's role in "Hook"
28 Start of an idea
29 Team manager
30 Ephron/Kerouac book about rest stop fast food?
35 Election night info
38 Computer grp.
39 You've seen them before
40 The "A" of 38-Across
41 React to gravity
42 Halloween supplies
43 A/C unit
46 Stoker/Wallace book about an unappreciated vampire?
53 Prized ones
55 Co. in a 2001 merger
56 Reveals
57 Say "y'all," say
59 Serves well done
60 19th-century literary inits.
61 ___ years (old)

62&63 Stele
65 Morrison/ Dinesen book about musical roots?
68 It's paid in el pais
71 Skedaddle
72 Y to the max?
73 Giant star of the 1930s–'40s
76 Church exchange?
77 Ball girl
78 Product introduced by a North Carolina pharmacist in 1898
79 ___ Spiegel
80 Total
83 Hailey/King book about flight delays?
86 Safety grp.
87 Switch extension
89 Naval intro
90 New money
91 Like some clocks
93 Atl. crosser, once
94 Member of a wedding party
97 Dershowitz/Shute book about badly fitting bikinis?
102 One who sees Ethiopia as the promised land
103 Old comics flapper
104 Lyricist Harbach
105 Farm female
108 Zeus' favorite child
110 Terkel/Updike book about two-income families?
113 From what source

114 Like a good argument
115 They're overcome
116 Pantry
117 007 foe
118 On the line

DOWN

1 OPEC units
2 Hot time on the Riviera
3 People who are practicing
4 Civic supporter
5 It blows off steam
6 Certain meter reader
7 Shows contempt
8 It may bring wisdom
9 More than a few words
10 Future resident
11 Unbending
12 Sign of nervousness
13 Lex. entry
14 Have no ___ for
15 Baloney
16 Perfumes
17 Animal followed by a tickbird
18 Atlanta's subway and bus system
19 Position
24 11/11 honoree
30 Old Red scare grp.
31 Depression
32 Novel
33 Sidewalk racer
34 Monster, so to speak
35 Weathercaster's tool
36 Film star Flynn
37 Sitting ducks

41 Constrict, as a passage
43 Call's partner
44 Part of a copse
45 SALT signatory
47 It may give a sinking feeling
48 Caruso player in "The Great Caruso"
49 Mex. neighbor
50 Copycat
51 Up
52 Mexican child
54 Professional prefix
58 Rebels
62 Smirnoff rival, informally
63 Divine name in showbiz
64 When Juliet is compared to the sun
65 Name in many a hymn
66 Five-time Rose Bowl winner
67 Weather info: Abbr.
68 "La Vie en Rose" singer
69 Old literary collection
70 Cream ___
73 Concert hall
74 Latin land
75 Author of "The Other"
77 "Yale ___" (1901 song)
78 Mail, in Marseille
81 Pirate's place
82 Big mouth
84 Bulletin board items
85 ___ Arnold's Balsam (old patent medicine)
88 "How wonderful!"

by Randolph Ross

72

SEE O_2

ACROSS

1 Impress firmly
5 Free (from)
11 Pitcher Reynolds who was called "The Chief"
16 Retreat
19 "__ Man" (1984 movie)
20 Roofer, at times
21 __ terrier
22 Neighbor of Ger.
23 Florist's concern?
26 What's that, Jaime?
27 E. C. Bentley detective
28 Done to __
29 Slot car
31 Rack
34 Antiquated ballpark?
38 Wimbledon winner Bueno and others
39 "It's déjà vu all over again" speaker
40 Reporting to
41 Actor who debuted in "The Men," 1950
42 Suffix with margin
43 Intimidates
46 Off
47 Lack of any desire for lunch?
50 Inits. for some pilots
54 A goner
56 Magician Jillette
57 Clinches
58 Mold source
59 Alias preceder
61 Reunion group
62 Word before reason or reach
63 Period preceding an expiration date?
71 Have a change of heart
72 Burn
73 Modern rest stop convenience, for short
74 Abrasive
75 TV actor Denver
76 Blubber
79 Addis __
84 1914 Belgian battle line
85 Auto plant employee?
88 Orsk's river
89 Son of Daedalus
91 It may be on a house
92 Weather warmer
94 Libreville's land
96 Cheese __
97 Nero's tutor
98 Diplomas?
102 Continues a visit
103 Paul Bunyan's dog
104 Explorer John and others
105 Kind of infection
106 Brouhaha
107 Funnies printed on packing materials?
115 Snowe or Byrd: Abbr.
116 Slip away
117 Kick out
118 Certain band member
119 Quash
120 Hannah of "Roxanne"
121 Treats vengefully
122 Four gills

DOWN

1 Time worth noting
2 '70s British P.M. Heath
3 Revival producer: Abbr.
4 Stale stand-up material?
5 Appearing live
6 Water conduits
7 Theater snack item
8 Last: Abbr.
9 Book before Esther: Abbr.
10 "__ the steamer bore him Eastward . . .": Kipling
11 Keen
12 Like some punch
13 Preferences
14 Provoke
15 Prize seeker
16 Coins
17 Phony
18 Auto option
24 Nymph in Greek myth
25 Eight-time Sugar Bowl champs
30 Totals
31 Scope
32 Elaine __ ("Taxi" role)
33 Bit of a merry refrain
34 Actor Alain
35 Nocturnal hunter
36 Port east of Gibraltar
37 It may be hard to carry
39 Ruination
43 Drink before bed?
44 Regarding
45 __ Arizona
48 A gem of a lady?
49 Storage place
51 London's __ Square
52 Unrainy
53 Bogs
55 Yellow-brown
58 Symbol of conductivity
60 Young fox
61 This answer's place: Abbr.
62 Rainy
63 It doesn't take much
64 Speech pauses
65 One-on-one sport
66 Loathsome
67 "All I Ever Need __" (Sonny & Cher hit)
68 Neuters
69 Hic, __, hoc
70 Sound
75 __ favor
76 Synopsis
77 Boroughs
78 [Just kidding!]
80 Snare set by Fudd?
81 Spring arrival
82 Place for dinero
83 Apply for __ (seek assistance)
85 Be dependent
86 High in the Andes
87 Opens again
90 Put the squeeze on
93 Sprung
94 Like some opportunities
95 Shade of brown
96 Average
98 "Cut it out!"
99 Reason for a reduced grade
100 Sight in China

by Con Pederson

101 One who's revolting
102 Gawp
105 ___-free
108 Constellation next to Telescopium
109 Some Web site features
110 Good name, for short
111 Meas. of computer scans
112 Band of geishas
113 Starter starter
114 Television

73

WORD FOR WORD

ACROSS

1 What to do after a vacation
7 Bathroom problem
13 Unit measured by a gauge
19 Longfellow's words before "O Ship of State!"
20 Peevish
21 Language named for a mathematician
22 Texas' ___ State University
23 Church donation?
25 "Arsenic and Old Lace" director, 1944
27 Rap sheet abbr.
28 Electrical bridge
29 Light-Horse Harry's surname
30 Corporate bribe?
37 Doctors' org.
38 Pell-___
39 Lithographer James
40 Apple of a sort
44 Increases
48 It may go across the board
51 Delicious leftover
52 Home of Pennsylvania's Lafayette College
53 Book of Samuel character
54 Like something written in 21-Across
55 Magazine stands?

59 Like some triangles
61 Hull sealant
62 Puts on a pedestal
63 Clinton cabinet member for all eight years
64 Outhouse?
67 Odysseus' father
69 A can of soda might contain one
70 ___ the Fifth (1910s auto)
73 Right
74 Garrote?
77 Had an eye (to)
78 Tide type
79 Like fingerprints
80 Pass quickly
81 Haddock's home
85 Possible result of pathological lying?
86 It's metered
87 Small bay
88 Informality
90 Italian article
91 Poker chips?
98 Variety
101 Put away
102 Simple card game
103 Modern-day Mesopotamian
104 Wedding band?
109 Took along
113 First name in cooking
114 Said word for word
115 About 30% of Africa
116 Cold sound
117 Carol starter
118 "Kansas City" director, 1996

DOWN

1 Inits. on a rocket
2 Photographer Goldin
3 Overeater
4 Smart ___
5 Fountain offerings
6 Publisher with a canine logo
7 Stat. for a pitch
8 ___ du Diable
9 '70s compact
10 Glimpse, in British slang
11 At home: Fr.
12 Neb. neighbor
13 Make aware
14 Polo, for one
15 Telepathy and such
16 Environmentalist's maj.
17 Reddish, perhaps
18 "Anything ___?"
20 Spook
24 Like bonds
26 Madcap comedy
30 Least honorable
31 Nelson Mandela's South African birthplace
32 Gallic Wars hero
33 Olympian Oerter and others
34 Bandage coating
35 Eggs
36 French artist Poussin
41 Example
42 It may be provided concessions
43 Give up
45 "The ___ Club"
46 Fused together
47 Topples
49 Garment under a doublet

50 Depress, with "out"
54 Something checked before answering
56 Bona ___
57 Does in
58 Guanabara Bay city
59 Bake in a shallow dish
60 Measure of an English firearm
63 "Begone!"
64 Freethinker, perhaps
65 Not so gloomy
66 "A Midsummer Night's Dream" extra
67 Antonio Fogazzaro novel
68 Blend
70 Seasoned stew
71 Never-ending, old-style
72 Cry of dismay
73 Item that may be blown up
74 Plant used as an astringent
75 Part of a split, perhaps
76 Mag. employees
81 France from France
82 Copying stuff
83 Write down
84 Russian Blue, e.g.
85 It has a head but no shoulders
89 Started
92 Muslim who knows the Koran by heart
93 Madcap comedy
94 Big name in fishing gear
95 Model's makeup, maybe

by Patrick Barry

96 Measure up to
97 Affording no leeway
98 Furies
99 Sketch
100 Kilt's stopping point
105 M.A. pursuer's test

106 Sp. title
107 Addams family relation
108 Rounded letter
110 Herd of whales
111 Block of time
112 Pitcher Quisenberry

ACROSS

1 Jack's love in "Titanic"
5 Bug
8 Certain school grade
12 First name in '50s TV
16 Rating
20 Words from 113-Across
22 Where 113-Across's creations may appear
23 Contents of the Uffizi Gallery
24 Like some refugees
25 It comes with strings attached
26 Suffix with persist
27 Calendario page
28 Devotes
30 Basketmaking need
35 Start of a quote
40 Hopping mad
44 Compares
45 Bonny lass's reply, maybe
46 In a state of reverence
47 Actor Bates
48 Compliments, as to the chef
49 Words
50 Kind of lock
51 Psychological manipulation
53 Head of England
55 Ornamental shrub
57 Buzzer
58 Soprano Moffo
59 "Stay!"
62 Doorkeeper's reply

63 Middle of the quote
66 See 71-Across
69 Surface
70 Salon job
71 With 66-Across, former New York politician
74 Swear (to)
76 Chemical suffix
77 Got through to
79 1988 platinum-selling country album
80 Out of control
83 It connects to the stem
84 Posterior
85 Mullah's land
86 Tube top
87 Was almost out of stock
89 Old ___ (Davy Crockett's rifle)
90 End of the quote
94 Melancholy, in music
95 Sore ankle application
96 "Whether times are good ___, happy . . ." (1971 song lyric)
100 Flock member
102 General Assembly topic
103 Shrimp, lobsters, etc.
107 Deli order
112 113-Across, e.g.
113 Speaker of the quote
114 "The Godfather" actress
115 "You said it!," in Sonora
116 Is idle
117 Farm outbuilding
118 Gush

DOWN

1 Account execs
2 Like lilac leaves
3 "Paradise Lost" figure
4 First-class
5 Cone makers
6 Novelist Gould
7 1981 film "___ Jeunesse"
8 Packing a punch
9 Literary olio
10 State capital?
11 Turn in many a children's game
12 TV site
13 In-flight info, for short
14 Charlie Chaplin title
15 Onetime communications giant
17 Log-on code
18 "Must be ___ news day"
19 Kind of shirt
20 Some gang members
21 Place for a grilling
25 ___ smoke
28 Spike Lee's "___ Gotta Have It"
29 Unit of force
31 Like palm trees in a storm
32 Foil
33 Actress Sobieski of "Joan of Arc"
34 Make beloved
36 Certain homecoming attendees
37 Pitching style
38 Fight enders, briefly
39 Soaks
40 Gentle one
41 "Would ___ to you?"

42 Windmill part
43 N.Y.C. subway
48 Philosophy 101 subject
49 Oz visitor
52 Subject of Avogadro's law
53 Rustic digs
54 Formerly
56 Prefix with -hedron
59 "Jurassic Park" actress
60 Crumble
61 Landing site of 4/1/45
63 "This is no joke!"
64 Shipbuilder's stock
65 Like the Olympics: Abbr.
66 Metal in witherite
67 Ceaseless, in poetry
68 Diamond stats
71 Plugging away
72 Uncle ___
73 Swirl
75 Sign of refinement
77 Warner Bros. inventory
78 What's that, Carlo?
81 Hawaiian foodfish
82 Syndicate since 1960
83 Tight
87 Bringing a blush to the cheek, maybe
88 Just open
89 Docking spots
91 Singer Luft
92 Posts on the stairs
93 Famed Leontyne Price role
97 German musical family

by Elizabeth C. Gorski

98 Like ___ off the old block
99 Plow pioneer
101 Rudiments
103 Suffix with techno-
104 Lean (on)
105 Prefix with colored
106 Not many
107 Bedwear
108 French men's magazine
109 Gore and others
110 It's right on a clock
111 "Skedaddle!"
112 Garrisons: Abbr.

ACROSS

1 Pop music's Salt-N-___
5 One experienced with running
8 It parallels a radius
12 Shield
18 Writer LeShan and others
19 Like bronze or tin
22 Certain ticket request
23 Daredevil's desire
24 Requesting shipments in wooden containers?
26 Rips out basting
28 Meets
29 Hidden
30 Venerable scholar of old England
31 Artist Gustave
33 Kind of room
35 Germinate
36 Chain hotel in Madrid?
42 Capital of Switzerland?
45 Scrap
46 1970s Tony Musante series
47 Old Germans
48 Certain sweater, informally
49 "Disgusting!"
50 Chopin piece
52 Dame ___
53 Classic 1953 27-Down
54 Monastic sites?
58 Biggest employer in Marysville, Ohio
59 Keg stopper
60 Addition column
61 Be careful

63 Captain in "Billy Budd"
65 Good lookers
67 Bittern, e.g.
70 1960s espionage show
71 Dissect, British-style
73 Fifth canonical hour
74 Word before "sweet land of liberty"
76 Marker
77 Supporter of sewer dwellers?
84 Philly player
85 Knee-slapper
86 Inveigled
87 Bill blocker
88 U.S.M.A. part: Abbr.
89 Contract parts
92 Utah's ___ Canyon
93 Babel
94 Space craft
95 Actor Pitt selling cosmetics?
97 One hopes for this in an I.C.U.
98 Cut short, maybe
99 Popular musical based on a Paul Gallico story
100 Spillane's "___ Jury"
102 Easy gait
105 Mysteries
110 Looks down on
112 Butting heads, charging other sheep, etc.?
116 Taunted
117 Chairman's need
118 Part of a demonstration

119 Actresses Murray and Clark
120 Just out
121 Cong. period
122 Sturdy pad
123 Basic French verb

DOWN

1 Home of the writer Mario Vargas Llosa
2 Castle Rock site
3 Was OK'd by Playtex?
4 Solicited
5 Masters
6 Tommy Dorsey's "___ Love"
7 It can have you seeing things
8 "A God in Ruins" novelist
9 Unattended
10 Thick drinks
11 ". . . to buy ___ pig"
12 1988 Dennis Quaid film
13 Live oak
14 Flowerless plants
15 McGregor of "The Phantom Menace"
16 "Big ___" (comic strip)
17 Salon worker
20 ___ Clark who sang "Poor, Poor Pitiful Me"
21 Druid, e.g.
25 "Death of a Salesman" salesman
27 See 53-Across
31 Block
32 Out at the prom, maybe
34 Publishers' hirees, for short

35 Spell
37 Soups
38 Scoundrels
39 1970s A's All-Star Joe
40 ___ time
41 Complain
42 Specialty in history as well as medicine?
43 Parody
44 Like gym clothes
48 More stifling
51 Anytime
53 Premium channel: Abbr.
55 Filled up
56 Office-holders
57 Traffic caution
62 Busy
63 Subordinate
64 Inveigle
66 "Uh-huh"
67 Baby cake
68 Form of acetylacetone
69 Nyet, e.g.
72 "___ out!"
73 Prominent
75 Pleasure-seeking
78 Fictional hunter
79 Period of duty
80 Santa ___
81 Fountain name
82 Worst lagger in a race
83 Together, after "in"
89 Comic Margaret
90 Pariah
91 Relief
95 Futurists' focus
96 Some boxes are made with them
98 Copy
101 "Careless Hands" singer, 1949
102 Simile center

by Robert H. Wolfe

103 Number of points?: Abbr.
104 Concoct
106 Down times
107 Nagy of Hungary
108 Mustang racers, once?
109 "Welcome" sights
110 Bygone pol. units
111 Zaire's Mobutu ___ Seko
113 Hood's arm
114 "___ time"
115 AT&T has one

ANSWERS

1

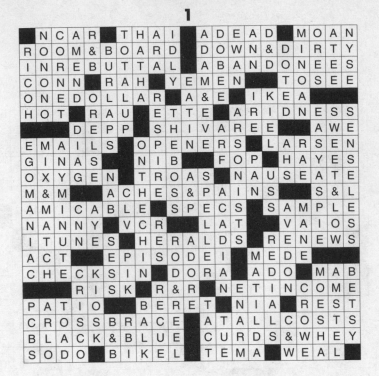

	N	C	A	R		T	H	A	I			A	D	E	A	D		M	O	A	N
R	O	O	M	&	B	O	A	R	D			D	O	W	N	&	D	I	R	T	Y
I	N	R	E	B	U	T	T	A	L			A	B	A	N	D	O	N	E	E	S
C	O	N	N		R	A	H		Y	E	M	E	N			T	O	S	E	E	
O	N	E	D	O	L	L	A	R		A	&	E		I	K	E	A				
H	O	T		R	A	U		E	T	T	E		A	R	I	D	N	E	S	S	
		D	E	P	P		S	H	I	V	A	R	E	E				A	W	E	
E	M	A	I	L	S		O	P	E	N	E	R	S		L	A	R	S	E	N	
G	I	N	A	S		N	I	B		F	O	P		H	A	Y	E	S			
O	X	Y	G	E	N		T	R	O	A	S		N	A	U	S	E	A	T	E	
M	&	M		A	C	H	E	S	&	P	A	I	N	S		S	&	L			
A	M	I	C	A	B	L	E		S	P	E	C	S		S	A	M	P	L	E	
N	A	N	N	Y		V	C	R		L	A	T		V	A	I	O	S			
I	T	U	N	E	S		H	E	R	A	L	D	S		R	E	N	E	W	S	
A	C	T		E	P	I	S	O	D	E	I		M	E	D	E					
C	H	E	C	K	S	I	N		D	O	R	A		A	D	O		M	A	B	
		R	I	S	K		R	&	R		N	E	T	I	N	C	O	M	E		
P	A	T	I	O		B	E	R	E	T		N	I	A		R	E	S	T		
C	R	O	S	S	B	R	A	C	E		A	T	A	L	L	C	O	S	T	S	
B	L	A	C	K	&	B	L	U	E		C	U	R	D	S	&	W	H	E	Y	
S	O	D	O		B	I	K	E	L		T	E	M	A		W	E	A	L		

2

	B	L	A	M	E	S		S	A	D	C	A	S	E		C	U	E	R	V	O
R	A	M	O	N	E		C	L	E	R	K	E	D		A	L	L	I	E	D
E	M	B	R	A	C	E	A	B	L	E	E	W	E		L	E	A	N	T	O
S	E	L	E	C	T	O	R		T	A	L	E	N	T			I	G	O	R
T	R	E	N	T		N	I	B		M	A	R		I	R	A	N	I		
			E	S	P		N	O	U	S			P	R	E	T	E	N	D	
S	U	B	S		R	I	G	H	T	O	N	Q	U	E	U	E		G	I	T
P	R	U	S	S	I	A		R	E	D	O	U	T		P	U	T	T	E	R
A	G	R		H	E	M	O		R	A	T	A		S	P	O	R	T	Y	
T	E	N	N	I	S	S	H	O	O		A	R	M	S		M	U	S		
		E	N	T	A	I	L			T	O	U	S	L	E					
	T	N	T		M	O	D	S		M	O	U	N	T	A	I	N	D	O	
P	R	O	W	A	R		B	E	T	A		E	D	E	L		O	E	D	
T	A	T	T	L	E		S	A	T	E	E	N		E	N	A	B	L	E	D
S	P	H		I	D	O	N	T	H	A	V	E	T	W	O		R	O	D	S
	P	I	S	C	O	P	O		R	E	M	O		S	A	O				
	N	T	E	S	T		B	R	A		O	N	A		D	W	A	R	F	
G	A	G	A		S	E	R	A	P	E		G	R	E	E	N	P	E	A	
A	N	G	L	E	E		R	U	N	A	R	O	U	N	D	S	I	O	U	X
I	N	N	E	E	D		A	T	T	R	I	T	E		E	T	E	R	N	E
L	A	U	D	E	D		S	E	S	T	E	T	S		R	E	S	T	E	D

3

```
T W O S ■ O V E N S ■ B O P S ■ U P B O W
H A L O ■ B A S I N ■ E D I T ■ P U P A E
A C D C ■ A L L B A S S E T S A R E O F F
W O E I S M E ■ S P O T T Y ■ D A R E S T
■ ■ ■ E V A N S ■ S L I T ■ B A I T ■ ■
C R E T E ■ S H U T T L E C A S S O C K S
L A R Y N X ■ I N O I L ■ A N T E ■ H A T
A R I P ■ A U R A ■ ■ E N G R ■ W I S E
M E T A ■ X K E ■ P R A T T ■ A P A C H E
P R U S S I A ■ S I E S T A S ■ O S K A R
■ ■ S A S S I N G T H E B L U E S ■ ■
D O R A G ■ E M I G R E S ■ I N T A I L S
C O O G A N ■ S P Y O N ■ C D C ■ I M I T
C O V E ■ E M U S ■ ■ D U E L ■ L I M A
A L E ■ O W A R ■ C O E D S ■ E L I N O R
B A R E F A C E D L A S S I E ■ A N G S T
■ ■ A N G E ■ R I T T ■ P A N D G ■ ■
C R U S O E ■ P A P E R Y ■ T O Y W I T H
C U L T U R A L M O R A S S E S ■ A D A M
L I N O S ■ D I A N ■ D E A R E ■ L E N O
I N A N E ■ M E S S ■ A R O S E ■ L A G S
```

4

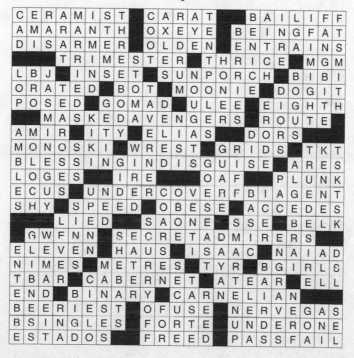

```
C E R A M I S T ■ C A R A T ■ B A I L I F F
A M A R A N T H ■ O X E Y E ■ B E I N G F A T
D I S A R M E R ■ O L D E N ■ E N T R A I N S
■ ■ T R I M E S T E R ■ T H R I C E ■ M G M
L B J ■ I N S E T ■ S U N P O R C H ■ B I B I
O R A T E D ■ B O T ■ M O O N I E ■ D O G I T
P O S E D ■ G O M A D ■ U L E E ■ E I G H T H
■ M A S K E D A V E N G E R S ■ R O U T E ■
A M I R ■ I T Y ■ E L I A S ■ D O R S ■ ■
M O N O S K I ■ W R E S T ■ G R I D S ■ T K T
B L E S S I N G I N D I S G U I S E ■ A R E S
L O G E S ■ I R E ■ O A F ■ P L U N K
E C U S ■ U N D E R C O V E R F B I A G E N T
S H Y ■ S P E E D ■ O B E S E ■ A C C E D E S
■ L I E D ■ S A O N E ■ S S E ■ B E L K
G W F N N ■ S E C R E T A D M I R E R S ■
E L E V E N ■ H A U S ■ I S A A C ■ N A I A D
N I M E S ■ M E T R E S ■ T Y R ■ B G I R L S
T B A R ■ C A B E R N E T ■ A T E A R ■ E L L
E N D ■ B I N A R Y ■ C A R N E L I A N ■
B E E R I E S T ■ O F U S E ■ N E R V E G A S
B S I N G L E S ■ F O R T E ■ U N D E R O N E
E S T A D O S ■ F R E E D ■ P A S S F A I L
```

5

```
A G A S P   E S T O P     M A I T R E D S
T O S I R   T H E W E B   O N T H E S E A
P L A C E C H E E S E O N T O S E E S A W
A D M   T A E     K N E E S O C K
R A I S E S L I T C A N D L E   L E G S
    T N T   O R A T E     L U D E N S
C D C A S E   N E S   T H E T A B   N E A
A E R I E   F I N A L   A N O N   S E L F
N A I R   H E A T S U P T E A K E T T L E
D T S   S A T     S T E R     T A I
W H I S T L E J O L T S D O Z I N G C A T
    S A L   A S I F     E S A   C I R
T I P S O V E R A Q U A R I U M   B O D Y
H M O S   A D O G   L E E D S   B I D E S
A M I   C R U D E S   O H O   A R R E S T
D I N G H Y     M A N E T   P E T
    X T R A   F L O O D S M O U S E H O L E
      I N L I E U O F     S E Z   R E X
B U I L D A B E T T E R M O U S E T R A P
A R T L O V E R   H E C T O R   B O I S E
G L O S S A R Y   S A V O Y   Y E N T L
```

6

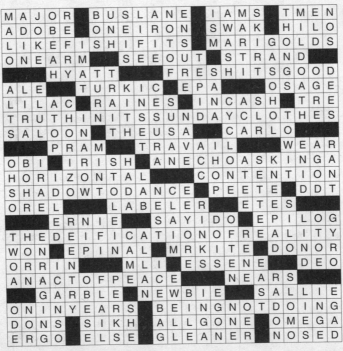

```
M A J O R   B U S L A N E   I A M S   T M E N
A D O B E   O N E I R O N   S W A K   H I L O
L I K E F I S H I F I T S   M A R I G O L D S
O N E A R M   S E E O U T   S T R A N D
    H Y A T T   F R E S H I T S G O O D
A L E   T U R K I C   E P A   O S A G E
L I L A C   R A I N E S   I N C A S H   T R E
T R U T H I N I T S S U N D A Y C L O T H E S
S A L O O N   T H E U S A   C A R L O
    P R A M   T R A V A I L   W E A R
O B I   I R I S H   A N E C H O A S K I N G A
H O R I Z O N T A L   C O N T E N T I O N
S H A D O W T O D A N C E   P E E T E   D D T
O R E L   L A B E L E R   E T E S
    E R N I E   S A Y I D O   E P I L O G
T H E D E I F I C A T I O N O F R E A L I T Y
W O N   E P I N A L   M R K I T E   D O N O R
O R R I N   M L I   E S S E N E   D E O
A N A C T O F P E A C E   N E A R S
    G A R B L E   N E W B I E   S A L L I E
O N I N Y E A R S   B E I N G N O T D O I N G
D O N S   S I K H   A L L G O N E   O M E G A
E R G O   E L S E   G L E A N E R   N O S E D
```

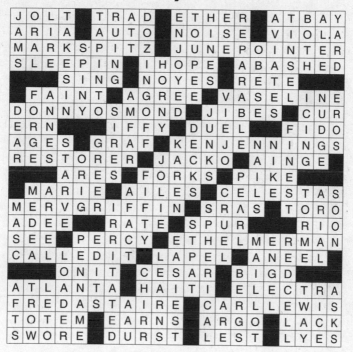

7

Grid 7 (across rows):

```
JOLT    TRAD    ETHER    ATBAY
ARIA    AUTO    NOISE    VIOLA
MARKSPITZ    JUNEPOINTER
SLEEPIN    IHOPE    ABASHED
    SING    NOYES    RETE
  FAINT    AGREE    VASELINE
DONNYOSMOND    JIBES    CUR
ERN    IFFY    DUEL    FIDO
AGES    GRAF    KENJENNINGS
RESTORER    JACKO    AINGE
    ARES    FORKS    PIKE
  MARIE    AILES    CELESTAS
MERVGRIFFIN    SRAS    TORO
ADEE    RATE    SPUR    RIO
SEE    PERCY    ETHELMERMAN
CALLEDIT    LAPEL    ANEEL
    ONIT    CESAR    BIGD
ATLANTA    HAITI    ELECTRA
FREDASTAIRE    CARLLEWIS
TOTEM    EARNS    ARGO    LACK
SWORE    DURST    LEST    LYES
```

8

Grid 8 (across rows):

```
  CREES    ICEAGES    SLAP
  HEAVE    FANWAVE    AWARE
 MENSAWEARDEPARTMENTS
HOC    INNS    RUSE    GRIDDLE
ANKLES    CAIRO    SEA    RAT
WOEIS    THREEMENINATUBA
SCRATCHER    EXE    SLR
ELEM    ROWERS    HABITABLE
RED    FIRSTAIDAKIT    COAL
   PILES    FOILED    MITZI
CRANES    REFUGED    DANTES
HOSTA    TALIAS    LINGO
UPTO    INDIANAOCEAN    MAC
BEATINGIT    STRAIN    ELIA
   ARC    ACI    ACCEPTERS
AWALKINTHEPARKA    ROSSI
RET    SEE    NOBEL    JONSON
CATSHOW    TATA    ELON    PUG
ARIVERARUNSTHROUGHIT
ROLEX    RATTIER    CLEAT
ONAN    KISSERS    HEDDA
```

9

```
S A S H E D   A D A M S   A B E   G R I T
I M P A L A   S A D A T   B E L G I A N S
T U R N S T O S T O N E   I S S U A N C E
A S I D E   S H A   S E A L E   T N G
R E G S   T H E S C A R L E T L E T T E R
  A T O   E E R   A N S E   A R A T
S H O W H O W I T S D O N E   T E N U R E
T E L   E L E V   S L O   S A T E S
R E A L M   L A N E   E N T   U R E
A D F E E   O N E N D   R E P L A C E
D E I S   S H O V E O V E R   T H E A
  R I S E S T O   B R I E R   H E A R D
  E S O   E E K   T I T O   A R N I E
  G U S T O   D I S   O L D S   D E L
H E N S O N   S I M P L E P L E A S U R E
I T B E   Y E A S   A A A   A T H
P A I N T I N T O A C O R N E R   A M B S
  A T E   G E N R E   F A O   A T Y O U
E L S I N O R E   M A R L I N L I N E U P
S T E A D M A N   A G O A L   E D E R L E
A D D L   E M S   S E E P S   V E R S E S
```

10

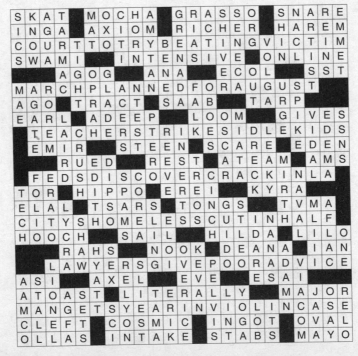

```
S K A T   M O C H A   G R A S S O   S N A R E
I N G A   A X I O M   R I C H E R   H A R E M
C O U R T T O T R Y B E A T I N G V I C T I M
S W A M I   I N T E N S I V E   O N L I N E
  A G O G   A N A   E C O L   S S T
M A R C H P L A N N E D F O R A U G U S T
A G O   T R A C T   S A A B   T A R P
E A R L   A D E E P   L O O M   G I V E S
T E A C H E R S T R I K E S I D L E K I D S
E M I R   S T E E N   S C A R E   E D E N
R U E D   R E S T   A T E A M   A M S
F E D S D I S C O V E R C R A C K I N L A
T O R   H I P P O   E R E I   K Y R A
E L A L   T S A R S   T O N G S   T V M A
C I T Y S H O M E L E S S C U T I N H A L F
H O O C H   S A I L   H I L D A   L I L O
R A H S   N O O K   D E A N A   I A N
L A W Y E R S G I V E P O O R A D V I C E
A S I   A X E L   E V E   E S A I
A T O A S T   L I T E R A L L Y   M A J O R
M A N G E T S Y E A R I N V I O L I N C A S E
C L E F T   C O S M I C   I N G O T   O V A L
O L L A S   I N T A K E   S T A B S   M A Y O
```

11

12

13

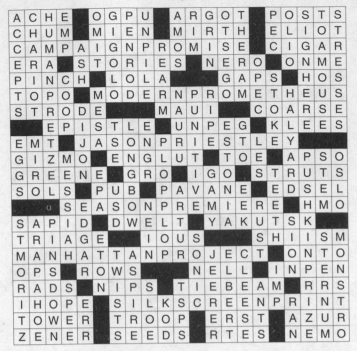

```
ACHE _ OGPU _ ARGOT _ POSTS
CHUM _ MIEN _ MIRTH _ ELIOT
CAMPAIGNPROMISE _ CIGAR
ERA _ STORIES _ NERO _ ONME
PINCH _ LOLA _ _ GAPS _ HOS
TOPO _ MODERNPROMETHEUS
STRODE _ _ MAUI _ COARSE
_ EPISTLE _ UNPEG _ KLEES
EMT _ JASONPRIESTLEY _
GIZMO _ ENGLUT _ TOE _ APSO
GREENE _ GRO _ IGO _ STRUTS
SOLS _ PUB _ PAVANE _ EDSEL
_ SEASONPREMIERE _ HMO
SAPID _ DWELT _ YAKUTSK _
TRIAGE _ IOUS _ SHIISM
MANHATTANPROJECT _ ONTO
OPS _ ROWS _ NELL _ INPEN
RADS _ NIPS _ TIEBEAM _ RRS
IHOPE _ SILKSCREENPRINT
TOWER _ TROOP _ ERST _ AZUR
ZENER _ SEEDS _ RTES _ NEMO
```

14

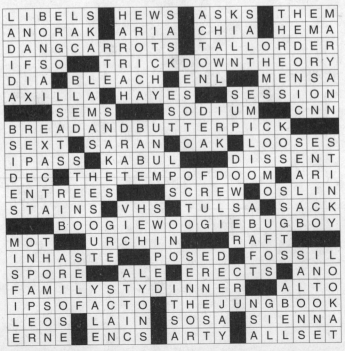

```
LIBELS _ HEWS _ ASKS _ THEM
ANORAK _ ARIA _ CHIA _ HEMA
DANGCARROTS _ TALLORDER
IFSO _ TRICKDOWNTHEORY
DIA _ BLEACH _ ENL _ MENSA
AXILLA _ HAYES _ SESSION
_ SEMS _ SODIUM _ CNN
BREADANDBUTTERPICK _
SEXT _ SARAN _ OAK _ LOOSES
IPASS _ KABUL _ DISSENT
DEC _ THETEMPOFDOOM _ ARI
ENTREES _ SCREW _ OSLIN
STAINS _ VHS _ TULSA _ SACK
BOOGIEWOOGIEBUGBOY
MOT _ URCHIN _ RAFT _
INHASTE _ POSED _ FOSSIL
SPORE _ ALE _ ERECTS _ ANO
FAMILYSTYDINNER _ ALTO
IPSOFACTO _ THEJUNGBOOK
LEOS _ LAIN _ SOSA _ SIENNA
ERNE _ ENCS _ ARTY _ ALLSET
```

15

```
A K I T A S ▮ E N D E D ▮ K A R L ▮ R H O
H E N R I K ▮ R A I S A ▮ A N T E ▮ O E D
S E C U R I T I E S A N A L Y S T ▮ T A I
I N A S E N S E ▮ C U L L ▮ ▮ S L A T E ▮
N E S T ▮ L A S S O ▮ E L O N G A T E ▮
▮ ▮ ▮ M E R ▮ M U S I C A L C O M E D Y
A M I N O S ▮ C A N E D ▮ N E O ▮ P I L E
F A M O U S L A S T W O R D S ▮ S O N Y S
T Y P E S ▮ U G H S ▮ I O S ▮ O E O ▮
R O U L E T T E ▮ F D A ▮ I V A N K A ▮
A R T ▮ T H E D O C T O R I S I N ▮ H T S
▮ S E A R E D ▮ P H D ▮ M A S E R A T I
▮ M A Y ▮ C E O ▮ S A N A ▮ T I K I S
A T E U P ▮ S H R I M P C O C K T A I L S
W E A L ▮ C I A ▮ C A R E T ▮ I L L S A Y
W A T E R S O F T E N E R ▮ A C E ▮ ▮
▮ D E T A I N E E ▮ A B A C K ▮ D A I S
F A R S I ▮ ▮ A M A D ▮ E R O D I B L E
A N I ▮ D E P A R T M E N T O F L A B O R
I C E ▮ E L A L ▮ S I R E N ▮ F I N E S T
L E S ▮ D I M E ▮ T E S L A ▮ S I E S T A
```

16

```
A S P I R A T O R S ▮ ▮ S T I M U L A N T
E L I M I N A T E D ▮ O P E R A S E R I A
F I E L D T R I P S ▮ P A R K R A N G E R
▮ P D A ▮ S O S ▮ E D ▮ L U G ▮
▮ S A T B Y ▮ A F T S ▮ N B A S T A R
O T T E R ▮ C A I R O ▮ L G A ▮ A H S O
M R E ▮ R A I N M A N ▮ S A R A ▮ I S O N
S E R B ▮ D I K ▮ M O L D I E R ▮ E I N E
K A R A T S ▮ A D E N O ▮ O N T A R G E T
▮ M E T H ▮ S R A ▮ E E R ▮ E O S ▮ N Y S
▮ E S T A T E ▮ W H O S O N ▮
A S A ▮ S I R ▮ A R M ▮ E H S ▮ A R T I
F O R G E T I T ▮ G O B A D ▮ S P U R N S
E L M O ▮ E A R L O B E ▮ E T S ▮ N A C L
W O O D ▮ S T Y E ▮ I N V A D E S ▮ C O O
▮ N U D E ▮ E M E ▮ L E H R S ▮ A S K M E
▮ G R E N A D E ▮ D E I S ▮ S I O M P
▮ S I P ▮ G O ▮ S K Y ▮ M E L
G R A S S S K I R T ▮ G R O U N D B E E F
N O V E L E T T E S ▮ S I L H O U E T T E
P O S S E S S E S ▮ U N E N D O R S E D
```

17

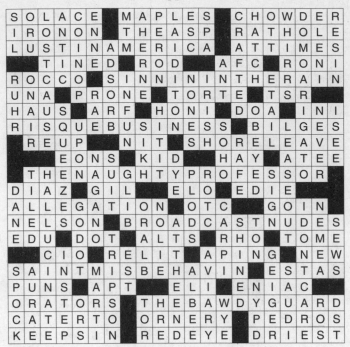

```
S O L A C E ■ M A P L E S ■ C H O W D E R
I R O N O N ■ T H E A S P ■ R A T H O L E
L U S T I N A M E R I C A ■ A T T I M E S
■ ■ T I N E D ■ R O D ■ A F C ■ R O N I
R O C C O ■ S I N N I N I N T H E R A I N
U N A ■ P R O N E ■ T O R T E ■ T S R ■
H A U S ■ A R F ■ H O N I ■ D O A ■ I N I
R I S Q U E B U S I N E S S ■ B I L G E S
■ R E U P ■ ■ N I T ■ S H O R E L E A V E
■ E O N S ■ K I D ■ H A Y ■ A T E E ■
■ T H E N A U G H T Y P R O F E S S O R ■
D I A Z ■ G I L ■ E L O ■ E D I E ■ ■
A L L E G A T I O N ■ O T C ■ G O I N
N E L S O N ■ B R O A D C A S T N U D E S
E D U ■ D O T ■ A L T S ■ R H O ■ T O M E
■ C I O ■ R E L I T ■ A P I N G ■ N E W
S A I N T M I S B E H A V I N ■ E S T A S
P U N S ■ A P T ■ E L I ■ E N I A C ■
O R A T O R S ■ T H E B A W D Y G U A R D
C A T E R T O ■ O R N E R Y ■ P E D R O S
K E E P S I N ■ R E D E Y E ■ D R I E S T
```

18

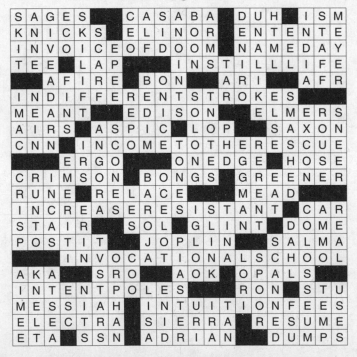

```
S A G E S ■ C A S A B A ■ D U H ■ I S M
K N I C K S ■ E L I N O R ■ E N T E N T E
I N V O I C E O F D O O M ■ N A M E D A Y
T E E ■ L A P ■ ■ I N S T I L L L I F E
■ A F I R E ■ B O N ■ A R I ■ A F R
I N D I F F E R E N T S T R O K E S ■ ■
M E A N T ■ E D I S O N ■ E L M E R S
A I R S ■ A S P I C ■ L O P ■ S A X O N
C N N ■ I N C O M E T O T H E R E S C U E
■ ■ E R G O ■ O N E D G E ■ H O S E
C R I M S O N ■ B O N G S ■ G R E E N E R
R U N E ■ R E L A C E ■ M E A D ■ ■
I N C R E A S E R E S I S T A N T ■ C A R
S T A I R ■ S O L ■ G L I N T ■ D O M E
P O S T I T ■ J O P L I N ■ S A L M A
■ I N V O C A T I O N A L S C H O O L
A K A ■ S R O ■ A O K ■ O P A L S ■
I N T E N T P O L E S ■ R O N ■ S T U
M E S S I A H ■ I N T U I T I O N F E E S
E L E C T R A ■ S I E R R A ■ R E S U M E
E T A ■ S S N ■ A D R I A N ■ D U M P S
```

19

MARYANN · CRAIGS · ROAST
ALOEVERA · REDCAP · ANKHS
JAMAICANMECRAZY · BERRA
ADE · TOP · ENE · INOUR
YOUDBESETONSTUNNING
SEAMY · BOOTSY · NOSE
AMELIA · CEE · ENC · THOS
ORISITJUSTYOU · SHIFT
ARC · NIC · CHACHA · OFA
KARL · HHH · LAUREATE
YOUREOUTOFTHISWORLD
COLORADO · ASS · NAES
APT · LITTLE · SSN · RBI
DEWEY · CANIHAVEYOURS
IRON · MLB · AXE · ICETEA
ARFS · MOESHA · SCOTT
YOURETHEONLYTENISEE
SCORE · OCT · EAU · NCO
NOTIE · YOUREMMMMMMGOOD
AMEND · TVROOM · POPSICLE
PORGY · DEEDEE · SHUSHED

20

PINGPONG · MAANDPA · HAM
EMOTICONS · OFFYEAR · ILE
NOTONESCUPOFTEETH · GIG
DUE · ELY · BOCA · TEACHER
STRATO · MEMOIRS · TAWNY
CATHODEWRAITH · DATA
PTER · ELIS · SIGHED · YON
MOHR · SLIT · NOMEAT
ISO · BAIN · HAMLET · AMORE
SSR · ESCAPEKEITH · RAHAL
SLOVAK · TRILL · ATHENA
IQUIT · DOUBLEYOUTH · ATT
SSGTS · ENISLE · TSOS · LEE
HAMILL · LOOP · CTRS
JEB · ENVOIS · SOON · AAIIS
AARP · SEATTLESLEUTH
CREAM · NOSIREE · NANANA
KHAYYAM · ITIS · LAN · LOC
MAD · BOTTOMOFTHEWEALTH
ART · ANGELOU · ORIENTATE
NTH · DESCENT · SADDENED

```
PETULA  BRAN  SHAD  CPAS
ARISEN  IDLE  COSI  LANA
NIGHTINGALEHAWKSLARKS
ACE  SOIE  USER  FRESCAS
MARTINPARROTSCOOTS
   ANS  TEEN  ARBORDAY
RASP  DENS  GRIME  IOLA
OBI  INERT  BEENE  ANGER
LOGICAL  ACTI  PIGGED
FINCHDUCKSCUCKOOS
ELSE  IGNIS  GHOST  PLEA
  WRENSWALLOWSRAILS
SENSES  SECY  AIMLESS
HUEYS  FLEES  BALES  GIA
ALEC  BOOST  COLD  SEEM
HADATALK  WHOA  CMI
  MERLINROOKSBOOBIES
YESORNO  AERO  KART  NUI
SPARROWGULLSCARDINALS
EINE  NEAT  DERN  ELOPES
RCAS  EROS  SRIS  DESTRY
```

```
 SHINING  SONTAG  ETHIC
CHEMICAL  MONACO  RHODE
NEWAGEMOVEMENTS  GETIN
NANCE  WEEP  TIEA  CPOS
  ROWEL  HARVESTHOME
ACHE  WORDS  RAE  TROTS
QUARTERSTAFF  ERES
UPLOADS  WASH  ROPETOW
ASFIT  TOADY  EAR  ANODE
  ACEY  BLUELAGOON  TEE
UCLA  MOOGS  IVORY  SHAD
ROO  PAPERTIGER  EPEE
GRADE  ESE  BANAL  EMMAS
ENFIELD  NEAT  EELPOUT
  SKIS  CRESCENTROLL
 LATIN  MST  DARCY  ENDO
WAXINGSALON  LEHAR
ARIL  OONA  OVUM  EMILE
NILLA  FULLMETALJACKET
DALEY  TROYES  TOODLEOO
STARE  CEMENT  ELYSIAN
```

23

WISP · TRASHY · SCARF · EWE
ASTA · VIRTUE · KOREA · VOL
ITIC · SPOKESPERSON · EOS
FOLK · PEA · OWN · BONDI
· LABORREPRESENTATIVE
GRABAT · MAAM · RIPSONE
IOTAS · MAORI · TSE · GNP
FLIGHTATTENDANT · ASEA
SET · RULED · AMOY · CUTER
· SLID · ODOR · BOGART
· WHITECOLLARWORKER
IMHOME · AGED · PIER
SUAVE · USED · NAFTA · INT
ALTE · THEATERDIRECTOR
WED · CHI · HOGAN · ROSIE
· TOEHOLD · XENO · PALTRY
PRIVATEINVESTIGATOR
OAKEN · SEI · NIT · RIDE
KIN · CIRCUITJUDGE · SCAN
ENO · ERROR · NATION · IKID
SSW · LASSO · TREATS · NYSE

24

SAHL · SCRIP · JOLLA · GTOS
ALOE · ELIDE · UNION · RANT
APPT · RATINCREASE · EPEE
REDSHIRT · ORONO · MIAMIS
· ILONA · TBIRD · PISTE
STAIRS · FUSE · MACADAMS
TAMPA · HATCRIMES · NASAL
ABO · SEENTO · NARC · NUKE
MONA · SANITARYCOD · RIP
PODIATRY · REBS · ABSENT
· DUHS · ABIDE · GMAN
POMADE · ARIE · HEADACHE
OCA · RUBGOLDBERG · PRAM
LADD · RIOT · OILMEN · YUM
ILIUM · INNAMONLY · AMITY
SANDALED · AMES · AMINES
· CRUEL · ALIST · STUNG
REHASH · FROND · STORESUP
ITIN · ICECREAMCON · OHSO
BANC · GOREN · YOUVE · LANE
SHAH · HONDA · SIDED · AMAT

```
D U K E ■ C H A R M ■ M A R C ■ A B L E
O N E A ■ H O S T A ■ C U R I O ■ P R E Y
O V E R C O M P E N S A T I O N ■ P E A R
D E P L O R E ■ S E W N U P ■ V O L A R E
L I P ■ Q U I T ■ D I V A ■ D E R E K ■
E L A L ■ S C A R ■ F A L L I N G S T A R
D E C A F ■ E R E C T S ■ A X E S ■ H B O
■ D E M O S ■ I P O ■ R I I S ■ B R I O
■ ■ B R I E F O U T L I N E ■ W O O L S
L A S ■ C L E F ■ P R I D E ■ M I N U E T
A T H L E T E ■ G L O B E ■ C O L O G N E
B L O O P S ■ S I E V E ■ C O W L ■ H E R
C U R B S ■ C E N T E R S P R E A D ■
O N T O ■ S E L A ■ T A S ■ D R I B S
A C C ■ A U D I ■ F L Y I N G ■ D A R L A
T H I R D D E G R E E ■ L O R D ■ Z O I C
■ R E E D S ■ O R T S ■ W I R E ■ U V A
A R C A N E ■ A D R O I T ■ D I T C H E D
S O U L ■ N O T H I N G T O D E C L A R E
T A I L ■ L I M A S ■ H O V E R ■ A H E M
A R T Y ■ Y L E M ■ S P A R S ■ M A D E
```

```
C I S C O ■ T A I L ■ C R O W ■ M E A R A
O N T A P ■ A T N O ■ L O C H ■ A X L E S
[HEN]R Y M A N C I N I ■ E A T I N K I T C[HEN]
■ E X P L O I T ■ S C A M ■ R E E L E D
■ F I S T ■ P L A N S ■ L A S E
E N G I N E ■ N E A R S ■ F E L D S P A R
L O R R E ■ P I A N O ■ V I D E O ■ A L E
I S E E ■ A R C[HEN]E M I E S ■ L I L T
T I E ■ E L I E ■ N I H ■ O P E N E R
E R N E S T O ■ H A R D L Y ■ R O D I N O
■ W A T E R ■ E E R I E ■ U N P I N
S L I V E R ■ M A S S E D ■ R E E N T R Y
C A T E R S ■ E T O ■ O A R S ■ [HEN]I E
A T[HEN]S ■ W[HEN]P I G S F L Y ■ D E L A
L E V ■ M A U L S ■ C R A M S ■ M O C K S
D R Y W A L L S ■ T E A S E ■ L O C K E T
■ O N B Y ■ S E I N E ■ T I N T ■
■ S U E D E S ■ H A N D ■ T Y C O O N S
A I R F R E S[HEN]E R ■ S T E P[HEN]C R A N E
H A G U E ■ E C R U ■ O H N O ■ L A T I N
S M E L L ■ S E E P ■ N O D S ■ E L O P E
```

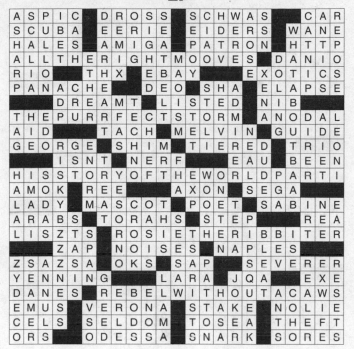

A	S	P	I	C		D	R	O	S	S		S	C	H	W	A	S			C	A	R
S	C	U	B	A		E	E	R	I	E		E	I	D	E	R	S		W	A	N	E
H	A	L	E	S		A	M	I	G	A		P	A	T	R	O	N		H	T	T	P
A	L	L	T	H	E	R	I	G	H	T	M	O	O	V	E	S		D	A	N	I	O
R	I	O			T	H	X		E	B	A	Y			E	X	O	T	I	C	S
P	A	N	A	C	H	E		D	E	O		S	H	A		E	L	A	P	S	E
		D	R	E	A	M	T		L	I	S	T	E	D		N	I	B			
T	H	E	P	U	R	R	F	E	C	T	S	T	O	R	M		A	N	O	D	A	L
A	I	D			T	A	C	H		M	E	L	V	I	N		G	U	I	D	E
G	E	O	R	G	E		S	H	I	M		T	I	E	R	E	D		T	R	I	O
		I	S	N	T		N	E	R	F			E	A	U		B	E	E	N
H	I	S	S	T	O	R	Y	O	F	T	H	E	W	O	R	L	D	P	A	R	T	I
A	M	O	K		R	E	E			A	X	O	N		S	E	G	A		
L	A	D	Y		M	A	S	C	O	T		P	O	E	T		S	A	B	I	N	E
A	R	A	B	S		T	O	R	A	H	S		S	T	E	P			R	E	A
L	I	S	Z	T	S		R	O	S	I	E	T	H	E	R	I	B	B	I	T	E	R
		Z	A	P		N	O	I	S	E	S		N	A	P	L	E	S		
Z	S	A	Z	S	A		O	K	S		S	A	P			S	E	V	E	R	E	R
Y	E	N	N	I	N	G				L	A	R	A		J	Q	A		E	X	E
D	A	N	E	S		R	E	B	E	L	W	I	T	H	O	U	T	A	C	A	W	S
E	M	U	S		V	E	R	O	N	A		S	T	A	K	E		N	O	L	I	E
C	E	L	S		S	E	L	D	O	M		T	O	S	E	A		T	H	E	F	T
O	R	S			O	D	E	S	S	A		S	N	A	R	K		S	O	R	E	S

S	T	A	R	T	O	F	F		T	I	M	P	A	N	I		H	I	Y	A
P	O	R	E	O	V	E	R		A	N	D	I	R	O	N		O	L	A	V
I	H	O	P	E	I	W	I	N	T	H	I	S	P	O	T		M	L	L	E
T	O	M				S	E	T	A			S	N	O	W	E	D	I	N	
S	E	A	N	S		A	B	S	O	L	V	E		E	T	A		R	E	G
			I	H	A	V	E	T	O	F	O	L	D		O	N	B	A	S	E
S	P	I	K	E	L	E	E				L	I	A	M		D	O	W		
H	E	R	O	E	S			G	A	P		H	B	O			S	T	D	S
I	W	A	N	T	A	F	U	L	L	H	O	U	S	E		H	O	W	I	E
I	T	I			T	U	N	E	D	I	N				S	A	M	O	S	A
T	E	S		F	I	N	D	E	R		F	E	I	N	T	S		C	C	S
A	R	E	O	L	A			I	N	O	R	D	E	R			A	R	I	
K	E	A	N	U		I	M	I	N	F	O	R	A	H	U	N	D	R	E	D
E	R	L	E		P	A	T		C	T	S			D	E	E	D	E	E	
		L	A	S		O	X	E	N			M	A	E	W	E	S	T	S	
S	T	I	L	T	S		I	M	T	H	E	D	E	A	L	E	R		
I	R	V		U	H	S		S	H	A	R	O	N	S		L	E	A	P	T
G	O	E	S	D	E	A	F		B	R	I	T					M	A	I	
N	O	G	O		I	D	L	I	K	E	A	N	O	T	H	E	R	A	C	E
A	P	O	P		L	A	O	T	I	A	N		R	E	A	S	O	N	E	R
L	S	T	S		A	T	W	O	R	S	T		S	A	W	S	T	A	R	S

29

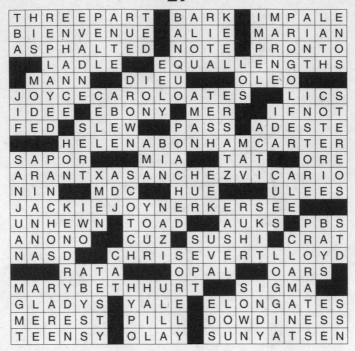

T	H	R	E	E	P	A	R	T		B	A	R	K		I	M	P	A	L	E
B	I	E	N	V	E	N	U	E		A	L	I	E		M	A	R	I	A	N
A	S	P	H	A	L	T	E	D		N	O	T	E		P	R	O	N	T	O
		L	A	D	L	E			E	Q	U	A	L	L	E	N	G	T	H	S
	M	A	N	N			D	I	E	U				O	L	E	O			
J	O	Y	C	E	C	A	R	O	L	O	A	T	E	S			L	I	C	S
I	D	E	E		E	B	O	N	Y		M	E	R			I	F	N	O	T
F	E	D		S	L	E	W			P	A	S	S		A	D	E	S	T	E
			H	E	L	E	N	A	B	O	N	H	A	M	C	A	R	T	E	R
S	A	P	O	R			M	I	A			T	A	T		O	R	E		
A	R	A	N	T	X	A	S	A	N	C	H	E	Z	V	I	C	A	R	I	O
N	I	N		M	D	C		H	U	E				U	L	E	E	S		
J	A	C	K	I	E	J	O	Y	N	E	R	K	E	R	S	E	E			
U	N	H	E	W	N		T	O	A	D		A	U	K	S		P	B	S	
A	N	O	N	O		C	U	Z		S	U	S	H	I		C	R	A	T	
N	A	S	D		C	H	R	I	S	E	V	E	R	T	L	L	O	Y	D	
		R	A	T	A			O	P	A	L			O	A	R	S			
M	A	R	Y	B	E	T	H	H	U	R	T		S	I	G	M	A			
G	L	A	D	Y	S		Y	A	L	E		E	L	O	N	G	A	T	E	S
M	E	R	E	S	T		P	I	L	L		D	O	W	D	I	N	E	S	S
T	E	E	N	S	Y		O	L	A	Y		S	U	N	Y	A	T	S	E	N

30

A	C	C	E	D	E		C	H	A	C	H	A		M	A	L	A	G	A	S
B	U	R	R	O	S		P	O	S	H	E	R		A	L	A	B	A	M	A
I	T	E	N	D	S	H	A	P	P	I	L	Y		N	A	T	U	R	E	L
D	E	A		G	O	O		H	E	L	L		S	I	C			B	L	T
E	S	S	A	Y		P	I	E	C	E	O	F	C	A	K	E		L	I	E
D	Y	E	S		S	W	A	T	S		A	R	C		S	T	E	A	D	
		H	A	M		A	D	S		P	T	A	S		P	E	D			
M	A	S		C	A	W	S		S	O	A	P				A	P	B		
A	T	H		C	R	E	A	M	F	I	L	L	E	D		A	S	H	E	N
O	T	O		E	L	I		D	I	L	L		I	N	T	E	R	N	E	
R	E	P	A	P	E	R		S	N	E	A	D		V	O	L	T	A	G	E
I	M	P	U	T	E	D		I	N	C	A		E	D	A		S	A	D	
S	P	I	N	S		O	N	B	A	C	K	W	A	R	D	S		E	L	L
	T	N	T			A	O	N	E			I	S	E	E		S	S	E	
	G	I	A		S	I	N	S		C	T	S		D	S	C				
R	A	C	E	R		A	L	E		S	A	U	L	T			A	B	C	S
A	G	E		F	I	R	E	S	T	A	R	T	E	R		A	L	O	H	A
D	E	N		R	A	D		A	R	N	O		O	U	R		L	E	S	
I	N	T	O	T	A	L		A	L	T	E	R	E	D	S	T	A	T	E	S
A	D	E	L	I	N	E		S	O	R	R	E	L		M	O	R	O	S	E
L	A	R	A	M	I	E		K	N	E	A	D	S		C	O	R	N	E	D

31

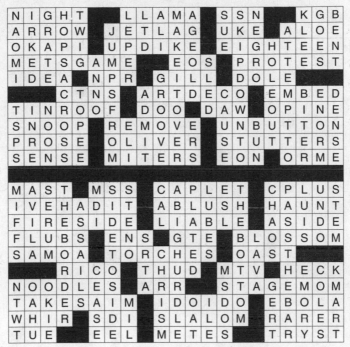

```
N I G H T     L L A M A     S S N       K G B
A R R O W   J E T L A G   U K E     A L O E
O K A P I   U P D I K E   E I G H T E E N
M E T S G A M E     E O S     P R O T E S T
I D E A     N P R   G I L L   D O L E
        C T N S     A R T D E C O     E M B E D
T I N R O O F     D O O     D A W     O P I N E
S N O O P     R E M O V E     U N B U T T O N
P R O S E   O L I V E R     S T U T T E R S
S E N S E   M I T E R S     E O N     O R M E
```

```
M A S T   M S S     C A P L E T     C P L U S
I V E H A D I T     A B L U S H     H A U N T
F I R E S I D E     L I A B L E     A S I D E
F L U B S   E N S     G T E     B L O S S O M
S A M O A     T O R C H E S     O A S T
        R I C O     T H U D   M T V     H E C K
N O O D L E S     A R R     S T A G E M O M
T A K E S A I M     I D O I D O     E B O L A
W H I R     S D I   S L A L O M     R A R E R
T U E     E E L   M E T E S       T R Y S T
```

32

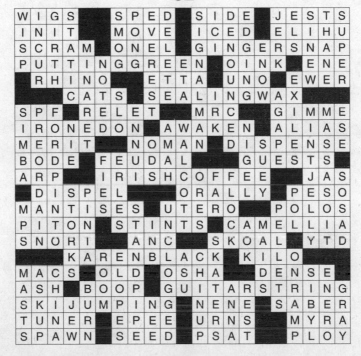

```
W I G S     S P E D     S I D E     J E S T S
I N I T     M O V E     I C E D     E L I H U
S C R A M   O N E L     G I N G E R S N A P
P U T T I N G G R E E N     O I N K     E N E
    R H I N O     E T T A     U N O     E W E R
        C A T S     S E A L I N G W A X
S P F     R E L E T     M R C     G I M M E
I R O N E D O N     A W A K E N     A L I A S
M E R I T     N O M A N     D I S P E N S E
B O D E     F E U D A L       G U E S T S
A R P     I R I S H C O F F E E     J A S
    D I S P E L       O R A L L Y   P E S O
M A N T I S E S   U T E R O     P O L O S
P I T O N     S T I N T S   C A M E L L I A
S N O R I     A N C     S K O A L   Y T D
    K A R E N B L A C K     K I L O
M A C S   O L D     O S H A     D E N S E
A S H   B O O P   G U I T A R S T R I N G
S K I J U M P I N G   N E N E     S A B E R
T U N E R   E P E E   U R N S     M Y R A
S P A W N   S E E D   P S A T     P L O Y
```

33

```
  A L I D A   S E A P O R T     C H O R D
S N O R E R   O N T A R I O   E L O P E R
I T S A L L R I G H T I F I M S O B U S Y
M A T E R I A L   R E L   A T T E S T S
      A S P   A B O N E   H E S
E N J O Y S   K N E L T   R A F   A L L I
S E E P     A O N E   S E R A   C L A D
T H A T I M S H O P P I N G I N A H A Z E
E R N   N E I L   S N A G S   N I M E S
S U S P E N D   P I T T I   Y E A S T
    A R S E N A L   R H E B O K S
S M E L T   A M A D O   A N I T R A S
H O V E L   S M I T E   G I A N   A N A
E V E R Y S E A S O N I T U R N D I Z Z Y
B E R M   E N T S   R O A D   L E I S
A S T O   R A H   G R O O M   H O O D O O
      F A T   O R A N T   P E R
P I S C O P O   L O G     P R E S A G E D
I N M Y C H R I S T M A S H O L I D A Z E
B R U T U S   T O T A L E D   E N D U R E
B E T E S   A N O N Y M S   D I A L A
```

34

```
  S A B O T   F E S S U P   C A T S U P
B E R A T E   A D E S T E   A L I E N E E
E L I S H A   R I T T E R   R O O T I E R
L E A S E L E A S T   S H I N E S H O W N
U N D E R   S W O O P   A D E S   N E E
G I N S   S T A N   A P P L Y   A S S E S
A C E   H U E Y   P U L S E   P I T
    B O E R   R U S E   P A R A P E T
S O A R E D   B O R E B O A R D   Y A L U
I N T E R   P E T E   E N D O R   S T A T
S T O W   R A G U     H A V E   T I T O
L I M B   O P I N E   N A P E   C A N E R
E M I R   S E N D S C E N T   T R I A D S
R E C O V E R   S L E D   J O A D
    O A S   T R E A D   C U R B   D S T
L E N D L   T O O N S   A I L S   S I T E
O R E   S O F A   S A U T E   A P S I S
T R U S S T R U S T   G R A P H G R A F T
T I T U L A R   T I N G O D   A R A B L E
O N E M O R E   E N T I R E   R O I L E D
  G R O P E S   R E H E A L   A N N E S
```

35

```
KNOB  PEAL  DANCER  SPAT
LINA  ACRE  SLOANE  YARE
ITIS  SLIT  OFMICEANDME
EROS  TACIT   REDBARON
GONEWITHTHEWIN   APERY
   TIC   GREER   SSS
ADS  THESOUNDANDTHEFUR
DEPOSERS   SNARE   ASA
ALEC   ANILS   CELLARED
MIDEAST  LATISH  LINERS
   ACLOCKWORKORANG
SHINTO  ASSUME  ARTEMIS
CASSAVAS   TAWNY   LONE
ATL   ARECA   NEBRASKA
THENAKEDANDTHEDEA  SYR
   ODS   LOUIE   DIT
IMAGE   IMNOTREALLYHER
NOSINESS   OMANI   COTE
CISFORCORPS  ITIN  ONUS
ARAT  SANEST  TATE  BODE
NAYS  TREATY  STAN  BRET
```

36

```
NEHI  OVERDO  STAS  SHEL
EXEC  HEREOF  ERLE  HARI
WASHINGTONFORALL   ERIN
ECO  MOSES  SAID  FLEECE
STUMP     JEFFERSONMAN
TATA  BEIRUT   OAKS
   SMELTED  SALAMI  SOC
LINCOLNALARMFIRE  JANA
ADO  ROIL  SEOUL  BARER
CERTAIN   NOLL   ANGIE
HAMILTONLITTLEINDIANS
ELATE   YODS   MOLESTS
SILLS   ACETO  SHOO  SEE
ISLE  JACKSONQUESTIONS
STY  BUCKET  EVEREST
   GUMM   SACRED  CRAT
GRANTPERCENT    SHUTE
RESETS  IOLE  ABBEY  NET
ANTI  FRANKLINYEARSWAR
SEIS  OINK  LATTER  HASA
PENS  ROTS  SNEERS  EYED
```

37

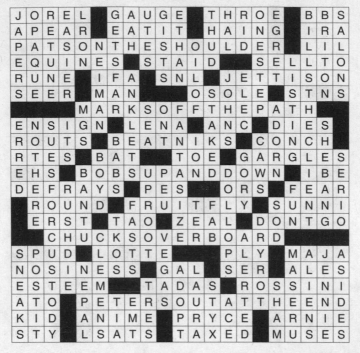

```
J O R E L ■ G A U G E ■ T H R O E ■ B B S
A P E A R ■ E A T I T ■ H A I N G ■ I R A
P A T S O N T H E S H O U L D E R ■ L I L
E Q U I N E S ■ S T A I D ■ ■ S E L L T O
R U N E ■ I F A ■ S N L ■ J E T T I S O N
S E E R ■ M A N ■ ■ O S O L E ■ S T N S
■ ■ ■ M A R K S O F F T H E P A T H ■
E N S I G N ■ L E N A ■ A N C ■ D I E S
R O U T S ■ B E A T N I K S ■ C O N C H
R T E S ■ B A T ■ T O E ■ G A R G L E S
E H S ■ B O B S U P A N D D O W N ■ I B E
D E F R A Y S ■ P E S ■ O R S ■ F E A R
■ R O U N D ■ F R U I T F L Y ■ S U N N I
■ E R S T ■ T A O ■ Z E A L ■ D O N T G O
■ C H U C K S O V E R B O A R D ■ ■ ■
S P U D ■ L O T T E ■ ■ P L Y ■ M A J A
N O S I N E S S ■ G A L ■ S E R ■ A L E S
E S T E E M ■ T A D A S ■ R O S S I N I
A T O ■ P E T E R S O U T A T T H E E N D
K I D ■ A N I M E ■ P R Y C E ■ A R N I E
S T Y ■ L S A T S ■ T A X E D ■ M U S E S
```

38

```
R E M A P ■ G A Z A ■ J E B ■ S M I T H
E A R N S ■ O W E D ■ A X E ■ B O O H O O
D R . K I L D A R E ■ N U I ■ I N V A I N
I L S A ■ A D I O S ■ E R R O R ■ I D L E
D E A R ■ M A T S ■ R E B U R D E N ■
■ N A M E R S ■ S A Y I T I S N ' T S O
E L D ■ A N D ■ M I C R A ■ D O R I S
G A M B I T ■ B A T H E S ■ L I O N I Z E
A V A I L S ■ R U S E ■ M I S R U L E S
D A N T E ■ C I V I L ■ R O B E ■ P L S
■ ■ R E U B E N , R E U B E N ■ ■
M R I ■ I R E S ■ R E P L Y ■ U P T O N
T E A C A R T S ■ A P E D ■ A T E A S E
I N V A D E S ■ C I C E L Y ■ D R I L L S
E L E N A ■ A G H A S ■ L E I ■ K O S
D O N ' T B E C R U E L ■ S A L A M I ■
■ T E E T O T A L ■ S I M P ■ E N D S
G L O W ■ S A R I N ■ A L E P H ■ A G U T
R E D A N T ■ R E O ■ D E R R I N G - D O
E D D I E S ■ A R I ■ D E R E ■ B E T E L
W A S T E ■ L S D ■ S T A Y ■ A R O S E
```

C	R	A	B		S	L	A	G		S	T	A	B		A	S	M	A	R	A
R	O	M	A		H	O	U	R		C	R	U	E		B	E	A	N	E	D
O	D	I	N		A	B	L	E		R	I	D	E		O	N	L	A	N	D
C	A	S	T	T	H	E	D	E	C	I	D	I	N	G	V	O	L	T		
E	N	S	U	E	D			K	O	B	E			E	E	R		U	P	I
			M	O	S	H		R	E	N	E	G	E			E	R	I	N	
	T	H	E	A	M	P	E	R	E	S	T	R	I	K	E	S	B	A	C	K
C	I	O	N		S	E	M	I			S	I	D		R	E	A	L	T	Y
O	M	N	I	S		D	A	N	Z	A		K	E	E	N	E	N			
R	E	D	A	C	T		S	E	L	A		O	R	E	S		A	N	E	
P	L	A	C	E	A	S	H	E	S	O	N	O	N	E	S	F	A	R	A	D
S	Y	S		N	I	K	E		T	E	N	S			T	I	L	I	N	G
			B	I	C	A	R	B		S	A	T	A	N		T	O	O	N	E
S	P	E	E	C	H		B	O	P		E	L	A	M		A	S	I	S	
W	A	T	T	S	I	T	A	L	L	A	B	O	U	T	A	L	F	I	E	
A	G	H	A			A	L	T	A	I	R		M	O	R	O				
P	E	I		I	R	S		T	R	I	S		A	L	T	H	E	A		
		O	H	M	I	M	P	R	O	V	E	M	E	N	T	L	O	A	N	S
S	E	P	I	A	S		T	U	N	E		O	P	A	H		R	U	T	S
T	W	I	N	G	E		A	D	I	N		T	I	N	O		A	T	E	E
L	E	A	D	E	N		S	E	C	T		E	C	O	N		H	E	R	S

H	A	I	G	H	T		S	A	B	R	A	S		Q	U	E	S	T	E	D
I	N	D	O	O	R		S	T	E	A	M	Y		U	N	B	O	R	N	E
E	G	Y	P	T	I	A	N	W	A	R	P	S	V	I	S	A	D	A	T	A
D	E	L		W	A	Y		O	N	E	S	T	E	P		N	A	G	E	L
			A	G	L	A	R	E			L	P	S			I	R	S		
M	A	N	D	R	E	A	D	S	R	I	G	I	D	E	T	H	I	C		
O	R	E	O	S		E	T	Y	M	O	N		R	O	O	F				
C	A	A	N		P	A	L		N	A	S	H		A	R	N	O	L	D	
	B	R	I	E	F	R	E	D	H	O	T	P	A	S	T	A	I	R	E	D
		T	A	C	T		O	U	T			L	A	S			B	A	A	
L	I	S	Z	T		F	I	N	D		C	A	L	L		H	U	S	S	Y
A	W	E			G	U	M		M	A	X		A	V	O	N				
D	I	E	T	H	E	L	P	S	C	O	M	E	R	M	A	N	A	G	E	
E	N	S	O	U	L		S	A	A	R		O	I	L		G	U	M	P	
			T	E	A	S		F	R	E	S	C	A			E	E	R	I	E
	H	O	S	T	E	V	E	R	S	H	A	L	L	E	N	D	U	R	E	
O	L	E			I	C	E			A	D	D	E	N	D					
B	O	R	E	R		L	A	S	C	A	L	A		A	R	P		R	P	I
E	G	O	R	E	P	U	L	S	E	S	A	V	I	D	A	L	L	I	E	S
L	I	E	A	B	E	D		S	T	O	L	E	N		P	A	T	T	O	N
I	N	S	T	A	T	E		S	A	F	A	R	I		T	Y	R	A	N	T

41

42

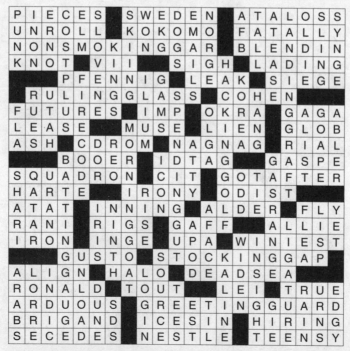

43

```
GASP  TAMALE   CRIPPLE
OVER  ARUGULA BOUNTIES
FIXESDAMAGES  INTHECAN
ELECTS   EMILE  AROSE
RADIO DISREGARDSNOTES
   POLISH NNW OLD
ADS PAGEANT PRO TREE
BEHEST  DISPLAYSVEILS
BAIL INTEL AYN HELDUP
ALPS SOU  ARROW NEELY
  WITHDRAWSDEPOSITS
LORNA STRIP  LEE HARE
AREOLE LES SAYSA OWED
INCREASESCUTS BANANA
COKE TIS NASTIER YOM
   LIT BAH TENETS
OBTAINSRELEASES FARSI
CRONE  AGORA  AUGEAN
TAKESFOR FOLLOWSLEADS
EVENTIME TITANIC SITE
TENDONS  COMETH TROT
```

44

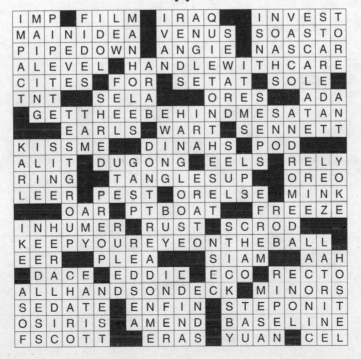

```
IMP FILM IRAQ INVEST
MAINIDEA VENUS SOASTO
PIPEDOWN ANGIE NASCAR
ALEVEL HANDLEWITHCARE
CITES FOR SETAT SOLE
TNT SELA ORES ADA
GETTHEEBEHINDMESATAN
 EARLS WART SENNETT
KISSME DINAHS POD
ALIT DUGONG EELS RELY
RING TANGLESUP OREO
LEER PEST ORELSE MINK
 OAR PTBOAT FREEZE
INHUMER RUST SCROD
KEEPYOUREYEONTHEBALL
EER PLEA SIAM AAH
DACE EDDIE ECO RECTO
ALLHANDSONDECK MINORS
SEDATE ENFIN STEPONIT
OSIRIS AMEND BASELINE
FSCOTT ERAS YUAN CEL
```

45

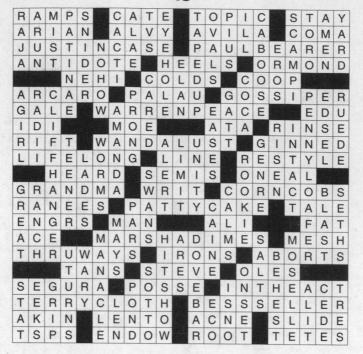

```
R A M P S   C A T E   T O P I C   S T A Y
A R I A N   A L V Y   A V I L A   C O M A
J U S T I N C A S E   P A U L B E A R E R
A N T I D O T E   H E E L S   O R M O N D
      N E H I   C O L D S   C O O P
A R C A R O   P A L A U   G O S S I P E R
G A L E   W A R R E N P E A C E   E D U
I D I   M O E   A T A   R I N S E
R I F T   W A N D A L U S T   G I N N E D
L I F E L O N G   L I N E   R E S T Y L E
    H E A R D   S E M I S   O N E A L
G R A N D M A   W R I T   C O R N C O B S
R A N E E S   P A T T Y C A K E   T A L E
E N G R S   M A N   A L I   F A T
A C E   M A R S H A D I M E S   M E S H
T H R U W A Y S   I R O N S   A B O R T S
    T A N S   S T E V E   O L E S
S E G U R A   P O S S E   I N T H E A C T
T E R R Y C L O T H   B E S S S E L L E R
A K I N   L E N T O   A C N E   S L I D E
T S P S   E N D O W   R O O T   T E T E S
```

46

```
T H O U   O P T   C H O O   R E A C T O R
R O A N   S L A M D U N K   O I L L I N E
O N K P   P I K E S P E A K O R B O A S T
D I S A G R E E D   C P O   E I S N E R
      I N E R T I A   A I D E   N E T T Y
A L L D A Y S O A K E R S   Q U O D
D O U B T   T I N   N U S   S T A B
O G R I S H   G O O D C L E A N P H O N E
B O I L   Y S E R   H A U L   L O R N E
E S E L   D O N   S T A I R   T I P T O P
    O R I E N T A L R O G U E
I B E R I A   R U A R K   S E C   T O D D
S A T I N   B A L I   B I L K   E R O O
B L A C K W A L L N O T E S   S K E I N S
N E T H   E L S   A A A   A T O N E
    T K T S   H O T C R O S S B O N E S
S A S H A   A S I F   T U N E O U T
A L M O N D   A R Y   P E T U L A N C E
N O I F S A N D S O R B O A T S   L A R A
Y O T E A M O   C R Y U N C L E   E N O S
O P E N S E A   H E E D   T E D   R A C Y
```

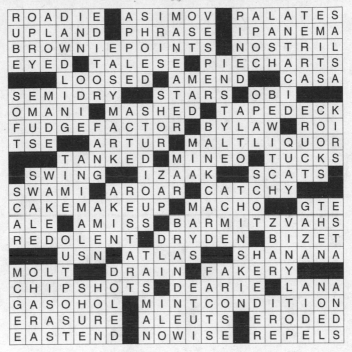

47

Grid 47:

R	O	A	D	I	E	█	A	S	I	M	O	V	█	P	A	L	A	T	E	S
U	P	L	A	N	D	█	P	H	R	A	S	E	█	I	P	A	N	E	M	A
B	R	O	W	N	I	E	P	O	I	N	T	S	█	N	O	S	T	R	I	L
E	Y	E	D	█	T	A	L	E	S	E	█	P	I	E	C	H	A	R	T	S
█	█	L	O	O	S	E	D	█	A	M	E	N	D	█	█	C	A	S	A	█
S	E	M	I	D	R	Y	█	S	T	A	R	S	█	O	B	I	█	█	█	█
O	M	A	N	I	█	M	A	S	H	E	D	█	T	A	P	E	D	E	C	K
F	U	D	G	E	F	A	C	T	O	R	█	B	Y	L	A	W	█	R	O	I
T	S	E	█	█	A	R	T	U	R	█	M	A	L	T	L	I	Q	U	O	R
█	█	█	T	A	N	K	E	D	█	M	I	N	E	O	█	T	U	C	K	S
█	S	W	I	N	G	█	█	I	Z	A	A	K	█	█	S	C	A	T	S	█
S	W	A	M	I	█	A	R	O	A	R	█	C	A	T	C	H	Y	█	█	█
C	A	K	E	M	A	K	E	U	P	█	M	A	C	H	O	█	█	G	T	E
A	L	E	█	A	M	I	S	S	█	B	A	R	M	I	T	Z	V	A	H	S
R	E	D	O	L	E	N	T	█	D	R	Y	D	E	N	█	B	I	Z	E	T
█	█	█	U	S	N	█	A	T	L	A	S	█	█	S	H	A	N	A	N	A
M	O	L	T	█	█	D	R	A	I	N	█	F	A	K	E	R	Y	█	█	█
C	H	I	P	S	H	O	T	S	█	D	E	A	R	I	E	█	L	A	N	A
G	A	S	O	H	O	L	█	M	I	N	T	C	O	N	D	I	T	I	O	N
E	R	A	S	U	R	E	█	A	L	E	U	T	S	█	E	R	O	D	E	D
E	A	S	T	E	N	D	█	N	O	W	I	S	E	█	R	E	P	E	L	S

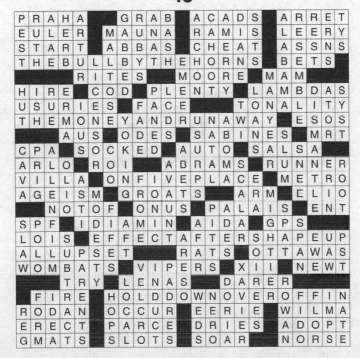

48

Grid 48:

P	R	A	H	A	█	G	R	A	B	█	A	C	A	D	S	█	A	R	R	E	T
E	U	L	E	R	█	M	A	U	N	A	█	R	A	M	I	S	█	L	E	E	R	Y
S	T	A	R	T	█	A	B	B	A	S	█	C	H	E	A	T	█	A	S	S	N	S
T	H	E	B	U	L	L	B	Y	T	H	E	H	O	R	N	S	█	B	E	T	S
█	█	█	R	I	T	E	S	█	M	O	O	R	E	█	M	A	M	█	█	█
H	I	R	E	█	C	O	D	█	P	L	E	N	T	Y	█	L	A	M	B	D	A	S
U	S	U	R	I	E	S	█	F	A	C	E	█	█	T	O	N	A	L	I	T	Y
T	H	E	M	O	N	E	Y	A	N	D	R	U	N	A	W	A	Y	█	E	S	O	S
█	A	U	S	█	O	D	E	S	█	S	A	B	I	N	E	S	█	M	R	T
C	P	A	█	S	O	C	K	E	D	█	A	U	T	O	█	S	A	L	S	A
A	R	L	O	█	R	O	I	█	A	B	R	A	M	S	█	R	U	N	N	E	R
V	I	L	L	A	█	O	N	F	I	V	E	P	L	A	C	E	█	M	E	T	R	O
A	G	E	I	S	M	█	G	R	O	A	T	S	█	A	R	M	█	E	L	I	O
█	N	O	T	O	F	█	O	N	U	S	█	P	A	L	A	I	S	█	E	N	T
S	P	F	█	I	D	I	A	M	I	N	█	A	I	D	A	█	G	P	S	█
L	O	I	S	█	E	F	F	E	C	T	A	F	T	E	R	S	H	A	P	E	U	P
A	L	L	U	P	S	E	T	█	█	R	A	T	S	█	O	T	T	A	W	A	S
W	O	M	B	A	T	S	█	V	I	P	E	R	S	█	X	I	I	█	N	E	W	T
█	█	T	R	Y	█	L	E	N	A	S	█	█	D	A	R	E	R	█	█	█
█	F	I	R	E	█	H	O	L	D	D	O	W	N	O	V	E	R	O	F	F	I	N
R	O	D	A	N	█	O	C	C	U	R	█	E	E	R	I	E	█	W	I	L	M	A
E	R	E	C	T	█	P	A	R	C	E	█	D	R	I	E	S	█	A	D	O	P	T
G	M	A	T	S	█	S	L	O	T	S	█	S	O	A	R	█	N	O	R	S	E

49

```
A L A S K A ■ S B A ■ ■ A S T R O ■ S P A
R E P A Y S ■ E A S T ■ O C H E R ■ O R R
F O R N O W ■ A T T Y ■ N O E L S ■ S U M
■ ■ ■ I T A ■ C H A P T E R I I ■ D O N A
B O N B O N B O O B O O ■ P R E F A C E D
O K I E ■ L A I ■ R A I ■ F E D O R A ■
W A L L A W A L L A Y O Y O ■ T A U S ■
L Y E ■ V I C ■ S I T I N ■ C O P S ■ ■
■ ■ M O N K S ■ S T D ■ H U A R A C H E
P E C A N ■ B E A L E ■ M A R K ■ W O O L
O A H U ■ D I N N E R P A R T Y ■ P U S S
P R I M ■ U R S A ■ B O O K I ■ P A S T A
E S C A P A D E ■ C I I ■ S C R E W ■ ■
■ H U L L ■ S H U L A ■ A I R ■ A G E
■ P I N A ■ M U U M U U F R O U F R O U
S E C O N D ■ I B M ■ T O I ■ I G O R
T R A N S I T S ■ P A G O P A G O D O D O
A R N O ■ C A R D S H A R P ■ A P E ■
B I C ■ M I M E O ■ A L A I ■ S A L T E D
L E A ■ S E P A L ■ S E C S ■ P R I O R Y
E R N ■ G R A D E ■ ■ N E H ■ S T O O G E
```

50

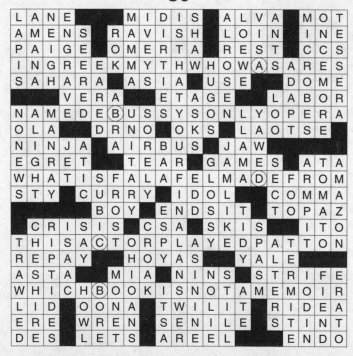

```
L A N E ■ ■ M I D I S ■ A L V A ■ M O T
A M E N S ■ R A V I S H ■ L O I N ■ I N E
P A I G E ■ O M E R T A ■ R E S T ■ C C S
I N G R E E K M Y T H W H O (A) S A R E S
S A H A R A ■ A S I A ■ U S E ■ D O M E
■ ■ V E R A ■ E T A G E ■ ■ L A B O R
N A M E D E (B) U S S Y S O N L Y O P E R A
O L A ■ D R N O ■ O K S ■ L A O T S E
N I N J A ■ A I R B U S ■ J A W ■ ■
E G R E T ■ T E A R ■ G A M E S ■ A T A
W H A T I S F A L A F E L M A (D) E F R O M
S T Y ■ C U R R Y ■ I D O L ■ C O M M A
■ ■ B O Y ■ E N D S I T ■ T O P A Z
C R I S I S ■ C S A ■ S K I S ■ I T O
T H I S A (C) T O R P L A Y E D P A T T O N
R E P A Y ■ H O Y A S ■ Y A L E ■ ■
A S T A ■ M I A ■ N I N S ■ S T R I F E
W H I C H (B) O O K I S N O T A M E M O I R
L I D ■ O O N A ■ T W I L I T ■ R I D E A
E R E ■ W R E N ■ S E N I L E ■ S T I N T
D E S ■ L E T S ■ A R E E L ■ E N D O
```

51

```
☀ D A Y P U N C H   C A P T   A S P I R E
R E M E A S U R E   O R L Y   S P A R E S
O B S T R U C T S   S O A P O P E R A ☆ S
O A T   C A L   R I M I E R   C E S T A
F R E D   L E A S E   A D D I C T S
    R E F   I T L L   S U G A R I E S T
M A D C A P   L O A D S   P I L A S T E R
T R A C E R S   S T E N O   N F L   H A Y
S T M A R Y S   H E L E N E S   L A B S
      I O S   I R E S   T E N E T
☽ R I V E R   ☀ ☽ A N D ☆ S   ☀ R I S E S
C O N E S   I L I E   O D E
H A V E   A N I M A T O   C A N A S T A
I D E   B E D   T E T O N   T E D I O U S
L I N S E E D S   E E R I E   S E R U M S
D E T E R G E N T   B O I L   D E L
    E N S N A R E   A N N U L   S T E P
A M A T I   D R O L L Y   P A S   R K O
T O T H E ☽ A L I C E   S H I R T T A I L
A P I E C E   A K I N   T A N G E R I N E
N E E D E D   T A D A   S H O O T I N G ☆
```

52

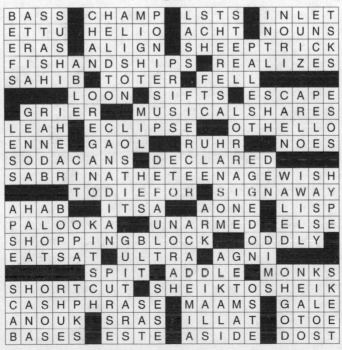

```
B A S S   C H A M P   L S T S   I N L E T
E T T U   H E L I O   A C H T   N O U N S
E R A S   A L I G N   S H E E P T R I C K
F I S H A N D S H I P S   R E A L I Z E S
S A H I B   T O T E R   F E L L
      L O O N   S I F T S   E S C A P E
  G R I E R   M U S I C A L S H A R E S
L E A H   E C L I P S E   O T H E L L O
E N N E   G A O L   R U H R   N O E S
S O D A C A N S   D E C L A R E D
S A B R I N A T H E T E E N A G E W I S H
    T O D I E F O H   S I G N A W A Y
A H A B   I T S A   A O N E   L I S P
P A L O O K A   U N A R M E D   E L S E
S H O P P I N G B L O C K   O D D L Y
E A T S A T   U L T R A   A G N I
      S P I T   A D D L E   M O N K S
S H O R T C U T   S H E I K T O S H E I K
C A S H P H R A S E   M A A M S   G A L E
A N O U K   S R A S   I L L A T   O T O E
B A S E S   E S T E   A S I D E   D O S T
```

53

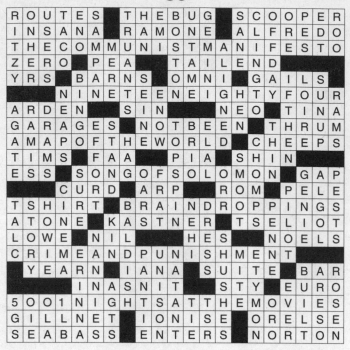

```
R O U T E S ■ T H E B U G ■ S C O O P E R
I N S A N A ■ R A M O N E ■ A L F R E D O
T H E C O M M U N I S T M A N I F E S T O
Z E R O ■ P E A ■ ■ T A I L E N D ■ ■
Y R S ■ B A R N S ■ O M N I ■ G A I L S ■
■ ■ N I N E T E E N E I G H T Y F O U R
A R D E N ■ S I N ■ ■ N E O ■ T I N A
G A R A G E S ■ N O T B E E N ■ T H R U M
A M A P O F T H E W O R L D ■ C H E E P S
T I M S ■ F A A ■ P I A ■ S H I N ■ ■
E S S ■ S O N G O F S O L O M O N ■ G A P
■ ■ C U R D ■ A R P ■ R O M ■ P E L E
T S H I R T ■ B R A I N D R O P P I N G S
A T O N E ■ K A S T N E R ■ T S E L I O T
L O W E ■ N I L ■ ■ H E S ■ N O E L S ■
C R I M E A N D P U N I S H M E N T ■ ■
■ Y E A R N ■ I A N A ■ S U I T E ■ B A R
■ ■ I N A S N I T ■ S T Y ■ E U R O
5 0 0 1 N I G H T S A T T H E M O V I E S
G I L L N E T ■ I O N I S E ■ O R E L S E
S E A B A S S ■ E N T E R S ■ N O R T O N
```

54

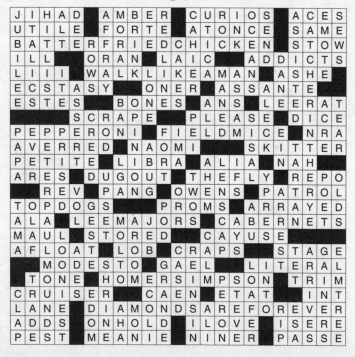

```
J I H A D ■ A M B E R ■ C U R I O S ■ A C E S
U T I L E ■ F O R T E ■ A T O N C E ■ S A M E
B A T T E R F R I E D C H I C K E N ■ S T O W
I L L ■ ■ O R A N ■ L A I C ■ ■ A D D I C T S
L I I I ■ W A L K L I K E A M A N ■ A S H E ■
E C S T A S Y ■ O N E R ■ A S S A N T E ■ ■
E S T E S ■ B O N E S ■ A N S ■ L E E R A T
■ ■ S C R A P E ■ P L E A S E ■ D I C E
P E P P E R O N I ■ F I E L D M I C E ■ N R A
A V E R R E D ■ N A O M I ■ ■ S K I T T E R
P E T I T E ■ L I B R A ■ A L I A ■ N A H ■
A R E S ■ D U G O U T ■ T H E F L Y ■ R E P O
■ R E V ■ P A N G ■ O W E N S ■ P A T R O L
T O P D O G S ■ ■ P R O M S ■ A R R A Y E D
A L A ■ L E E M A J O R S ■ C A B E R N E T S
M A U L ■ S T O R E D ■ C A Y U S E ■ ■
A F L O A T ■ L O B ■ C R A P S ■ S T A G E
■ M O D E S T O ■ G A E L ■ L I T E R A L
■ T O N E ■ H O M E R S I M P S O N ■ T R I M
C R U I S E R ■ C A E N ■ E T A T ■ ■ I N T
L A N E ■ D I A M O N D S A R E F O R E V E R
A D D S ■ O N H O L D ■ I L O V E ■ I S E R E
P E S T ■ M E A N I E ■ N I N E R ■ P A S S E
```

55

C	A	L	F	■	D	U	E	■	B	R	A	N	C	H	■	G	A	M	E	R
I	D	E	A	L	I	S	T	■	R	E	V	I	L	E	■	O	P	I	N	E
D	E	G	R	A	D	E	R	■	A	V	A	T	A	R	■	L	A	N	D	S
E	L	O	■	G	E	R	E	■	C	E	N	T	S	O	F	F	C	O	U	P
R	A	F	T	E	R	S	■	T	H	A	T	I	S	■	O	P	E	R	E	■
■	■	M	I	R	O	■	S	O	I	L	■	■	■	A	R	R	■	■	■	■
S	T	U	N	■	T	H	E	D	A	■	T	W	I	S	T	O	F	L	E	M
K	I	T	E	S	■	A	R	A	L	■	H	A	T	H	■	J	A	V	A	■
Y	E	T	■	E	S	S	A	Y	■	T	O	K	A	Y	■	S	O	B	I	G
■	■	■	T	A	T	■	■	A	R	M	E	N	■	■	P	R	O	T	O	■
S	A	I	N	T	G	E	O	R	G	E	A	N	D	T	H	E	D	R	A	G
A	G	R	E	E	■	■	P	O	L	E	S	■	■	U	A	W	■	■	■	■
L	A	R	G	E	■	O	R	B	E	D	■	B	I	L	G	E	■	O	L	D
E	M	E	R	■	■	B	A	I	T	■	S	E	M	I	■	■	D	R	U	I	D
M	A	G	I	C	J	O	H	N	S	■	T	R	A	P	P	■	O	T	I	S
■	■	■	H	I	E	■	■	L	I	E	N	■	H	A	L	O	■	■	■	■
■	S	C	O	R	N	■	P	A	T	E	N	T	■	B	E	N	E	F	I	T
I	L	L	F	I	X	H	I	S	W	A	G	■	A	R	N	O	■	S	R	I
N	A	I	F	S	■	A	C	T	I	V	E	■	G	O	O	D	D	E	A	L
R	I	V	E	T	■	L	O	A	N	E	R	■	T	O	L	E	R	A	T	E
E	N	E	R	O	■	S	T	R	E	S	S	■	S	D	S	■	Y	S	E	R

56

W	O	L	F	■	B	O	N	A	M	I	■	D	E	L	L	■	T	A	T	A
E	M	I	R	■	O	V	I	S	A	C	■	E	P	E	E	■	E	V	A	N
F	A	C	I	A	L	E	X	P	R	E	S	S	I	O	N	■	L	A	N	G
T	R	E	A	S	U	R	E	S	■	B	O	I	L	■	A	M	E	N	D	S
■	■	R	I	S	E	S	■	R	A	N	C	O	R	■	O	C	T	E	T	■
B	I	D	■	S	E	A	■	B	A	G	G	A	G	E	C	L	A	I	M	■
U	S	E	S	■	S	T	A	I	D	■	■	R	O	D	S	■	■	■	■	■
L	A	C	E	S	■	L	O	A	D	E	D	Q	U	E	S	T	I	O	N	■
K	A	L	A	H	A	R	I	■	R	E	D	O	U	N	D	■	■	N	R	A
S	C	A	L	A	W	A	G	■	P	A	R	E	■	■	C	A	M	R	Y	■
■	R	U	N	N	I	N	G	C	O	M	M	E	N	T	A	R	Y	■	■	■
A	G	A	P	E	■	I	O	U	S	■	R	O	U	L	E	T	T	E	■	■
A	N	N	■	H	E	N	R	E	I	D	■	I	M	P	L	O	R	E	S	■
A	U	T	O	S	U	G	G	E	S	T	I	O	N	■	A	L	I	S	T	■
■	P	A	N	G	■	■	■	M	A	G	I	C	■	A	B	L	E	■	■	■
■	C	O	U	N	T	E	R	O	F	F	E	R	■	S	H	H	■	E	A	R
C	H	I	L	D	■	D	E	M	U	R	S	■	U	S	A	I	R	■	■	■
H	A	L	E	S	T	■	V	A	N	E	■	I	N	U	N	D	A	T	E	S
E	R	I	N	■	B	L	A	N	K	E	T	S	T	A	T	E	M	E	N	T
A	L	E	C	■	S	E	M	I	■	S	A	L	I	N	E	■	B	E	V	Y
P	Y	R	E	■	P	I	P	S	■	T	W	E	E	T	Y	■	O	N	Y	X

57

```
B U S H   ■   B U B ■ H A A G ■   S C O O P ■
A B O U T ■   E L I G I B L E ■   W I N N I E
C O M M A N D T O A D O G S L E D T E A M
H A M I T U P ■ L I E U ■ T A L E ■ A F T
■ T E D ■ M O R O N S ■ P A S T R Y ■ ■
■ ■ L I E ■ S A G S ■ C O P S E ■ P L A N
G A I T S ■ T H Y ■ C L I O O R E R A T O
A G E I S T S ■ ■ N O E L ■ ■ G E T T O
B U R E A U ■ R E E L O U T ■ W Y S T A N
S A S S ■ T H E R M O ■ ■ O S I P ■ E R E
■ ■ ■ S T U B B O R N B E A S T ■ ■ ■
Y E R ■ T U T U ■ F A M I N E ■ B S M T
A R A R A T ■ S T R A P I N ■ S C O T I A
D R O O L ■ ■ R U S E ■ ■ S T A B I L E
D O U B L E A G E N T ■ B E E ■ L T C O L
A R L O · C L O V E ■ C A G E ■ L A K ■
■ ■ T A H I T I ■ O H I O A N ■ I S A
C A M ■ B E B E ■ A U E L ■ F E L L I N I
W H A T O L I V E R T W I S T W A N T E D
T E J A N O ■ E N T R Y F E E ■ N A T A L
■ M A V E N ■ N O S E ■ F A R ■ G O R E
```

Bush, Mush, Muse, Mule, Mole, More, Gore

58

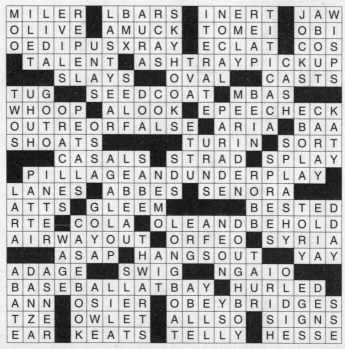

```
M I L E R ■ L B A R S ■ I N E R T ■ J A W
O L I V E ■ A M U C K ■ T O M E I ■ O B I
O E D I P U S X R A Y ■ E C L A T ■ C O S
■ T A L E N T ■ A S H T R A Y P I C K U P
■ ■ S L A Y S ■ O V A L ■ ■ C A S T S
T U G ■ · S E E D C O A T ■ M B A S ■ ■
W H O O P ■ A L O O K ■ E P E E C H E C K
O U T R E O R F A L S E ■ A R I A ■ B A A
S H O A T S ■ ■ ■ T U R I N ■ S O R T
■ ■ C A S A L S ■ S T R A D ■ S P L A Y
■ P I L L A G E A N D U N D E R P L A Y ■
L A N E S ■ A B B E S ■ S E N O R A ■ ■
A T T S ■ G L E E M ■ ■ ■ B E S T E D
R T E ■ C O L A ■ O L E A N D B E H O L D
A I R W A Y O U T ■ O R F E O ■ S Y R I A
■ ■ A S A P ■ H A N G S O U T ■ Y A Y
A D A G E ■ S W I G ■ N G A I O ■ ■
B A S E B A L L A T B A Y ■ H U R L E D
A N N ■ O S I E R ■ O B E Y B R I D G E S
T Z E ■ O W L E T ■ A L L S O ■ S I G N S
E A R ■ K E A T S ■ T E L L Y ■ H E S S E
```

59

```
MAINE   SARA   APTER    RAT
OSSIE   KNIT   PRONE   PELE
THINGPIECE   PINGSALMON
TOTO   LMNO   SAMI   TRAINS
STINGUPTHEPLACE   RINSE
      AMY    TALL   XSANDOS
WARBLE   AHA    EGAN
ATOLLS   GETTHEKINGSOUT
THOUS   CAL   HAVE   DEANNA
ELM   WHIM   URI   RESPECT
REMI   HANSBRINGER   SLOT
STARMAN   MOB   COPS   LIL
KITKAT   WANE   IRS   DEANE
ICESKATINGRING   HEMMER
      EMIT   AGE   OCTADS
DEALSIN   BIOG    SHA
INLAW   THATTOUCHOFMING
FRACAS   URIS   NOAH   EROO
FORTYWINGS   SINGORSWIM
ELMO   ANTES   STAG   BOISE
RLS   BASSO   NYNY   INNER
```

60

```
CORPSE   POLL   CACAO   FADES
OPIATE   OBEY   ORALS   EXIST
PENCILSLOSEPOINTS   RIATA
UNSER   AYES   ELENA   PULPER
LEER   ALPS   DEITY   SELLERS
ADD   ELI   BURST   APPEAR
   KNIVESUPSHARPLY   SAC
SALAD   ARETE   ARAS   GUSH
EDITOR   OTT   SHOT   MENSA
TAG   FEATHERSDOWN   CANCAN
ASHE   WWI   SHEENA   ONEHIT
   TABASCO   OTB   YESHIVA
GASSER   ZADORA   STE   ANTS
REWELD   BANANASSPLIT   GOA
AGIRL   CORN   PAR   RACERS
PITS   COOK   RELIC   WIDTH
ESC   HORSESBUCKTREND
   HABITS   CHEST   AMY   DAM
OVERATE   CHUTE   SOFT   POLE
SISALS   ALIST   EMIT   TROLL
ADOBE   LEADHEAVILYTRADED
KAFIR   BORNE   BITE   OUTAGE
ALFAS   SNEAD   SLED   WEEDED
```

61

R	O	B	B		C	O	M	B	O		I	H	A	D		S	N	E	A	D
E	M	I	R		L	I	A	R	S		N	A	V	E		R	A	L	L	Y
M	A	N	I	F	E	S	T	O	S		T	H	E	T	R	O	U	B	L	E
I	N	S	T	O	N	E		W	I	S	E	A	C	R	E		S	A	S	S
		A	R	C		O	N	A	I	R			A	C	M	E				
	W	I	T	H	B	E	I	N	G	P	U	N	C	T	U	A	L	I	S
J	O	H	N	D	E	E	R	E		M	O	N	I	T	O	R		E	S	P
E	L	I		I	S	H		B	A	S	I	C	S		I	N	D	I	A
F	E	L	I	X		E	U	R	O		E	S	E		B	L	E	A	T	S
F	O	S	S		O	S	G	O	O	D			T	A	L	E				
	T	H	A	T	T	H	E	R	E	I	S	N	O	B	O	D	Y		
	T	U	T	S			F	L	E	E	C	E		L	O	S	E
E	L	P	A	S	O		A	P	R		K	R	O	C		R	E	U	P	S
R	E	A	R	S		F	L	O	U	T	S			A	W	E		B	A	P
A	C	C		I	S	O	T	O	P	E		A	R	T	I	L	L	E	R	Y
T	H	E	R	E	T	O	A	P	P	R	E	C	I	A	T	E	I	T
		A	S	O	F		A	R	L	E	N		C	A	B		
C	H	U	G		O	A	K	T	R	E	E	S		S	H	R	I	M	P	S
H	A	R	O	L	D	R	O	M	E		C	O	M	P	E	N	D	I	U	M
A	R	G	U	E		A	T	A	N		T	U	B	E	R		O	N	C	E
D	I	E	T	S		W	O	N	A		S	T	A	C	Y		S	T	E	W

62

P	A	B	S	T		T	O	L	E	D	O		F	A	V	A		B	A	G
A	L	L	E	R		E	L	O	P	E	D		I	M	A	M		A	D	O
S	L	I	C	E	A	N	D	D	I	C	E		R	E	L	A	T	I	V	E
H	U	N	T	A	N	D	P	E	C	K		J	E	D	I		U	T	E	S
A	R	K		S	T	E	R			S	I	T	E	D		B	A	R	B
S	E	E	T	O		R	O	C	K	A	N	D	R	O	L	L		N	S	A
	D	R	A	N	O		M	A	S	A	D	A		Y	A	R	D	E	D
	B	O	W	A	N	D	S	C	R	A	P	E		R	E	S	
P	A	K		U	N	D	O		B	O	K		R	I	D	G	W	A	Y
A	M	I	S	S		M	O	W	A	T		L	A	N	D		G	I	B	E
B	A	S	E		D	I	N	A	H		G	E	N	E	S		A	T	R	A
L	I	S	A		O	X	E	N		S	U	I	T	S		P	E	C	A	N
O	N	A	D	A	T	E		S	C	I		I	T	O	R		H	M	S
	N	O	V		D	U	C	K	A	N	D	C	O	V	E	R	
C	A	D	G	E	R		S	O	I	R	E	E		A	T	E	A	T
R	P	M		C	U	T	A	N	D	P	A	S	T	E		E	M	I	R	S
A	R	A	B		N	O	T	E	S			O	L	1	N		R	E	A
Y	O	K	E		T	W	O	S		P	L	U	G	A	N	D	P	L	A	Y
O	P	E	N	M	I	N	D		S	L	I	P	A	N	D	S	L	I	D	E
L	O	U		A	S	I	A		S	O	L	O	E	D		T	O	N	E	R
A	S	P		W	H	E	Y		S	T	A	N	D	S		O	P	E	D	S

63

A	D	D	E	D		E	D	I	C	T	S		A	N	T	I	W	A	R
B	E	A	R	E	R		C	A	M	E	R	A		C	O	U	R	A	G	E
O	F	F	I	C	E	C	O	M	P	L	E	X		A	D	R	E	N	A	L
R	E	F	E	R	T	O		P	O	L	E			B	I	N		D	R	Y
T	R	Y		E	A	R	P		S	A	L	K	S		C	I	A		
			V	E	R	N	E		T	R	I	N	I		E	N	R	O	L
J	A	P	E		D	I	E	M		S	K	U	N	K		G	I	R	L	S
A	M	O	R		C	R	A	M		E	C	C	E		R	E	G	A	L
K	E	E	N	S		E	A	S	E		K	E	A		A	L	A	M	O
E	X	T	O	L	S		G	O	S	P	E	L		N	O	D		N	A	P
	I	N	A	T	T	E	N	T	I	V	E	P	U	P	I	L	S		
D	S	C		T	U	B		R	A	M	A	D	A		S	U	I	T	U	P
R	I	F	L	E		I	V	Y		N	O	R	A		S	T	O	L	E
I	D	E	A	S		R	E	N	A		S	W	I	G		O	P	E	N
B	E	E	C	H		D	R	A	N	O		N	A	R	C		U	S	E	D
	A	T	E	I	N		V	I	T	U	S		H	E	I	S	T		
	D	N	A		E	L	I	T	E		S	E	T	H		A	P	E
G	A	S		G	T	O		D	O	T	E		T	R	A	I	N	E	D
O	B	E	R	L	I	N		S	O	F	T	S	H	O	U	L	D	E	R	S
R	E	L	I	E	V	E		O	T	I	O	S	E		S	O	L	A	C	E
E	L	A	P	S	E	S		L	E	T	S	O	N		M	E	R	Y	L

64

P	I	C	A	B	O		A	B	O	I	L		S	O	W	S		J	C	T
I	N	D	I	R	A		M	U	N	R	O		P	R	O	S	P	E	R	O
C	A	R	R	Y	F	I	S	S	U	R	E		H	A	R	R	O	W	E	D
			N	I	N	T	H	S		W	R	E	C	K	S	R	E	A	D
	P	R	E		S	K	E	E		P	E	A	R	L		E	L	M
J	E	A	N	S	H	A	L	L	O	T		P	E	E	R	E	S	S
A	K	I	T	A			D	A	B		S	I	X		F	A	N
M	O	T	O	R		A	E	R	O	S	O	L	S		A	T	T	I	L	A
B	E	T	M	I	D	D	L	E	R		Z	E	A	L		O	R	F	E	O
		R	O	O	T		R	O	B	B	I	N	L	E	E	C	H
	M	C	N	A	I	R		I	N	U	S	E		M	E	S	S	R	S
F	I	L	L	S	P	E	C	T	E	R		A	M	I	E
O	M	A	R	S		S	A	L	E		C	U	R	T	R	U	S	T	L	E
N	E	W	B	I	E		R	E	D	R	A	F	T	S		R	E	O	I	L
Z	O	E		G	E	R		S	U	P				A	T	A	L	L
	D	A	N	K	E	S	T		D	O	C	K	H	O	L	I	D	A	Y
	A	R	B		D	H	A	B	I		L	O	O	M		N	Y	C
K	N	E	E	L	S	B	O	R	E		C	O	R	N	E	T
A	G	I	T	A	T	O	R		G	Y	M	N	E	I	G	H	B	O	R	S
R	U	N	S	R	I	O	T		E	A	V	E	S		A	R	A	R	A	T
O	S	S		A	R	K	S		T	R	I	S	H		S	U	R	R	E	Y

65

66

67

68

69

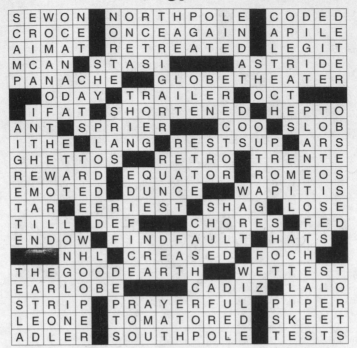

S	E	W	O	N	■	N	O	R	T	H	P	O	L	E	■	C	O	D	E	D
C	R	O	C	E	■	O	N	C	E	A	G	A	I	N	■	A	P	I	L	E
A	I	M	A	T	■	R	E	T	R	E	A	T	E	D	■	L	E	G	I	T
M	C	A	N	■	S	T	A	S	I	■	■	■	A	S	T	R	I	D	E	■
P	A	N	A	C	H	E	■	■	G	L	O	B	E	T	H	E	A	T	E	R
■	O	D	A	Y	■	T	R	A	I	L	E	R	■	O	C	T	■	■	■	■
■	I	F	A	T	■	S	H	O	R	T	E	N	E	D	■	H	E	P	T	O
A	N	T	■	S	P	R	I	E	R	■	■	C	O	O	■	S	L	O	B	■
I	T	H	E	■	L	A	N	G	■	R	E	S	T	S	U	P	■	A	R	S
G	H	E	T	T	O	S	■	R	E	T	R	O	■	T	R	E	N	T	E	■
R	E	W	A	R	D	■	E	Q	U	A	T	O	R	■	R	O	M	E	O	S
E	M	O	T	E	D	■	D	U	N	C	E	■	W	A	P	I	T	I	S	■
T	A	R	■	E	E	R	I	E	S	T	■	S	H	A	G	■	L	O	S	E
T	I	L	L	■	D	E	F	■	■	C	H	O	R	E	S	■	F	E	D	■
E	N	D	O	W	■	F	I	N	D	F	A	U	L	T	■	H	A	T	S	■
■	■	■	N	H	L	■	C	R	E	A	S	E	D	■	F	O	C	H	■	■
T	H	E	G	O	O	D	E	A	R	T	H	■	■	W	E	T	T	E	S	T
E	A	R	L	O	B	E	■	■	■	C	A	D	I	Z	■	L	A	L	O	■
S	T	R	I	P	■	P	R	A	Y	E	R	F	U	L	■	P	I	P	E	R
L	E	O	N	E	■	T	O	M	A	T	O	R	E	D	■	S	K	E	E	T
A	D	L	E	R	■	S	O	U	T	H	P	O	L	E	■	T	E	S	T	S

70

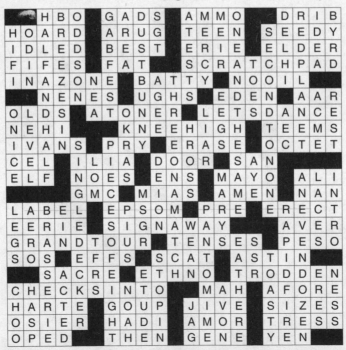

■	H	B	O	■	G	A	D	S	■	A	M	M	O	■	■	D	R	I	B
H	O	A	R	D	■	A	R	U	G	■	T	E	E	N	■	S	E	E	D	Y
I	D	L	E	D	■	B	E	S	T	■	E	R	I	E	■	E	L	D	E	R
F	I	F	E	S	■	F	A	T	■	S	C	R	A	T	C	H	P	A	D	■
I	N	A	Z	O	N	E	■	B	A	T	T	Y	■	N	O	O	I	L	■
■	N	E	N	E	S	■	U	G	H	S	■	E	D	E	N	■	A	A	R
O	L	D	S	■	A	T	O	N	E	R	■	L	E	T	S	D	A	N	C	E
N	E	H	I	■	■	K	N	E	E	H	I	G	H	■	T	E	E	M	S
I	V	A	N	S	■	P	R	Y	■	E	R	A	S	E	■	O	C	T	E	T
C	E	L	■	I	L	I	A	■	D	O	O	R	■	S	A	N	■	■	■
E	L	F	■	N	O	E	S	■	E	N	S	■	M	A	Y	O	■	A	L	I
■	■	G	M	C	■	M	I	A	S	■	A	M	E	N	■	N	A	N	■
L	A	B	E	L	■	E	P	S	O	M	■	P	R	E	■	E	R	E	C	T
E	E	R	I	E	■	S	I	G	N	A	W	A	Y	■	■	A	V	E	R
G	R	A	N	D	T	O	U	R	■	T	E	N	S	E	S	■	P	E	S	O
S	O	S	■	E	F	F	S	■	S	C	A	T	■	A	S	T	I	N	■
■	S	A	C	R	E	■	E	T	H	N	O	■	T	R	O	D	D	E	N
C	H	E	C	K	S	I	N	T	O	■	M	A	H	■	A	F	O	R	E
H	A	R	T	E	■	G	O	U	P	■	J	I	V	E	■	S	I	Z	E	S
O	S	I	E	R	■	H	A	D	I	■	A	M	O	R	■	T	R	E	S	S
O	P	E	D	■	T	H	E	N	■	G	E	N	E	■	Y	E	N	■	■

71

```
B A D E G G S ■ A L I S T S ■ U N A R M S
B O O L E A N ■ G A N T R Y ■ S O T H A T
L U C K Y S E V E N T E E N ■ E N T I R E
S T S ■ S M E E ■ G E R M ■ ■ S A N T A
■ ■ H E A R T B U R N O N T H E R O A D
R E T U R N S ■ L A N ■ R E R U N S ■
A R E A ■ ■ S A G ■ ■ W I G S ■ B T U
D R A C U L A T H E M A N ■ K E E P E R S
A O L ■ B A R E S ■ E L I D E ■ A C E S
R L S ■ O N I N ■ S T O N E ■ M A R K E R
■ ■ J A Z Z O U T O F A F R I C A ■ ■
P E S E T A ■ S C O O T ■ I E S T ■ O T T
I D O S ■ ■ B E L L E ■ P E P S I ■ D E R
A D D U P T O ■ A I R P O R T M I S E R Y
F A A ■ E R O O ■ ■ U S S ■ ■ E U R O
■ ■ A N A L O G ■ S S T ■ B E S T M A N
C H U T Z P A H O N T H E B E A C H ■ ■
R A S T A ■ ■ B O O P ■ O T T O ■ E W E
A T H E N A ■ W O R K I N G C O U P L E S
W H E N C E ■ C O G E N T ■ H U R D L E S
L A R D E R ■ S M E R S H ■ A T S T A K E
```

72

```
E T C H ■ I M M U N E ■ A L L I E ■ S P A
R E P O ■ N A I L E R ■ C A I R N ■ P O L
A D R O O P I N T H E B U C K E T ■ E S A
■ ■ T R E N T ■ ■ A T E E ■ R A C E R
A N T L E R S ■ D O O M E D S T A D I U M
M A R I A S ■ B E R R A ■ ■ U N D E R ■
B R A N D O ■ A L I A ■ D A U N T S ■
I D L E ■ N O N O O N S E N S E ■ U S A F
T O A S T ■ P E N N ■ I C E S ■ S P O R E
■ ■ A K A ■ ■ C L A N ■ W I T H I N
T H E T W I L I G H T O F T H E G O O D S
R E P E N T ■ S E A R ■ ■ A T M ■ ■
E M E R Y ■ P Y L E ■ B A W L ■ A B A B A
Y S E R ■ H O O D C A R R I E R ■ U R A L
■ ■ I C A R U S ■ L I E N ■ E L N I N O
■ G A B O N ■ ■ S T E A K ■ S E N E C A
C O L L E G E P R O O F S ■ S T A Y S O N
E L M E R ■ R A E S ■ ■ S T A P H ■ ■
A D O ■ C A R D B O A R D C A R T O O N S
S E N ■ E R O D E ■ D E P O R T ■ O B O E
E N D ■ D A R Y L ■ S P I T E S ■ P I N T
```

73

```
U N P A C K   ■   M I L D E W   ■   A M P E R E
S A I L O N   ■   S P L E E N Y   ■   P A S C A L
A N G E L O   ■   C H E C K F O R P R I O R S
■   ■   ■   C A P R A   ■   A K A   ■   A R C   ■   L E E
B U C K S F O R A P R O M O T I O N   ■   ■
A M A   ■   ■   M E L L   ■   ■   I V E S   ■   I M A C
S T E P S U P   ■   S A W B L A D E   ■   C O R E
E A S T O N   ■   ■   S A U L   ■   ■   C O D E D
S T A L L S F O R T I M E   ■   S C A L E N E
T A R   ■   D E I F I E S   ■   ■   S H A L A L A
■   ■   H E A D F O R T H E H I L L S   ■   ■
■   L A E R T E S   ■   ■   C A L O R I E   ■   R E O
R E D R E S S   ■   S T O P F O R B R E A T H
A I M E D   ■   ■   N E A P   ■   ■   R I D G E D
F L I T   ■   A T L A N T I C   ■   B E D S O R E
T A X I   ■   N O O K   ■   ■   E A S E   ■   ■   U N A
■   ■   C H A N G E F O R T H E B E T T E R
I L K   ■   A T E   ■   W A R   ■   ■   I R A Q I   ■   ■
R I N G F O R S E R V I C E   ■   L U G G E D
E M E R I L   ■   R E C I T E D   ■   S A H A R A
S N E E Z E   ■   A D E S T E   ■   A L T M A N
```

74

```
R O S E   ■   ■   F L U   ■   P A S S   ■   D E S I
E V A L U A T I O N   ■   B O N A P P E T I T
P A T I S S E R I E   ■   I T A L I A N A R T
S T A T E L E S S   ■   U K E   ■   E N T   ■   ■   ■
■   E N E R O   ■   ■   S P E N D S   ■   I S T L E
■   ■   I W A S T H I R T Y T W O W H E N
L I V I D   ■   L I K E N S   ■   N A E   ■   A W E D
A L A N   ■   K U D O S   ■   T E X T   ■   Y A L E
M I N D G A M E S   ■   L O O   ■   ■   S P I R E A
B E E   ■   A N N A   ■   D O N T G O   ■   E N T E R
■   ■   I S T A R T E D C O O K I N G   ■
B E A M E   ■   E M E R G E   ■   T I N T   ■   A B E
A T T E S T   ■   A N E   ■   C O N T A C T E D
R E B A   ■   A M O K   ■   S E P A L   ■   H I N D
I R A N   ■   C A P   ■   R A N L O W   ■   B E T S Y
U N T I L T H E N I J U S T A T E   ■   ■
M E S T O   ■   I C E B A G   ■   ■   O R B A D
■   ■   R A M   ■   W A R   ■   C R U S T A C E A
P L A I N B A G E L   ■   F R E N C H C H E F
J U L I A C H I L D   ■   T A L I A S H I R E
S I S I   ■   S I T S   ■   S T Y   ■   ■   S P E W
```

```
P E P A ■ P O L ■ ■ U L N A ■ D E F E N D
E D A S ■ R U S T P R O O F ■ O N E W A Y
R I S K ■ O R D E R I N G A L A ■ C R A T E
U N S E W S ■ ■ R I S E S T O ■ I N N E R
■ B E D E ■ D O R E ■ ■ ■ M E N S ■ ■
B U D ■ S P A N I S H R A M A D A ■ E S S
O R T ■ T O M A ■ T E U T O N S ■ C R E W
U G H ■ E T U D E ■ E D N A ■ ■ S H A N E
T H E F R A P A V I L I O N S ■ H O N D A
■ B U N G ■ T E N S ■ ■ L O O K O U T
V E R E ■ E Y E R S ■ H E R O N ■ I S P Y
A N A L Y S E ■ N O N E ■ T H E E ■ ■
S T E L E ■ P A T R O N O F T H F R A T S
S I X E R ■ H O O T ■ L U R E D ■ N A Y
A C A D ■ C L A U S E S ■ S E G O ■ D I N
L E M ■ T H E B R A D O F A V O N ■ T L C
■ ■ C R O P ■ ■ L I L I ■ I T H E
A M B L E ■ E N I G M A S ■ S C O R N S
S T R O N G R A M T A C T I C S ■ R O D E
A G E N D A ■ P R O T E S T E R ■ M A E S
N E W E S T ■ S E S S ■ S O S ■ E T R E
```

The New York Times

Crossword Puzzles

The #1 name in crosswords

Available at your local bookstore or online at nytimes.com/nytstore

Coming Soon!

Rise and Shine Crossword Puzzles	0-312-37833-5	$7.95/$8.95 Can.
Coffee, Tea or Crosswords	0-312-37828-9	$7.95/$8.95 Can.
Crosswords for Two	0-312-37830-0	$12.95/$14.50 Can.
Will Shortz Presents		
I Love Crosswords Vol. 2	0-312-37837-8	$7.95/$8.95 Can.
Crosswords to Keep Your Brain Young	0-312-37858-8	$8.95/$9.95 Can.
Sweet Dreams Crosswords	0-312-37836-X	$9.95/$10.95 Can.
Easy Crossword Puzzles Vol. 9	0-312-37831-9	$9.95/$10.95 Can.
Sunday at Home Crosswords	0-312-37834-3	$7.95/$8.95 Can.
Easy to Not-So-Easy Crosswords		
Puzzle Omnibus Vol. 2	0-312-37832-7	$12.95/$14.50 Can.
Crosswords for a Relaxing Weekend	0-312-37829-7	$12.95/$14.50 Can.
Sunday at Home Crosswords	0-312-37834-3	$7.95/$8.95 Can.

Special Editions

Little Black (and White)		
Book of Crosswords	0-312-36105-X	$12.95/$14.50 Can.
The Joy of Crosswords	0-312-37510-7	$9.95/$10.95 Can.
Little Red and Green Book		
of Crosswords	0-312-37661-8	$13.95/$16.25 Can.
Little Flip Book of Crosswords	0-312-37043-1	$10.95/$11.95 Can.
How to Conquer the New		
York Times Crossword Puzzle	0-312-36554-3	$9.95/$10.95 Can.
Will Shortz's Favorite		
Crossword Puzzles	0-312-30613-X	$9.95/$10.95 Can.
Will Shortz's Favorite Sunday		
Crossword Puzzles	0-312-32488-X	$9.95/$10.95 Can.
Will Shortz's Greatest Hits	0-312-34242-X	$8.95/$10.50 Can.
Will Shortz Presents Crosswords		
for 365 Days	0-312-36121-1	$9.95/$10.95 Can.
Will Shortz's Funniest Crossword Puzzles	0-312-32489-8	$9.95/$10.95 Can.
Will Shortz's Funniest		
Crossword Puzzles Vol. 2	0-312-33960-7	$9.95/$10.95 Can.
Will Shortz's Xtreme Xwords	0-312-35203-4	$7.95/$8.95 Can.
Vocabulary Power Crosswords	0-312-35199-2	$10.95/$11.95 Can.

Daily Crosswords

Fitness for the Mind Crosswords Vol. 1	0-312-34955-6	$10.95/$11.95 Can.
Fitness for the Mind Crosswords Vol. 2	0-312-35278-6	$10.95/$11.95 Can.
Crosswords for the Weekend	0-312-34332-9	$9.95/$10.95 Can.
Daily Crossword Puzzles Vol. 71	0-312-34858-4	$9.95/$10.95 Can.
Daily Crossword Puzzles Vol. 72	0-312-35260-3	$9.95/$10.95 Can.

Volumes 57-70 also available

Easy Crosswords

Easy Crossword Puzzles Vol. 8	0-312-36558-6	$9.95/$10.95 Can.
Easy Crossword Puzzles Vol. 7	0-312-35261-1	$9.95/$10.95 Can.
Easy Crossword Puzzles Vol. 6	0-312-33057-7	$9.95/$10.95 Can.

Volumes 2-5 also available

Tough Crosswords

Tough Crossword Puzzles Vol. 13	0-312-34240-3	$10.95/$11.95 Can.
Tough Crossword Puzzles Vol. 12	0-312-32442-1	$10.95/$11.95 Can.
Tough Crossword Puzzles Vol. 11	0-312-31456-6	$10.95/$11.95 Can.

Volumes 9-10 also available

Sunday Crosswords

Simply Sunday Crosswords	0-312-34243-8	$7.95/$8.95 Can.
Sunday in the Park Crosswords	0-312-35197-6	$7.95/$8.95 Can.
Sunday Morning Crossword Puzzles	0-312-35672-2	$7.95/$8.95 Can.
Everyday Sunday Crossword Puzzles	0-312-36106-8	$7.95/$8.95 Can.
Sunday Brunch Crosswords	0-312-36557-8	$7.95/$8.95 Can.
Sunday at the Seashore Crosswords	0-312-37070-9	$7.95/$8.95 Can.
Sleepy Sunday Crossword Puzzles	0-312-37508-5	$7.95/$8.95 Can.
Sunday's Best	0-312-37637-5	$7.95/$8.95 Can.
Sunday Crossword Puzzles Vol. 33	0-312-37507-7	$9.95/$10.95 Can.
Sunday Crossword Puzzles Vol. 32	0-312-36066-5	$9.95/$10.95 Can.
Sunday Crossword Puzzles Vol. 31	0-312-34862-2	$9.95/$10.95 Can.

Large-Print Crosswords

Large-Print Big Book of Holiday Crosswords	0-312-33092-8	$12.95/$14.50 Can.
Large-Print Crosswords for a Brain Workout	0-312-32612-2	$10.95/$11.95 Can.
Large-Print Crosswords for Your Coffee Break	0-312-33109-6	$10.95/$11.95 Can.
Large-Print Will Shortz's Favorite		
Crossword Puzzles	0-312-33959-3	$10.95/$11.95 Can.
Large-Print Crosswords to Boost		
Your Brainpower	0-312-32037-X	$10.95/$11.95 Can.
Large-Print Daily Crossword Puzzles	0-312-31457-4	$10.95/$11.95 Can.
Large-Print Daily Crossword Puzzles Vol. 2	0-312-33111-8	$10.95/$11.95 Can.
Large-Print Crosswords for Your Bedside	0-312-34245-4	$10.95/$11.95 Can.
Large-Print Big Book of Easy Crosswords	0-312-33958-5	$12.95/$14.50 Can.
Large-Print Easy Crossword Omnibus Vol. 1	0-312-32439-1	$12.95/$14.50 Can.
Large-Print Crossword Puzzle Omnibus Vol. 8	0-312-37514-X	$13.95/$15.50 Can.
Large-Print Crossword Puzzle Omnibus Vol. 7	0-312-36125-4	$12.95/$14.50 Can.
Large-Print Crossword Puzzle Omnibus Vol. 6	0-312-34861-4	$12.95/$14.50 Can.

Omnibus

Easy to Not-So-Easy Crossword Omnibus Vol. 1	0-312-37516-6	$12.95/$14.50 Can.
Crosswords for a Lazy Afternoon	0-312-33108-8	$12.95/$14.50 Can.
Lazy Weekend Crossword Puzzle Omnibus	0-312-34247-0	$12.95/$14.50 Can.

Lazy Sunday Crossword Puzzle Omnibus	0-312-35279-4	$12.95/$14.50 Can.
Big Book of Holiday Crosswords	0-312-33533-4	$12.95/$14.50 Can.
Giant Book of Holiday Crosswords	0-312-34927-0	$12.95/$14.50 Can.
Ultimate Crossword Omnibus	0-312-31622-4	$12.95/$14.50 Can.
Tough Crossword Puzzle Omnibus Vol. 1	0-312-32441-3	$12.95/$14.50 Can.
Crossword Challenge	0-312-33951-8	$12.95/$14.50 Can.
Crosswords for a Weekend Getaway	0-312-35198-4	$12.95/$14.50 Can.
Biggest Beach Crossword Omnibus	0-312-35667-6	$12.95/$14.50 Can.
Weekend Away Crossword Puzzle Omnibus	0-312-35669-2	$12.95/$14.50 Can.
Weekend at Home Crossword Puzzle Omnibus	0-312-35670-6	$12.95/$14.50 Can.
Holiday Cheer Crossword Puzzles	0-312-36126-2	$12.95/$14.50 Can.
Crosswords for a Long Weekend	0-312-36560-8	$12.95/$14.50 Can.
Crosswords for a Relaxing Vacation	0-312-36694-9	$12.95/$14.50 Can.
Will Shortz Presents Fun in the Sun		$12.95/$14.50 Can.
Crossword Puzzle Omnibus	0-312-37041-5	$12.95/$14.50 Can.
Sunday Crossword Omnibus Vol. 9	0-312-35666-8	$12.95/$14.50 Can.
Sunday Crossword Omnibus Vol. 8	0-312-32440-5	$12.95/$14.50 Can.
Sunday Crossword Omnibus Vol. 7	0-312-30950-3	$12.95/$14.50 Can.
Easy Crossword Puzzle Omnibus Vol. 5	0-312-34859-2	$12.95/$14.50 Can.
Easy Crossword Puzzle Omnibus Vol. 4	0-312-33537-7	$12.95/$14.50 Can.
Easy Crossword Puzzle Omnibus Vol. 3	0-312-36123-8	$12.95/$14.50 Can.
Crossword Puzzle Omnibus Vol. 16	0-312-36104-1	$12.95/$14.50 Can.
Crossword Puzzle Omnibus Vol. 15	0-312-34856-8	$12.95/$14.50 Can.
Crossword Puzzle Omnibus Vol. 14	0-312-33534-2	$12.95/$14.50 Can.
Supersized Book of Easy Crosswords	0-312-35277-8	$14.95/$16.25 Can.
Supersized Book of Sunday Crosswords	0-312-36122-X	$15.95/$17.95 Can.

Previous volumes also available

Variety Puzzles

Acrostic Puzzles Vol. 10	0-312-34853-3	$9.95/$10.95 Can.
Acrostic Puzzles Vol. 9	0-312-30949-X	$9.95/$10.95 Can.
Sunday Variety Puzzles	0-312-30059-X	$9.95/$10.95 Can.

Portable-Size Format

Crosswords for Your Coffee Break	0-312-28830-1	$7.95/$8.95 Can.
Sun, Sand and Crosswords	0-312-30076-X	$7.95/$8.95 Can.
Weekend Challenge	0-312-30079-4	$7.95/$8.95 Can.
Crosswords for the Holidays	0-312-30603-2	$7.95/$8.95 Can.
Crosswords for the Work Week	0-312-30952-X	$7.95/$8.95 Can.
Crosswords for Your Beach Bag	0-312-31455-8	$7.95/$8.95 Can.
Crosswords to Boost Your Brainpower	0-312-32033-7	$7.95/$8.95 Can.
Cuddle Up with Crosswords	0-312-37636-7	$7.95/$8.95 Can.
C Is for Crosswords	0-312-37509-3	$7.95/$8.95 Can.
Crazy for Crosswords	0-312-37513-1	$7.95/$8.95 Can.
Crosswords for a Mental Edge	0-312-37069-5	$7.95/$8.95 Can.
Favorite Day Crosswords: Tuesday	0-312-37072-5	$7.95/$8.95 Can.
Afternoon Delight Crosswords	0-312-37071-9	$7.95/$8.95 Can.
Crosswords Under the Covers	0-312-37044-X	$7.95/$8.95 Can.
Crosswords for the Beach	0-312-37073-3	$7.95/$8.95 Can.
Will Shortz Presents		
I Love Crosswords	0-312-37040-7	$7.95/$8.95 Can.
Will Shortz Presents Crosswords to Go	0-312-36695-7	$7.95/$8.95 Can.
Favorite Day Crosswords: Monday	0-312-36556-X	$7.95/$8.95 Can.
Crosswords in the Sun	0-312-36555-1	$7.95/$8.95 Can.
Expand Your Mind Crosswords	0-312-36553-5	$7.95/$8.95 Can.
After Dinner Crosswords	0-312-36559-4	$7.95/$8.95 Can.
Groovy Crossword		
Puzzles from the '60s	0-312-36103-3	$7.95/$8.95 Can.
Piece of Cake Crosswords	0-312-36124-6	$7.95/$8.95 Can.
Carefree Crosswords	0-312-36102-5	$7.95/$8.95 Can.
Fast and Easy Crossword Puzzles	0-312-35629-3	$7.95/$8.95 Can.
Backyard Crossword Puzzles	0-312-35668-4	$7.95/$8.95 Can.
Easy Crossword Puzzles for		
Lazy Hazy Crazy Days	0-312-35671-4	$7.95/$8.95 Can.
Brainbuilder Crosswords	0-312-35276-X	$7.95/$8.95 Can.
Stress-Buster Crosswords	0-312-35196-8	$7.95/$8.95 Can.
Super Saturday Crosswords	0-312-30604-0	$7.95/$8.95 Can.
Café Crosswords	0-312-34854-1	$7.95/$8.95 Can.
Crosswords for Your Lunch Hour	0-312-34857-6	$7.95/$8.95 Can.
Easy as Pie Crossword Puzzles	0-312-34331-0	$7.95/$8.95 Can.
Crosswords to Soothe Your Soul	0-312-34244-6	$7.95/$8.95 Can.
More Quick Crosswords	0-312-34246-2	$7.95/$8.95 Can.
Beach Blanket Crosswords	0-312-34250-0	$7.95/$8.95 Can.
Crosswords to Beat the Clock	0-312-33954-2	$7.95/$8.95 Can.
Crosswords for a Rainy Day	0-312-33952-6	$7.95/$8.95 Can.
Crosswords for Stress Relief	0-312-33953-4	$7.95/$8.95 Can.
Cup of Crosswords	0-312-33955-0	$7.95/$8.95 Can.
Crosswords to Exercise Your Brain	0-312-33536-9	$7.95/$8.95 Can.
Crosswords for Your Breakfast Table	0-312-33535-0	$7.95/$8.95 Can.
More Crosswords for Your Bedside	0-312-33612-8	$7.95/$8.95 Can.
T.G.I.F Crosswords	0-312-33116-9	$7.95/$8.95 Can.
Quick Crosswords	0-312-33114-2	$7.95/$8.95 Can.
Planes, Trains and Crosswords	0-312-33113-4	$7.95/$8.95 Can.
More Sun, Sand and Crosswords	0-312-33112-6	$7.95/$8.95 Can.
Crosswords for a Brain Workout	0-312-32610-6	$7.95/$8.95 Can.
A Cup of Tea Crosswords	0-312-32435-9	$7.95/$8.95 Can.
Crosswords for Your Bedside	0-312-32032-9	$7.95/$8.95 Can.
Coffee Break Crosswords	0-312-37515-8	$9.95/$10.95 Can.

Other volumes also available

St. Martin's Griffin